PRAISE FOR *LEADING WITH EMOTIONAL INTELLIGENCE*

"Measuring quantifiable results is mandatory in our business. Our company has realized an ROI that exceeded our expectations because of the training and coaching from Relly Nadler captured in *Leading with Emotional Intelligence*. We have improved our ability to promote from within, have improved employee retention, and our leaders have integrated many of the tools explained in Relly's book into their management technique."

Jim Snell, President
Shield Healthcare Inc.

"Relly is the best I have seen at leadership development. Our executives use his leadership tools every day."

Myron Jones, President
NMB Technologies Company

"I read *Leading with Emotional Intelligence* and I was quite impressed. You did a great job presenting the material in a straightforward, credible way; more important, your process for building the EI competencies is both very practical and sensible. Nice job."

Bill Tredwell, Vice President
Hay Group, Inc.

"Relly Nadler, one of the world's foremost executive coaches, provides the reader with detailed and easy-to-use practices to make you and your leaders superstars. One of the most valuable leadership books available!"

Jeffrey E. Auerbach, Ph.D., President
College of Executive Coaching
Author of Personal and Executive Coaching

"Dr. Relly Nadler is continually on the cutting edge when it comes to Leadership Development. His innovative ideas and tools in *Leading with Emotional Intelligence* are the reason our localized Leadership Development efforts have been so successful year after year."

Lynda Hollens, Director of Employee Development
Wholesale Operations, Anheuser-Busch, Inc.

"One of the most practical and useful books on the topic that I've seen. The user-friendly layout makes it easy to find useful tips and ideas. The book is full of vivid examples that bring the issues to life."

David B. Peterson, Ph.D., Senior Vice President
Personnel Decisions International
Author of Leader as Coach *and* Development First

"Reldan S. Nadler scores big with this wonderful book, *Leading with Emotional Intelligence.* His promise is that here is a book about how to understand and apply Emotional Intelligence. He delivers. He offers keys to improving our leadership potential as well. Relly's work is smart, practical, and easy to use. He delivers a solid and comprehensive presentation of Emotional Intelligence in a manner that suits the reading audience that is looking for clear information quickly. His assessments, evaluations, and inventories point clearly to behaviors worth noting."

David J. Mahoney, Ph.D.
Psychologist, Consultant, Executive Coach

"Dr. Nadler's book *Leading with Emotional Intelligence* is an easy book to read and also to apply the EI techniques and tools. I have used the book in both my coaching practice and as a university professor in my MBA courses on leadership. My clients and students enjoyed the assessment profile on being a Star Performer. Wonderful book with practical lessons on Emotional Intelligence. A 'must have' for every executive."

Dr. Tammy Wong
Fostering Executive Leadership, Inc.

"*Leading with Emotional Intelligence* is a treasure trove of actionable strategies to develop Emotional Intelligence. If you want to improve self-control, self-confidence, teamwork, collaboration, interpersonal communication, and empathy, this great resource will show you how. It is the most clear, precise, and pragmatic book on how to enhance performance by developing key Emotional Intelligence competencies that I have read.

"Whether you are a company leader, coach, consultant, or individual performer, *Leading with Emotional Intelligence* wisely provides essential tips to help you excel. My executive coaching and leadership development clients love this book."

Dr. Maynard Brusman
Consulting Psychologist and Executive Coach

"While there are hundreds of references, books, and articles based on Daniel Goleman's conceptualization of Emotional Intelligence (EI), I found Dr. Nadler's *Leading with Emotional Intelligence* to be one of the most practical and helpful. Not only does he include detailed discussions of EI 'stars' and the competencies that make them stars, but more important he also includes specific tools and strategies that coaches, managers, counselors, and others can use to help turn others into EI stars. Additionally, there are excellent assessment tools (e.g., EI Star Profile, Derailer Detector) that leaders or executive coaches and others will want to include in their toolboxes. His discussion of the Assumption Ladder and the Emotional Audit are two techniques/tools that I have personally added to my 'toolbox,' used, and I have found this material, as well as so much more, extremely helpful."

Ed Nottingham, Ph.D.
Author, It's Not as Bad as It Seems: A Thinking Straight Approach to Happiness

"The EI Star Profile and Derailer Detector in *Leading with Emotional Intelligence* have provided great insights for my clients. These tools give leaders an opportunity to improve their understanding of Emotional Intelligence competencies and gain insight into their own Emotional Intelligence strengths and weaknesses."

Guy Summers, President
Farrell Group, LLC

"Relly, I believe, is one of the world's foremost Executive Coaches. I believe that by providing us with *Leading with Emotional Intelligence*, Relly readily shares his wisdom and experience not only with his readers, but also, by his practical 'realistic applications' approach, to help both new leaders and successful business leaders. Relly shows and teaches us how to close the gap between concepts and applications time and time again. Rather than being limited by the boundaries of their previous knowledge; now my clients are already achieving immediate results from some of the fantastic tools and techniques Relly offers his readers. The Assumption Ladder has been readily embraced by a number of my clients as a 'must have' in the preparation and planning and communication of their decisions."

Ann-Marie Docherty, Master Industrial Relations
Graduate, Australian Institute of Company Directors
2001 Telstra Business Women of the Year

"Nadler's *Leading with Emotional Intelligence* is a great way for both leaders and coaches to learn and grow. EI is powerful. It is an essential element for both business and coaching, and when integrated with wellness is a strong formula for success. Read this book, apply it, and the positive effects for you and your firm will be the reward."

Cathy L. Greenberg, Ph.D., Co-author of
What Happy Companies Know, What Happy Women Know,
What Happy Working Mothers Know
Managing Partner, h2c, LLC, Happy Companies, Healthy People

"Relly Nadler's *Leading with Emotional Intelligence* provides the kind of real-world guidance that is so often missing from leadership books. The tools and techniques are immediately applicable, and it has become the primary text I use for my training and coaching work."

Nick Rothenberg
OD Consultant and Owner, 2Be, LLC

"Dr. Reldan Nadler has provided a useful tool for women seeking to advance their careers and themselves. Few women are lucky enough to have a personal coach, but the content of this book is going to be very helpful, particularly the worksheets, inventories, and templates. *Leading with Emotional Intelligence* can only encourage women to have confidence in these skills and motivate women to stretch themselves in new directions—including reaching for top executive leadership positions."

Lois Phillips, Ph.D., Co-author of Women Seen and Heard: Lessons Learned from Successful Speakers

"I was able to apply how the stages of a team's development can be used for building trust and cohesion even in the midst of conflict. The strategies for developing others outlined in the book are full of practical take-aways and valuable for any leader's coaching toolbox."

Steve Romano
Director of Organizational Development and Training
The Kleinfelder Group

"All coaches know that a practical, hands-on guide to how you actually improve EI is critical to building this competency. This is the 'field guide' we needed."

Diane Foster, Certified Master Coach
M.A. Career Development
Principal, Diane Foster & Associates

"*Leading with Emotional Intelligence* and the *Leadership Keys* are not for 'short-ball-hitter' leaders. They are practical and insightful tools for leaders who know that blind spots and things that go bump in the night are what cause failure. These tools bring insight and therefore awareness that can support overall success."

T. H. Stevenson, President/CEO
Cleveland Consulting Group, Inc.

"Relly Nadler's *Leading with Emotional Intelligence* represents a very rich starter toolkit for new coaches and a great reference for the experienced coach. I was impressed by the strategies' simplicity and how quickly I was able to integrate them into my coaching practice."

Brigadier-General (Retired) Charles Lemieux
OMM, MSC, CHRP, MPEC
President, CNSL Consultants, Inc.

"Relly Nadler, in *Leading with Emotional Intelligence*, shares 100+ strategies for leaders to turn 'just-another-player' employees into Star Performers. With *Leading with Emotional Intelligence*, you're never at a loss for ideas. Pick up this book, open to any page, and you will find a key lesson in leadership."

Sylva K. Leduc, M.Ed., MPEC
Leadership Specialist

"Emotional Intelligence behaviors can be learned, and *Leading with Emotional Intelligence* combines practical techniques for improvement with real-life experiences of leaders in business and politics. This is an essential resource for everyone interested in how leaders can improve their relationships with others, and ultimately achieve greater business results."

Anna Hinder
Searl Street Consulting, Australia

LEADING
WITH
EMOTIONAL
INTELLIGENCE

**HANDS-ON STRATEGIES
FOR BUILDING CONFIDENT and
COLLABORATIVE
STAR PERFORMERS**

Reldan S. Nadler, Psy.D.

New York Chicago San Francisco Lisbon London Madrid Mexico City
Milan New Delhi San Juan Seoul Singapore Sydney Toronto

The *McGraw·Hill* Companies

3 4 5 6 7 8 9 10 11 12 13 14 15   QFR/QFR   1 9 8 7 6 5 4 3

ISBN   978-0-07-175095-0
MHID   0-07-175095-9

Library of Congress Cataloging-in-Publication Data

Nadler, Reldan, S., 1951–
    Leading with emotional intelligence : hands-on strategies for building confident and collaborative star performers / by Reldan S. Nadler.
        p.   cm.
    ISBN: 978-0-07-175095-0 (hardback : acid-free paper)
    1. Leadership.   2. Emotional intelligence.   I. Title.

    BF637.L4N33   2011
    658.3'14—dc22   2010027285

Interior design by Patricia Bacall

*This book is dedicated to Martin S.
and Patricia S. for their inspiration, years of teamwork,
and love of the written word.*

*Also in memory of Ann Nadler, L.O.M.,
for her teachings on love, nurturance, fun, and
the art of giving and relationship-building.*

*To Dillon and McKensey for your abundant gifts,
talents, and opportunities for Juli and me
to grow our Emotional Intelligence.*

CONTENTS

CHAPTER TWO: EMOTIONAL SELF-CONTROL
TOOLS AND STRATEGIES   83

PREFACE

s a psychologist doing executive coaching, leadership development training, and consulting in organizations, I have found the research, concepts, and application of Emotional Intelligence (EI), also called Emotional Quotient (EQ), to be a powerful selling tool and validation for this important work. The additional knowledge sets of Social Intelligence, brain neuroscience, and "mindsight" have added intrigue and hard science to business performance. What CEO or organization doesn't want more Star Performers—successful leaders—in their ranks? But as I began using the EI research and the Emotional Competence Inventory (ECI) tool, I identified a significant gap between the big concepts and how to apply them. Like you, leaders, managers, trainers, consultants, and coaches want to know what will make them more successful today and are less interested in the rigmarole of organizational and personality theory. Simply put, when I began training people in EI, I heard a lot of, "I think the concepts and goals are great. Now, what can I do today to help raise my Emotional Intelligence?"

Numerous books and papers have been written on the topic, but most are either too general or theoretical. I needed a resource that was practical, accessible, and filled with specific strategies that could easily be applied to help executives and their direct reports raise their Emotional Intelligence without a lot of fuss or muss. When I read a business or leadership book, I want to get one or two "hard-hitting" actions that I can immediately apply. If successful, these strategies can enrich the individuals' and organization's life and effectiveness. In addition, then I have a tried-and-true practice I can use in my next consulting engagement.

Not finding this kind of book, I was inspired to create *Leading with Emotional Intelligence* (an update of *Leaders' Playbook*) to fill the gap between theory and practice. This book, I hope, will raise Emotional Intelligence for you, your direct reports or clients, and your organization. It will add strategies and actions to your toolbox, augment your work, and promote Star Performance in all of your endeavors.

Over the last 30 years I have worked with more than 15,000 leaders in corporations, organizations, groups, and teams, always looking for what works to separate the great from the good. What are the specific endeavors that make them successful? Here you will read the secrets of Star Performers, plus have me as your coach to move into the top 10% of your field. Just doing a few of these "micro-initiatives" can create "macro impacts" on your performance.

Leading with Emotional Intelligence is part of a series of resources for leaders to use to improve Emotional Intelligence. Other resources and tools explore different competencies and the secrets of Stars and successful coaches. The website www.leading withei.com has *free* EI assessments, tools, and articles.

Leading with Emotional Intelligence allows you to discover the secrets of Stars from a cross section of different industries and helps you use the powerful strategies of a seasoned executive coach. Like a successful coach's playbook from professional sports, this book should become well-worn and guarded from your competitors!

—*Reldan S. Nadler, Psy.D., MCC*

ACKNOWLEDGMENTS

I would like to first thank my family—my wife, Juli, for her creative touch, warmth, enthusiasm, love, and support; my son, Dillon, for his curiosity, cleverness, creativity, and critical eye on parts of the book; and my daughter, McKensey, for her creative spark, story listening, big heart, and love for people.

To my main men, Lux and Gregg, for being on the Board, for their humor, ideas, ski trips, and for helping me to keep my perspective of what is really important in life.

A sincere thanks to the executives profiled in *Leading with Emotional Intelligence*—Henrik, Paulette, Mark, and John—for their time sharing their life stories and the help they gave in weaving together the fabric of what makes them Stars.

I also want to thank all of the executives and companies who have allowed me to learn and practice my ideas, and who continue to teach me how to be effective in the corporate and organizational world.

Thanks, too, to my colleagues at the College of Executive Coaching (CEC) and Jeff Auerbach, for the stimulating conversations about the theory, research, and practice of developing Star Performers. Also to all of the students at CEC who gave me feedback, ideas, and support for the tools presented in *Leading with Emotional Intelligence*.

To my other esteemed colleagues: Nick Rothenberg, for his insightful feedback, camaraderie, and support of these tools; Steve Roberts, for his facilitation expertise, creativity, and ease to work with; Patricia Schwartz, for her help with the manuscript and enthusiasm; and Michelle Loomis, for her excitement and encouragement for this book.

A special thanks to Dr. Cathy Greenberg, my co-host on "Leadership Development News," our VoiceAmerica top business Internet radio show bringing cutting edge leadership tools and concepts to our listeners. Her happiness, wisdom, and experience have made interviewing leadership gurus very educational and delightful.

I want to thank the Emotional Intelligence community. To Daniel Goleman, for his initiative, leadership, and integration of all of the theory and research. To Richard Boyatzis and the Hay Group, for their expertise in identifying and developing competencies and for the creation of the Emotional Competency Inventory (ECI). To Bill Tredwell of the Hay Group, for his ideas, enthusiasm, and support.

Thank you to my friends and colleagues at Outward Bound and the Association of Experiential Education, who gave me the "best practice field" to learn about Star Performance as well as an abundance of tips, strategies, and tools.

To my Confluent Education mentors—George Brown, Stu Shapiro, and Mark Phillips—for teaching me about Emotional Intelligence before it was formally named.

To my extended family—Nancy, Larry, Michael, Katherine, Van, Martine, and all the Nadlers and Hayeses—for their years of support and love.

To Ilene Segalove, for her clarity, insight, and support.

To Ellen Reid and the Star book team of Laren Bright, Patricia Bacall, Brookes Nohlgren, and Natalie Gibency—for their expertise, perfection, calmness under fire, and professionalism in creating this book. To Julie Simpson for her proofreading and attention to detail.

To the UCSB students who contributed to the creation of this book—Ian Farr, Steve Hall, Tony Muna, Martin Young, and Brenton Gieser. Westmont students Ralph Walton and Trevor Alleman, who contributed research, are on their way to successful careers.

And lastly, I want to thank my friends Roger, Charlie, the Santa Barbara bunch, and the Paramus crowd for teaching me the foundation, specifics, and practice of Emotional Intelligence.

INTRODUCTION

WHY EMOTIONAL INTELLIGENCE?

Jim bumbled his way through his first presentation to the board in his new role as CFO. The CEO, Steve, was very disappointed and surprised by Jim's performance. Jim had forgotten to bring his memory stick to the presentation, but only discovered his oversight as he set up and all the board members were filing into the room. Kicking himself, and obviously thrown off, Jim had to talk about the slides from his handout. His performance reflected this—by his nervousness, disorganization, and lack of poise. Steve, who had supported Jim for the CFO position, exclaimed afterward, "What happened? I was counting on you. Now you are going to have an uphill battle to get back your credibility with this group, if you can."

Dejected and miffed, Jim asked himself the same thing: "What happened?" Half a dozen scenes replayed through his head:

1. On the way to the meeting, Mary, one of his best employees, had told him she was very disappointed in her review and was going to write a rebuttal. He was taken aback at her comments and at the bad timing, as Mary knew he was going to a big meeting. Jim was very short and defensive with her, which was not like him, and he immediately regretted his reaction.

2. He had raced to work this morning, as he had to drop off his daughter, McKensey, at school on the way. She was late getting out of the house because she was looking for one of her shoes.

1

3. Driving to work, he was thinking about the two people from his department he would have to let go at the end of the day. He still wasn't sure how he was going handle this, and it added to his feeling of being overwhelmed.

4. He had gotten only four and a half hours of sleep the night before, as he was worried about the presentation. In addition, he was anxious about telling his wife about two upcoming business trips he would have to take with the new position. He knew she would be upset as she worried this new position would have him traveling more and she was concerned about the impact on the family.

5. He had left the house in a rush this morning with his mind full of all the tasks ahead of him and "mindlessly" walked right past his memory stick, even though he had placed it by the front door with his notes so he would not forget anything.

All of these emotional events influenced each other, and they impacted Jim's cognitive functioning and his performance. His brain was spent, his emotions were fragile, and his ability to control them and perform at his best was impaired.

Warren Bennis, the founding father of leadership writings and insights, has called for "the field of leadership studies to attend to how we can develop leaders who understand relationships and communication, who can manage themselves and others with wisdom, creativity, and values." He identified resilience as the most important quality of a leader or anyone wanting to lead a healthy and meaningful life.[1]

Jim failed to manage himself or successfully manage others in these interactions. He was like a quarterback who threw two interceptions for touchdowns in the first half of the game and couldn't shake it or recover to perform in the second half. He didn't have the plays or strategies to rebound, recover, stay flexible, and continue to perform at his best. He needed more Emotional Intelligence to prevent this catastrophe in his first big activity in his new role.

All of us have experienced days and moments like this. We need a game plan and strategies to better manage ourselves, develop resilience, and creatively manage others for top performance. This is even more necessary when the stress and rigors of work and life compromise our brain functioning and performance. We need an Emotional Intelligence playbook.

WHY NOW: CONVERGING CHAOS

We are in the middle of a leadership "double whammy."

First, we are in the midst of what is being called the Great Recession. The country lost 8.4 million jobs from 2007 to 2009, four times the net losses in the recession of the 1980s and 1.2 million more than previously estimated. These losses are continuing in 2010. The *LA Times* reports, "The severe destruction of jobs since December 2007, when the recession began, means that it will take years for millions of distressed families—and the economy as a whole—to climb back from what is being called the Great Recession."[2]

On top of this recession, we are approaching the largest turnover of human capital in our history, as 40% of the American workforce will be eligible to retire in 2010. Leaders will have to contend with a projected shortfall of 10 million workers in the next few years.[3]

The questions leaders have to face today are abundant:

- Will I have a job?
- Will my people have jobs?
- How do I motivate the ones who are here?
- How do I keep my best people from leaving and finding more secure work?
- How do I train the ones who are here for the next challenge and to be our new Stars?
- How do we deal with more work and fewer people?
- How do we all manage our stress and enjoy work more?
- How do we do our best work with all that is going on?

- How do I hire the best people who can be our next Stars?
- How do I manage myself to keep all this in perspective and perform at my best?

David Rock has said the brain knows only two states: Is this situation a *threat* to me (with the inherent fear)? Or does this situation offer *reward* (with possible release of pleasurable brain chemicals, such as dopamine)? As you read the questions above, which state does your brain go into?[4]

EQ, IQ BRAIN DRAIN LOOP

Over my years of doing leadership training in corporations, I have run, with hundreds of people, a business scenario simulation that produces the same results every time. The basic components of the activity mirror the stress in the daily workday, which accentuates a *threat* to the brain. The lack of immediate answers and the complexity of the task result in a brain freeze of sorts, where less oxygen and blood flow are going to the brain's executive functioning area. As a result, both the EQ and IQ (Intelligence Quotient) capacity are lowered, with unintended consequences that impact the leader's style and then the team climate. As you read this, ask yourself if you experience these reactions and emotions daily.

The components of the scenario include the following:

1. **Complexity:** You have challenging problems without simple solutions. There are new systems, new people and technology, different cultures, differing needs to please, and interdependencies on others to get your job done.

2. **Urgency:** Everything is important and has to be done now, and you don't know how to get it all done.

3. **Individual performance pressure:** You want to make sure you do your job right and don't see the bigger system issues or problems that may be affecting you and others, or how you are impacting others.

The results equal overwhelm and chaos, which lead to the following consequences for the leaders and the team.

LEADERS' CONSEQUENCES

Leaders have less executive functioning brainpower operating or lower EQ and IQ going into solving the problems and therefore exhibit poorer leadership. There is more overwhelm, frustration, confusion, impatience, poor communication, blaming, and defensiveness.

In the search to solve the problems, the brain becomes reductionist: "*What* is the problem?" becomes a search for "*Who* is the problem?"

TEAM CONSEQUENCE

Team members' emotions may include feeling blamed, defensive, unacknowledged, and confused and the desire to avoid or withdraw from the process. This affects their engagement, morale, retention, and performance. Team EQ and IQ are decreased, and this result can then bring others down, as shown in Figure I.1.

The dynamic shown in Figure I.1 occurs in almost every organization unless the leader is very aware, intentional, and disciplined. The way out of this loop is to enhance your Emotional Intelligence, being aware of your reactions and your team's reactions and then modifying the plays or strategies as needed. Dan Siegel, a psychiatrist and neuroscience researcher, calls this skill mindsight, a combination of insight into yourself and empathy toward others.[5]

We have all watched football coaches pacing the sidelines of an exciting game, avidly referring to their well-worn playbooks. Like most coaches in the world of sports, leaders* in business also need an official playbook to get out of the EQ, IQ Brain Drain Loop and provide just the right strategies to enhance their success and produce more wins. A playbook is a compilation of vital strategies developed to utilize each player's unique capabilities and strengths.

---

*The term *leader* is used in this book to describe a vast cross section of roles including but not limited to individual performers, managers, coaches, trainers, and consultants. "Leaders" are either leading themselves or others to maximize their potential and capabilities.

FIGURE I.1   EQ, IQ BRAIN DRAIN LOOP

ORGANIZATIONAL DAILY DYNAMICS
Complexity, urgency, individual performance
pressure (IPP)

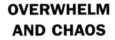

TEAM CLIMATE
Defensive about being
blamed, frustration, unsure
of what to do, withdrawal
or checking out, minimal
engagement, spreading
decreased EQ and IQ to
others on the team

**OVERWHELM
AND CHAOS**

**LEADERS' EQ
AND IQ DECREASE**

POOR LEADERSHIP
Confusion, impatience, frustration, lack
of clarity and direction, blaming others,
defensiveness, over- or under-managing

Great leaders, like superior coaches, know their players and need to have access to specific strategies to increase Star Performance. Whether you are a CEO, manager, coach, trainer, or consultant, *Leading with Emotional Intelligence* is the official hands-on guide that takes you and your team to the leading edge.

Some of the practices in this book were developed over the many years I worked closely with a variety of executive clients; others were gleaned from organizational, success, and peak performance literature. They are listed under *Coach's Corner*. Filled with specifically designed resources, tools, strategies, stories, and practices, *Leading with Emotional Intelligence* informs and inspires you to increase your Emotional Intelligence. It also features a selection of what I call "Star Profiles." These condensed interviews with important leaders illustrate a set of principles and practices that help each Star shine in one or more areas of Emotional Intelligence. Often Stars are not cognizant of exactly what they are doing that makes them so effective, and through the interview process these actions became more visible.

Leading with Emotional Intelligence focuses on *six* of the 20 key competencies of Emotional Intelligence: Emotional Self-Control, Self-Confidence, Teamwork and Collaboration, Developing Others, Communication, and Empathy. A competency is a learned ability, and each one contributes uniquely to making a leader more effective. I have chosen to focus on these six competencies because they are the ones I find executives consistently want to master first. I also believe these six competencies give leaders tools that not only help them but also guide and inspire those they lead. (See page 25 for the list of 20 competencies.)

EI VS. IQ

"Emotional Intelligence" was first coined in 1990 by Peter Salovey and John Mayer and became popularized by Daniel Goleman in his 1995 book, *Emotional Intelligence.* "Emotional Quotient," or EQ, was first termed by Dr. Reuven Bar-On in 1985. There was a time when

IQ was considered the primary determinant of success, but our IQ-idolizing view of intelligence is far too narrow. Instead, "Emotional Intelligence" is now considered the strongest indicator of success in the work world.

IQ, or Intelligence Quotient, and technical expertise help you get your job. EI, or Emotional Intelligence, is what makes you a Star Performer. IQ contributes only 4-10% toward a leader's success. But the higher up you are in an organization, the more Emotional Intelligence determines your leadership success, contributing as much as 85-90%.[6]

Emotional Intelligence, aside from being the key ingredient for success, can also protect an IQ drain or dive when either stress or emotionality can affect cognitive functioning. Leaders with more Emotional Intelligence are more adaptable, resilient, and optimistic. Emotional Self-Control will be explored more in Chapter 2.

Today there are three main schools of Emotional Intelligence, each with its own unique models and tools for measuring EI. Mayer, Salovey, and Caruso's abilities-based concept uses a self-assessment instrument called the Mayer, Salovey and Caruso Emotional Intelligent Test, or MSCEIT. The Bar-On model, developed by Reuven Bar-On, uses the Emotional Quotient Inventory (EQi). And the Goleman, Boyatzis and Hay Group model uses the 360-degree assessment Emotional Competence Inventory (ECI) and Emotional and Social Competence Inventory (ESCI). (See the Additional Resource section for more information about these assessments and others.)

Now with advances in new fields such as Social Neuroscience, Cognitive Social Neuroscience, and NeuroLeadership, we have added "Social Intelligence" to the Emotional Intelligence concept and vernacular to capture what Goleman calls "two person psychology: what transpires as we connect."[7] PET scans and functional MRIs have added data to the dance between people's brains when they interact. These advances are adding to what we know about leadership, "followship," innovation, emotional regulation, creativity, and decision-making. Leadership is accomplished through social relationships, and we are "wired to connect."[8]

The term Social Intelligence was first coined by Edward Thorndike in 1920 and defined as the ability to understand and manage men and women. Reuven Bar-On, a psychologist and one of the founding fathers of Emotional Intelligence, has used the term Emotional and Social Intelligence from his start. Goleman, in his book *Social Intelligence*, expanded the working definitions to call the personal side of the equation Emotional Intelligence and the social side Social Intelligence.

For the purpose of this book, I will use the generic term Emotional Intelligence to incorporate the advances of Social Intelligence, brain neurosciences, and the new field of NeuroLeadership.

The Emotional Intelligence definition I will use is the two-by-two model shown in the following chart from the Goleman, Boyatzis and Hay Group model. EI can be defined in terms of understanding yourself, managing yourself, understanding others, and managing others. People who possess high Emotional Intelligence are the ones who truly succeed in work—building flourishing careers and long-lasting relationships as well as having a balanced work and home life.

	SELF	OTHERS
Awareness	Self-Awareness	Other Awareness
Management	Self-Management	Relationship Management

STAR PERFORMERS SHINE AND SO CAN YOU

The corporate world became enamored with EI, which led to Goleman's writing of a second book, *Working with Emotional Intelligence* in 1998, and then, in 2006, *Social Intelligence*. As EI research and theory grew in popularity and impact, Goleman helped found the creation of the Consortium for Research on Emotional Intelligence in Organizations with Cary Cherniss; Richard Boyatzis, from Case

Western Reserve University; the Hay Group, a consulting firm; and others who collaborated on in-depth research. Goleman, Boyatzis, and the Hay Group developed a useful application, a 360-degree assessment to measure Emotional Intelligence, called the Emotional Competence Inventory (ECI).

A Star Performer is defined as a person performing in the top 10% of an organization . . .

They have recently added the Emotional Social Competency Inventory (ESCI), which has fewer competencies and is used more for research. In addition, Goleman, Boyatzis, and McKee wrote *Primal Leadership*, and Boyatzis and McKee wrote *Resonant Leadership*. The Additional Resources section lists quality resources that highlight the big three EI models, other important EI models, neuroscience, and NeuroLeadership. The research generated from these sources is rich, compelling, and invaluable. It is now possible to confidently identify the key competencies that make Star Performers. A Star Performer is defined as a person performing in the top 10% of an organization, while average performers make up 60-80% of the workforce.[9]

Here are some brief examples that describe the critical benefits of developing Emotional Intelligence:

Boyatzis and Ratti did a study in 2009 with managers and leaders in Italy and found that emotional, social, and cognitive intelligence competencies predict performance. More specifically, in the EI competency cluster, effective executives showed more initiative, while effective middle level managers showed more planning than their less effective counterparts. Similarly, in the Social Intelligence competency cluster, effective executives were more distinguished in networking, self-confidence, persuasiveness, and oral communication.[10]

Dries and Pepermans, in a study with 102 managers conducted in 2007, found that high-potential managers had higher scores on the Emotional Quotient Inventory (EQi) than "regular" managers. They had high scores in specific subscales that included Assertiveness, Independence, Optimism, Flexibility, and Social Responsibility. Many of the EQi competencies correlate with the model presented here and the EI Star Profile used as a self-assessment in this book.[11]

The Yale EI group, in a study conducted in 2006 with 44 analysts and clerical employees from the finance department of a Fortune 400 insurance company, found that emotionally intelligent individuals received greater merit increases and held higher company rank than their counterparts. They also received better peer and supervisor ratings than their counterparts on interpersonal facilitation and stress tolerance. In the study, the Yale EI group used the MSCEIT self-assessment and the EQi 360-degree feedback, plus company indicators of work performance.[12]

Steve Stein, in a study of 76 CEOs in 2002, found the CEOs had higher than average scores on Independence, Assertiveness, Optimism, Self-Regard, and Self-Actualization using the EQi.[13]

TalentSmart, an EI consultancy that uses a modification of the Goleman, Boyatzis, and Hay Group model, has given over 500,000 EI surveys. Travis Bradberry and Jean Greaves report the following findings in their 2009 book *Emotional Intelligence 2.0*:

1. EI scores had gone up from 2003 till 2007 and then went down in the hard times of 2008.

2. There was little difference in EI scores between the genders.

3. Of males who ranked in the top 15% in decision-making, 70% also scored the highest in Emotional Intelligence skills. Bradberry and Greaves point out that "paying attention to your emotions is the most logical way to make good decisions."

4. Middle managers had the highest EQ scores; for titles of directors and above the scores went down, with CEOs having the lowest EQ scores. The authors assume this may be because

people are promoted more for what they know or how long they have worked for a company than for their skill in managing others. They reassert, though, that "EQ skills are more important to job performance than any other skill. The same holds true for every job title; those with the highest EQ scores within any position outperform their peers."

5. EQ and age showed a big gap in self-management between the older generations, Traditionalists (born 1922-1944) and Baby Boomers (born 1945-1964), and the younger generations, Generation X (born 1965-1976) and Generation Y (born 1977-1998). The biggest gap was between the Boomers and Generation Y. Self-management and overall EQ both increase with age: 60-year-olds scored higher than 50-year-olds, who scored higher than 40-year-olds, and so on.

6. In examining the rise of China as an economic power, Talent-Smart studied 3,000 Chinese executives. They found that American executives scored 15 points lower than the Chinese executives in self-management and relationship management. This makes sense considering that in Chinese culture, business is personal and executives regularly meet over dinner to discuss business and family, which is part of the relationship management competencies. They also see personal outbursts as shameful and have learned to manage their impulses in contrast to the lack of impulse control we have seen with some Americans (see Chapter 2).[14]

For 515 senior executives analyzed by the search firm Egon Zehnder International, those who were primarily strong in Emotional Intelligence were more likely to succeed than those who were strongest in either relevant previous experience or IQ.[15]

"Analyses done by dozens of different experts in close to five hundred corporations, government agencies, and non profit organizations worldwide have arrived at remarkably similar conclusions . . .

all point to the paramount place of emotional intelligence in excellence on the job—in virtually all jobs."[16]

Competency research in over 200 companies and organizations worldwide suggests that about one-third of this difference is due to technical skill and cognitive ability, while two-thirds is due to emotional competence.[17]

"In general the higher a position, 85 percent of their competencies for success were in the EI domain."[18]

WHO IS THIS BOOK FOR?

This book is for everyone who wants to move up or perform better in his or her role by applying Emotional Intelligence strategies and tools.

If you are:

- An Individual Performer, you can use *Leading with Emotional Intelligence* to see what competencies you need to focus on to become a Star Performer. You don't have to supervise someone else, but can use the tools to improve your own performance in a safe, well-paced manner.

- An Executive or Manager in an organization, you usually have development plans in place for the people you supervise to bring them to the next level. The problem arises when you don't have the training, experience, or time to help your people know *what* to do differently after helping them identify their development areas. *Leading with Emotional Intelligence* provides you with a map and proven tools to support positive changes as you guide your direct reports toward becoming Star Performers.

- A Coach of any kind—whether working with business executives and leaders or life, personal, and career coaching—you can effectively use all of the tools in *Leading with Emotional Intelligence* to enhance your work. The strategies included will raise the Emotional Intelligence of your clients and will promote Star Performance in all of your respective fields of work.

- A Trainer or Consultant who wants to bring Emotional Intelligence concepts into your organizations, you will find ideas and practices that will instantly integrate into your established practice or curriculum.

WHAT YOU'LL LEARN TO DO

Following are the key benefits you will receive from *Leading with Emotional Intelligence.*

- Assess yourself (and your direct reports or clients) to determine how you rate in all 20 key competencies necessary for being a Star Performer.

- Identify possible derailers for yourself (and your direct reports or clients) on various career paths.

- Review the research that validates and supports specific Emotional Intelligence competencies to become a Star Performer.

- Read Star Profiles of successful leaders and discover their secrets and daily practices in particular areas of competency.

- Select specific development actions for yourself, your direct reports, or your clients to start the Star Journey.

- Present materials to your teams or clients to raise their Emotional Intelligence.

- Become more conversant in giving solid and specific answers to the following leadership questions as you mobilize toward becoming a Star Performer in your chosen field:
    - ▲ How can I become more effective as a leader?
    - ▲ How do I best manage my emotions?
    - ▲ How do I develop my people to be our next leaders?
    - ▲ How can I communicate to be more successful?

▲ What can I do at my next team meeting to improve morale and performance?

▲ How do I increase my confidence to take the steps to be a Star?

GETTING STARTED: THE IDEAL PLAN

Here is an overview and plan to enhance your Emotional Intelligence and that of the people you work with.

- First read Chapter 1: Are You a Star Performer or Just Average? to understand what Emotional Intelligence is all about.

- Then take the two self-assessments in Chapter 1 to evaluate your current Star Performance:

  ▲ The EI Star Profile

  ▲ The Derailer Detector

- Fill out the Star Performer Action Plan, highlighting your strengths.

- Choose one of the following five chapters featuring the six competencies that you or your clients/team need today. You need not work in chronological order!

  ▲ Chapter 2: Emotional Self-Control

  ▲ Chapter 3: Self-Confidence

  ▲ Chapter 4: Teamwork and Collaboration

  ▲ Chapter 5: Developing Others

  ▲ Chapter 6: Communication and Empathy

- Read and re-read the *Secrets & Practices* of a Star Performer and review the *Coach's Corner* of Star strategies in your chosen chapter. In this section you will learn a number of tools and action steps to improve your performance. It is written as if I were your coach, helping you face-to-face. All the plays, or strategies, are compiled in the Table of Contents and Chapter 7, with page numbers to allow for easy searching.

- Choose two or three strategies outlined from *Secrets & Practices* of a Star Performer and the *Coach's Corner* that you believe will help raise your or your clients'/team's Emotional Intelligence.

- Focus on these actions for one to two months until you develop mastery. Then integrate other strategies that will benefit you.

- Read, practice, and practice some more.

- Share your plan with a peer and your team, which will help solidify your commitment and immediately engender support for your goals.

- If you are working with a leader, show him or her your Star Performer Action Plan and set aside time to review your learning and experiences with him or her.

- You can write your responses to the questions in the book or use a notebook to record your work.

CHAPTER ONE

ARE YOU A STAR PERFORMER
OR JUST AVERAGE?

W hy be a Star Performer? Research has shown that Stars, those who fall in the top 10% of performance, produce twice as much revenue for the organization as managers in the 11th through 89th percentiles.[1] The 90th percentile is a "tipping point" where the amount of change in performance is drastic. Imagine if you had the strategies and plays to move yourself and your team into the top 10%.

This chapter gives an overview of basic concepts and practical applications of Emotional Intelligence to be a Star Performer, illustrated by a collection of Star Profiles, interviews, coaching tips, and analyses of well-known Star Performers such as Warren Buffett, President Bill Clinton, Meg Whitman (past CEO of eBay), Jeffrey Immelt (CEO of GE), and USC and NFL Seattle Seahawks football coach Pete Carroll, plus many more. You will learn more about why it is so important for leaders to develop their EI and how you and your direct reports or clients can develop it as well. Chapters 2 through 6 will build on this foundation with more in-depth discussion of the four cluster areas of EI and the key competencies necessary to be a Star.

An EI assessment called the "EI Star Profile" is included to help you and your direct reports gauge your current abilities. The influence of leaders is depicted in the section "Are You or Your Boss Debilitating?" Following that is the Derailer Detector assessment to identify in yourself or in other key players behavior that may lead to derailment. You are also invited to complete your own Star

Performer Action Plan at the end of this chapter and each of the following chapters.

LEADERSHIP SKILL GAP

Warren Bennis said one of the four major threats to our world is the current level of leadership of our human institutions, and only exemplary leadership can solve the other three key threats: nuclear/biological catastrophe, pandemic, and tribalism/assimilation.[2]

Developing strong leadership is essential for our world and our organizations to deal with the current threats and opportunities, and it is also critical in order to develop the next level of leaders or "bench strength." In normal times this is a major endeavor; now with the converging chaos of the "Great Recession" and huge human capital turnover, it is a greater challenge for both new and seasoned leaders.

Unfortunately, I have found that most leaders underperform. Certainly not on purpose, but they stay average for the same basic reasons:

1. They don't have the time to develop leadership in others.
2. They don't have the requisite skills or training to lead a team.
3. Once in a leadership position, they underestimate just how much influence they really have over their direct reports.
4. They don't employ the necessary strategies frequently enough to be successful. It is easier to put out the fire of the day than to take the time to develop their bench strength or team.

If the leader underperforms, so does the team and the organization. Some basic foundational skills or activities just don't happen with regularity with today's leaders.

This issue is highlighted by the results of recent research. For example, the Ken Blanchard Companies did four separate studies from 2003 through 2006 with 2,004 respondents, and these respondents cited developing leadership bench strength as their number one issue.

In order to understand and define the most critical components of effective leadership, the Blanchard Companies launched a follow-up study in 2006 in which more than 1,400 leaders, managers, and executives shared their views on the critical skills and common mistakes connected to leadership. The top five things leaders admitted they fail to do were the following:

1. Failing to provide appropriate feedback (praise, redirection)—82% of respondents
2. Failing to listen to or involve others in the process—81% of respondents
3. Failing to use a leadership style appropriate to the person, task, and situation (over-supervising or under-supervising)—76% of respondents
4. Failing to set clear goals and objectives—76% of respondents
5. Failing to train and develop their people—59% of respondents[3]

These are basic skills or tasks that leaders fail to do. Yet, they are critical today for leaders due to the converging chaos and double whammy leaders are hit with. We have all heard of "work-life balance"; what is needed to be a Star Performer is more "work-leadership balance." These basic leadership tasks get relegated, neglected, or ignored in favor of the crisis of the day or until it's too late and a serious problem emerges. Some 66% of employees today report they have too little interaction with their bosses.[4]

On a daily basis leaders need to be aligning brains by inspiring, delegating, giving feedback, coaching, holding accountabilities, and setting clear direction.

HOW CAN LEADERSHIP HELP AT THIS TIME?

In 2009, the Center for Creative Leadership stated that numerous in-depth studies have reached the same conclusion: organizations that invest in leadership development perform better than those that don't. In short, they found investment in leadership development programs does the following:

- Improves bottom-line financial performance
- Attracts and retains talent
- Drives a performance culture
- Increases organizational agility[5]

Bersin & Associates, an independent research firm, found that it is hard to find a company that has survived many economic cycles that does not have a sophisticated leadership development strategy in place.[6]

A study in *Harvard Business Review* by Laurie Bassie and Daniel McMurrer showed a strong link between leadership skill and the bottom line. The study looked at 11 publicly traded financial service firms and their stock price. They found that companies with higher scores for their investment in human capital delivered stock returns that were five times higher than those of companies with less emphasis on human capital.[7]

What we want and need from our leaders today is drastically different from what we needed in the past. In a 2006 *Fortune* article, Tom Neff, a top CEO recruiter, stated, "Companies don't want dictators or kings or emperors. Instead of someone who gives orders, they want someone who asks probing questions that force the team to think and find the right answers—a subtle technique."[8] In this "unprecedented war for top talent" that is raging in the global economy, a new profile of a leader is beckoned.[9]

Fortune has stated: "Talent of every type is in short supply, but the greatest shortage of all is skilled, effective managers."[10] Noel Tichy, a University of Michigan Business School professor and former chief of GE's leadership development program, says, "The leadership pipeline is broke."[11] Right Management Consultants, a major outplacement firm, found that "77% of companies say they don't have enough successors to their current senior managers."[12] From a survey Right also found that "the number one skill companies seek in managers is 'the ability to motivate and engage others.' Ranking a close second is the ability to communicate."[13]

All of the above data, situations, and events raise important leadership questions and point to the essential need for Emotional Intelligence answers and training.

- How can we maximize our influence as leaders?
- What lessons can we learn from our fallen or derailed leaders?
- What do Star Performers have to teach us?
- What plays or strategies can we follow to develop a company of Stars?
- What can we learn about Emotional Intelligence from profiles about some of our most public leaders?

Emotional Intelligence is often *the* missing piece of the skillset and behavior of today's leadership crisis. It is obviously crucial for organizations to promote the development of high Emotional Intelligence with all of their leaders to avoid serious problems such as lack of impulse control and employees underperforming because their leader is not clear, motivating, or acknowledging their efforts.

EQ, IQ, OR TECHNICAL EXPERTISE?

Just about every manager in the boardroom or conference room is smart, with a typical IQ score of 115 or above. IQ is actually an equalizer in corporate environments, and being a few IQ points above or below isn't really noticeable (although much meeting time is wasted as executives argue to demonstrate their few extra IQ points and "smarts"). As performers move up in their organizations, the truth is, no matter how smart they are, they inevitably leave their expertise behind. As they become managers and beyond, more of their success comes from leadership skills rather than from their IQ points or technical acumen. That means they need to cultivate many new abilities, including motivating others to new levels, coordinating efforts between team members and departments, managing deadlines, and resolving conflicts.

There is an obvious gap between the skill set needed to be a supervisor or a manager and a leader. At DreamWorks Animation (creators of *Shrek*, *Madagascar,* and *Kung Fu Panda*), for example, talented animators who excel in their craft have the opportunity to move up. They often leave the work they trained years to excel at and are promoted to lead other animators who were once their peers. Often they show up with little or no experience or expertise in this important new leadership position. This challenge is common in many career paths where individuals find themselves moving up the corporate ladder. What do they do? What do they need to learn to lead and lead well? This is where Emotional Intelligence can provide the skills to help them succeed in their new leadership position. The good news is EI can be learned and enhanced, where IQ is fixed. *Leading with Emotional Intelligence* will provide the plays to advance.

> As they become managers and beyond, more of their success comes from leadership skills rather than from their IQ points or technical acumen.

HOW TO BE A STAR PERFORMER—NEW RULES FOR SUCCESS

	INDIVIDUAL	SUPERVISOR/MANAGER
Motivation	Self	Diverse group
Communication	Few people	Team & cross teams
Rewards	Own effort & immediate	Success of the team, longer term
Accountability	Self	Team
Quality	Self	Diverse group
Time management	Self	Team

Martin Moskovits was a good example of a man who came into his job with a high IQ and great technical skill who was challenged to rise up to a leadership position. Moskovits was the Dean of Mathematics, Physical and Life Sciences, for the University of California at Santa Barbara (UCSB). He had a Ph.D. in Chemistry and led 13 departments, 250 professors, 4,000 undergraduates, and 600 graduate students. Fifty percent of research funding for UCSB came to his programs, and in the last few years three professors from his departments were awarded the Nobel Prize. How much of his day-to-day work was involved with his technical expertise, chemistry? Not much. But Moskovits was a great leader because he had many strengths in the competencies of Emotional Intelligence. He could manage relationships with professors and donors, had empathy for others and elicited trust, was an inspiring speaker, and knew how to use his influence to get things done.

Generation X, born from 1965 to 1976, has been documented to have lower EI than the Baby Boomers because of all the hours they have spent interacting with technology including computers, electronic games, and TV versus being in a social situation dealing with others. Also fewer and fewer X-ers are entering the workplace to replace the Boomers. There are 78 million Boomers retiring in the next 10-15 years and only 45 million X-ers to replace them. This data points to the beginning of a crisis phase in the corporate milieu, where Emotional Intelligence is needed for leadership at the highest positions in organizations. In the near future there will certainly be an "Emotional Intelligence drain as Gen Yers move to senior leadership."

> The good news is EI can be learned and enhanced, where IQ is fixed.

The Millennials, born between 1977 and 1998, are a generation nearly as large as the Baby Boomers. They are full of potential and very high maintenance. They're variously called the Internet Generation, Echo Boomers, Nexters, Generation Y, the Nintendo Generation, and the Trophy Generation.

Just as the X-ers and Boomers finalize their own negotiations for an uncertain workplace peace, optimistic Millennials find themselves at the mercy of X-er skepticism. Gen-Xers complain the Millennials are another indulged generation like the Boomers—they say they are self-absorbed. Millennials charge that Gen-Xers are cynical and aloof—that they can be a wet blanket on fresh ideas and idealism.[14]

Now, with Traditionalists (born between 1922 and 1944) over 66 years old, we have all four generations in the workforce. To be a successful leader in this social milieu demands that you have insight into yourself and empathy for others. Having a flexible leadership style and high Emotional Intelligence will help you navigate the generational differences.

Robert Kelley of Carnegie-Mellon University has interviewed people across the nation, asking this important question: "What percentage of the knowledge to do your job is stored in your own mind?" In his book, *How to Be a Star at Work*, he states that in 1986 the typical answer was "75% of the time." By 1997 the percentage had slid 15-20 points, to 55%. One company's staff members admitted that only 10% of the knowledge they needed to do their jobs was still stored in their minds![15] What does this tell us? Collaboration, teamwork, empathy, communication, networking, and initiative are vital to complete the tasks at work. The shift from IQ and technical expertise to EI and the ability to lead in many ways from the head and heart together is obvious.

> In the near future there will certainly be an "Emotional Intelligence drain."

THE FOUR AREAS OF EMOTIONAL INTELLIGENCE

In *The Emotionally Intelligent Workplace*, Cherniss and Goleman have identified the key competencies of Star Performers. This model has changed over time and is constantly being updated to correspond with current research on exactly what makes a Star. The following list is from Cherniss and Goleman.[16] A Star, again, is defined as someone who is in the top 10% of performance. The easiest definition of *Emotional Intelligence* is "exhibiting a good balance of personal and social competencies in four distinct areas or clusters:

Self-Awareness—Understanding yourself

Self-Management—Managing yourself

Social Awareness—Understanding others

Relationship Management—Managing others"

Again, the goal is not to be a Star in every competency inside of each of the four clusters, but to have a good balance of competencies across the four areas listed above. Typically having 9 or 10 competencies across the four clusters is what it takes to be a Star Performer.[17] The following diagram represents the four distinct areas and lists the 20 competencies:

THE 20 COMPETENCIES OF EMOTIONAL INTELLIGENCE [18]

PERSONAL	SOCIAL
Self-Awareness	**Social Awareness**
Emotional Self-Awareness	Empathy*
Accurate Self-Assessment	Organizational Awareness
Self-Confidence*	Service Orientation
Self-Management	**Relationship Management**
Emotional Self-Control*	Influence
Trustworthiness	Inspirational Leadership
Conscientiousness	Developing Others*
Adaptability	Building Bonds
Achievement Orientation	Teamwork and Collaboration*
Initiative	Conflict Management
	Communication*
	Change Catalyst

*You'll notice that these six competencies are addressed in this book. Emotional Self-Control, Self-Confidence, Teamwork and Collaboration, Developing Others, Communication, and Empathy were chosen because they are the key areas executives ask for support with first and foremost. They are also core abilities that will help you successfully introduce EI into your organization. Although these six will also help create resonance in others quickly, all the competencies are important.

PROFILES OF STAR PERFORMERS

The following profiles feature leaders who are Star Performers. You will have a chance to examine a diagram of their successes (and weaknesses) by reviewing how they exhibit their EI strengths on the key clusters. You will see not only what competencies have contributed to their successes but also which competencies have led some to derail and become fallen heroes. Sometimes you will notice that a competency overused can become a weakness. So that you can identify them more easily, many of the competencies are pointed out in parentheses inside of the profile and at the end of each profile.

> Because of the person's visibility and potential impact on others, one derailer can undermine or trump a whole set of EI competencies.

All of the leaders profiled have many Star competencies; otherwise, they wouldn't be as successful in their careers. What is interesting to note, though, is the power and influence of their particular derailers. A "derailer" is defined as a behavior or attitude that curtails an individual's performance or advancement. It gets that person off the track to success. Because of the person's visibility and potential impact on others, one derailer can undermine or trump a whole set of EI competencies. These "fatal flaws" must be attended to and ameliorated for a leader to sustain his or her success.[19]

The determination of what competencies these leaders excel in is from a variety of sources written about them in the public domain. The depictions are inferred rather than established from interviews or assessments. The aim is to illustrate, inform, and match which behaviors to focus on to be a star in your organization.

Everyone has different opinions of public figures, and you may disagree with how these leaders are profiled on the EI competencies. The goal is to look at them through the lenses of Emotional and Social Intelligence competencies and assess which behaviors are effective and which aren't, irrespective of your political persuasion, your ideology, or opinion of the leaders. Behavior is always interpretive, and with high-profile leaders we have an opportunity to know more about their behaviors and patterns than we do with other leaders, even though these portrayals are highly influenced by the media. My hope is that the specific behaviors of Stars that are salient in these profiles will serve as a view of Emotional Intelligence in action and be useful to you and others in developing leaders.

In reading these profiles and the profiles of other successful leaders in this book, you will see their ability to be resilient after a failure or a derailer. These became turning points for their resurrection and return to Starhood. Pay attention to which parts of their stories impress or attract you, as that will be a sign that there is information for you and your development in that story.

HOW STAR PERFORMERS SHINE

The charts for each profile illustrate and clarify the components of Star Performers. Notice how Stars are able to demonstrate the personal and social competencies in each of the boxes. True Stars know and manage themselves and understand and motivate others. Goleman has stated that one needs to focus on the personal side of emotional competencies first in order to successfully enhance the social competencies. A star (★) indicates that the profiled person is a Star Performer in that cluster of competencies, while a noose (🪢)

may indicate a derailer or potential problem for the individual. The EI competency or competencies that are illustrated are indicated in parentheses following each example.

WARREN BUFFETT

Warren Buffett is one of the most successful investors in America's history and exemplifies a Star Performer in Emotional Intelligence. In 2008 he became the richest man in the world, and he was runner-up in 2009 with $37 billion of net worth (he lost $25 billion between 2008 and 2009).[20] In 2010 Forbes has him as #3 with $47 billion and Carlos Slim Helu of Mexico the new #1 with $53.5 billion and Bill Gates #2 with $53 billion.

Buffett employs roughly 233,000 people in more than 88 businesses.[21] He is truly a leader and a manager's manager as he is one of the few people Fortune 50 CEOs go to for advice. His holding company Berkshire Hathaway has major stock ownership in many companies and was voted the #3 World's Most Admired Company by *Fortune* magazine for 2010. In 2009 Berkshire Hathaway purchased Burlington Northern Railroad—a self-described all-in bet—and purchased a $5 billion stake in Goldman Sachs. This makes Buffett "a major stakeholder in the global economic recovery, with tentacles that span from coal to collateral debt obligations," according to *BusinessWeek*.[22] (Initiative, Achievement Orientation)

People have spent more than $1 million just to have lunch with Buffett. Chief executives of companies in which he has a stake laud his patience, foresight, and ability to capture the essence of complex financial situations in just a few words.[23] (Emotional Self-Control, Communication)

Buffett was born in Omaha, Nebraska, in 1930 as a middle child and the only son of three children. His father was a businessman and later a congressman. Buffett started school in Washington, D.C., and then went to Wharton School of Business and the University of

Nebraska for his B.A. He later received a M.S. in Economics from Columbia University.

Buffett's initiative, confidence, and interest in business were apparent at an early age. He filed his first tax return at 13 while working in his grandfather's grocery store and deducted his watch and bicycle as expenses for his newspaper route. At 15 years old he and a friend paid $25 for a pinball machine to be placed in a barbershop, and within months they had three pinball machines in different barbershops. Buffett uses his history as a measuring stick to determine a manager's passion for business. He says he can tell more about a manager's success if he had a lemonade stand as a child than by where he went to college. This is an indication of passion and love of business for him.[24]

To amass his empire Buffett first had to gain partnerships and trust with other companies and then manage those under him. Buffett's ability to accomplish these tasks demonstrates many of the competencies of Emotional Intelligence. Early in his career he took a Dale Carnegie course, considered one of the first true leadership training programs and full of EI concepts and skills. Buffett credits this training with giving him the confidence and people skills to teach investment principles at the University of Nebraska to people twice his age. (Building Bonds)

One of the competencies that Warren Buffett is known for is his hands-off management style. It is his belief that if you find the right managers and deal with them correctly, companies can run themselves. Buffett knows that the people who run the companies he owns understand the social and logistical makeup of those companies better than he does. They were hired to run them due to their aptitude for running the type of companies that they are in charge of. When Jim Kilts came out of retirement to turn Gillette around as its CEO, Buffett paid what Kilts considered the ultimate compliment. He resigned from Gillette's board and said, "If you have the right person running the business then you don't need me."[25] (Developing Others)

Buffett checks in just once a year with each company he has major ownership in and otherwise lets managers do what they do best while he suppresses the urge to micro manage the entire operation.[26] (Emotional Self-Control) He does have them update yearly who their successor would be if something happened to them.

How Warren Buffett treats these managers under his authority is particularly telling of his leadership prowess. He is a big advocate of bringing forth a positive attitude from the start and continuing that with positive reinforcement for those who perform well. An example of his Inspirational Leadership and Optimism was with American Express CEO Kenneth Chenault, who had to ask for help from Buffett when Buffett's stake in American Express had just lost $8 billion because of credit losses. Chenault knew that Buffett would be his "confidence booster." In the midst of the financial meltdown, Buffett's style was unwavering and predictable. Chenault said Buffett was "objective, direct and he knows what he believes."[27] (Self-Confidence)

Mary Buffett and David Clark have several bestselling books about Warren Buffett, including *Buffettology*, and have chronicled his "management secrets." Several other Emotional Intelligence competencies are also included in the management secrets they ascribe to him:

- Motivating others to achieve. They describe Buffett's ability to motivate others to hit one business home run after another. (Developing Others, Teamwork and Collaboration)
- Are you a victor or victim? Buffett learned to take control of his life from his father's actions in the face of adversity; for example, in the Great Depression his father started a new business. (Adaptability)
- The power of honesty. Admitting mistakes is the hallmark of trustworthiness.
- The power of praise and the dangers of criticism. Buffett believes leaders should praise by name and never misses

an opportunity to praise managers in private, at Berkshire Hathaway's annual meetings, or by announcing the praise in annual reports. If you have to criticize, criticize the category: for example, by saying the report could have been better, the sales numbers are low. (Communication, Developing Others)

- Listening well to avoid arguments and manage conflict. Buffett learned from Dale Carnegie to listen well and respect people's opinion even if they are different than his. He was also influenced by Benjamin Franklin's biography, where Franklin says he forbade himself from using language that communicated a fixed opinion, like "certainly" or "obviously," and instead adopted "I imagine" or "it appears to me."[28] (Conflict Management)

For self-renewal, Buffett plays bridge 12 hours a week and is an avid University of Nebraska football fan. Warren Buffett's successes in business, in understanding and managing himself, and in managing other high-powered individuals reflect his mastery of many of the Emotional Intelligence competencies. He is also a notable philanthropist, having pledged to give away 85% of his fortune to the Gates Foundation. (Service Orientation)

Below are the EI competencies for Warren Buffet, which show stars shining across all four clusters.

Key Strengths/Competencies
- Accurate self-assessment
- Confidence
- Initiative
- Achievement orientation
- Adaptability
- Service orientation
- Trustworthiness
- Inspirational leadership

- Communication
- Influence
- Building bonds
- Developing others
- Conflict management
- Teamwork and collaboration

Derailers

- No major ones noticed

EI Ratings: Warren Buffett

	PERSONAL	SOCIAL
Understanding	Self	Others
	★	★
Managing	Self	Others
	★	★

CARLY FIORINA

Carly Fiorina is a good example of the resiliency that Warren Bennis said is the key attribute of a leader. Since leaving the CEO position of Hewlett Packard (HP) in 2005 under pressure from her board of directors, Fiorina has reemerged into the spotlight—one, as a breast cancer survivor, and two, as a candidate for the Senate from the state of California. She said her breast cancer experience steeled her for a rough-and-tumble campaign against Barbara Boxer.

In 2008 Fiorina also showed that she could follow the lead of others in a new realm as she supported John McCain. During McCain's run for office, Fiorina acted as his chairman of fundraising.[29] This political experience has led her to venture out on her own in politics. She has secured a total of $2.7 million for her campaign to replace California Democratic Senator Barbara Boxer in the 2010 election.

Fiorina's desire to serve and give back in politics will test her Emotional and Social Intelligence. She demonstrates many of the EI competencies across the personal and social clusters. She was the first woman to head a Dow 30 company and the first "outsider" of HP in 60 years to take the reins of the computer giant. Hewlett-Packard today is a $72 billion company and Fiorina helped orchestrate the biggest tech merger to date, with Compaq. She set her initial objectives on building a new vision for HP as an Internet company—jump-starting its innovation and recalibrating HP's vaulted culture. *Fortune* magazine said Fiorina is "a world-class risk taker."[30] Her strategy failed, though, in the eyes of her board. The stock price during her tenure was down 50%, where Dell was only down 9%.[31]

In *Fortune* Fiorina was rated #1 of the 50 most powerful women in American business.[32] She is a charismatic leader known for a personal touch. A standard practice of hers is giving balloons and flowers to employees who land big contracts, which inspires intense loyalty and appreciation. (Developing Others/ Empathy)

The *Wall Street Journal* said, "She was an alluring, controversial new breed of CEOs who combine grand visions with charismatic but self-centered and demanding style." She was decisive and had crisp presentation skills and was "accused of valuing boldness over precision and follow-through."[33] Her overused confidence may have turned into a weakness. Inside HP she was a polarized figure who could be abrupt and autocratic. Many high-level executives had quit recently and that concerned the board. Fiorina was becoming more irritated and defensive about her strategy. She failed to empower others as much as she could, and in January 2005 the board wanted to distribute her power and she initially disagreed.

Before HP, Fiorina was at Lucent Technologies, a spin-off of AT&T. She took them public and launched a flashy marketing campaign that repositioned them from a maker of phone equipment to an Internet company. She landed on *Fortune's* cover in 1998 with the caption, "The Most Powerful Woman in American Business." "Affable and strikingly confident, she is a natural leader. At Lucent, she is said to have won the hearts as well as the minds of her staff," (Confidence and Leadership) said Louise Kehoe of the *Financial Times*.[34] Fiorina always said leadership was gender-neutral.

She was selected out of 300 potential CEOs for her ability to:

- Conceptualize and communicate new strategies
- Deliver on quarterly financial goals with operational savvy
- Bring urgency to the organization with powerful vision
- Drive a new net vision through the company with strong management skills (Leadership, Change Catalyst, Influence, and Communication)

She is very customer-focused and understands that what the customer needs is not always what he or she asks for (Service Orientation). She is up at 4 A.M. to feed her birds and work out. "It's a good thinking time," she says. (Self-Management)

Fiorina's father is a federal court judge and law professor. Her mother was a painter and was the strongest person she knew. Fiorina has a B.A. from Stanford and went to law school at UCLA, before dropping out. As a child, Fiorina moved frequently. "I always landed in a whole new place . . . You learn to be self-reliant. It didn't scare me anymore."[35]

Fiorina spends a lot of time boating with her husband of 17 years, who is retired, and she has two stepdaughters and a 3-year-old granddaughter.

Key Strengths/Competencies

- Developing others
- Empathy
- Confidence
- Change catalyst

- Influence
- Communication
- Service orientation
- Leadership
- Initiative
- Achievement orientation

Derailers

- Confidence (overused)
- Initiative (overused)
- Drives others too hard
- Self-promotion

From above, Carly Fiorina is clearly a Star in three clusters, but her overused confidence, an inability to accurately assess her strengths and weaknesses, and not delegating authority to others may have led to her resignation. Whether her stardom will rise again in politics will be determined by voters versus a board.

EI Ratings: Carly Fiorina

	PERSONAL	SOCIAL
	Self	Others
Understanding	👎	★
	Self	Others
Managing	★	★

JEFFREY IMMELT

Jeffrey Immelt was appointed Chairman of the Board and CEO of General Electric (GE) on September 7, 2001. Founded in 1892, GE is one of the most powerful and respected companies in the world, with over 300,000 employees in 160 countries, representing 11 financial, services, and technology businesses. GE is the country's biggest exporter with 60% of their revenue from outside the U.S.[36]

In 2006 *Fortune* reported that GE was rated #1 in the World's Most Admired Companies for the sixth time in eight years.[37]

During the Great Recession it dropped to #9 in 2009 and #16 in 2010. John Chambers, CEO of CISCO, rated Immelt as the CEO he most admires and stated, "The job that GE and Jeff Immelt have done is the best in business. You learn a lot about a person and a company during the tough times."[38] Immelt is on President Obama's economic recovery advisory board.

Immelt's initial entry into GE was challenging. Not only did he follow the legendary Jack Welch, who had been CEO for twenty years, but he also took his new position only four days before 9/11 and the collapse of the World Trade Center. His leadership has been highlighted by weathering many storms and much criticism, but Immelt has pulled through and shined because he has demonstrated many of the EI competencies in his long and distinguished career.

In 1994, when Immelt was vice president of GE Plastics American, he almost got fired for poor performance. Instead of reaching his 20% profit goal, he delivered only 7% in earnings growth with a missed income of approximately $50 million!

In an interview with *Fast Company*, Immelt recalled the dramatic subsequent events. During the annual leadership meeting in 1995, he was actively avoiding having the "tough talk" with Welch and tried to escape the auditorium. Welch grabbed him as he was slipping away and said, "Jeff I am your biggest fan, but you just had your worst year in the company. Just the worst year. I love you and I know you can do better. But I'm going to take you out if you can't get it fixed."[39] (This is a good example of tough empathy from Welch.)

"Even though I came close to being fired," Immelt added, "I never considered quitting. I knew the issues were my fault and I didn't want to let my people down." He described this experience as the most painful time in his entire career. But Immelt is highly adaptable, and he reflected, "Surviving a failure gives you more self-confidence. Failures are great learning tools—but they must be kept at a minimum."[40] (Trustworthiness, Confidence, Adaptability)

"There was only one person who thought I had a future at GE then, and it was me." He stated that at meetings people thought he was a "dead man walking." Immelt learned that no one was going to define who he was and only he could get himself out of the fix.[41] (Initiative, Achievement Orientation)

Immelt had been in training for the CEO position for 20 years. He started working at GE in 1982 and held global leadership roles in many of GE's businesses. He earned a B.A. from Dartmouth, where he also played football, and an M.B.A. from Harvard University. He worked at Proctor and Gamble in 1978, where Steven Ballmer, now CEO of Microsoft, was his office mate.

Immelt can be a firm leader but not the bully Welch was. He has fired friends, but did it in a nice way, even calling them after they left to see how they were doing.[42] (Conflict Management) Since being named Chairman-elect in 1999, Immelt also made it a point to engage a wider spectrum of people; now 50% of all senior executives and 54% of new corporate officers are women, minorities, or foreign employees.[43]

Immelt is highly optimistic and keeps his focus on the future and how to make it better. "I've always believed the future is going to be better than the past . . . and I believe I have a role in that."[44] In talking about how to motivate others to get through tough times, Immelt emphasizes the need to be straight with people. "You need to let them know where you are and communicate how the road looks for them."[45] (Inspiring Leadership, Change Catalyst) His father worked at GE for 38 years, and Immelt personally experienced the effects of a good or bad boss on his father's motivation and the whole family's sense of well-being. (Empathy)

In a talk Immelt gave to the Military Academy at West Point in 2009, he emphasized, "The agenda for our country and the complexity of our challenges require us to rethink what aspects of leadership we need to emphasize. . . . It takes courage to rethink your leadership paradigm. But I recognized that if I wanted the company to change, that I would have to change myself. And, a good leader is never too old to learn"[46] (Accurate Self-Assessment)

One of the best practices he identified to improve on and shared with the cadets was listening. "I decided that I needed to be a better listener coming out of the crisis. I felt like I should have done more to anticipate the radical changes that occurred. To that end, about twice each month, I invite one of our top 25 leaders to a Saturday session where we talk about the company, the future, and each other. At that session, we are 'two friends talking.' I encourage an open critique of each other. Listening in this way has built trust and commitment. My top leaders want to be in a company where their voice is heard."[47] (Building Bonds, Developing Others)

Immelt spends four to five days a month with customers as well as attending two town-hall meetings per month with hundreds of customers. He initiated "dreaming sessions" with them. Together, Immelt and customers brainstorm where the business will be in five to ten years. (Service Orientation) In 2010 GE will spend almost $6 billion to launch 100 new products.

GE spends more than $1 billion a year on training and education programs. Immelt says he spends 30% of his own time teaching and coaching. This is a huge commitment to leadership development and follows a practice of Welch's, who was known to spend more than 50% of his time teaching leadership to his people.[48] (Developing Others)

Immelt's ritual around self-management and renewal includes getting up every morning at 5:30 and working out for an hour on the treadmill, stair stepper, and elliptical trainer while watching the news and sports.[49]

Following are the EI competencies for Jeffrey Immelt, shining with stars across all four clusters.

Key Strengths/Competencies

- Accurate self-assessment
- Confidence
- Initiative
- Inspirational leadership
- Achievement orientation
- Adaptability
- Change catalyst
- Service orientation
- Empathy
- Trustworthiness
- Conflict management
- Influence
- Organizational awareness
- Developing others
- Building bonds

Derailers

- No major ones noticed (. . . yet!)

EI Ratings: Jeffrey Immelt

	PERSONAL	SOCIAL
Understanding	Self ★	Others ★
Managing	Self ★	Others ★

SERGEY BRIN

Sergey Brin is one of the founders of Google, Inc. (along with Larry Page). Google started in 1998 in a garage in Menlo Park, California, 106 years after GE began. In August 2004 Google went public in an unconventional initial public offering (IPO) at $85 and raised $2 billion, which was the largest IPO ever. Google has been on a hot streak. Its fortune went up $5.5 billion in 12 months. Google was #4 of the World's Most Admired Companies in 2009, and it was #2 in 2010.[50]

In reviewing Google's meteoric rise, I wanted to examine what EI competencies supported its huge success and chose to profile Sergey Brin to find out more. Much of what is determined for him is also true for Larry Page, and many of the EI competencies can be inferred from the environment they created together at Google.

Brin and Page are both listed as #24 in the 2010 *Forbes Magazine* featuring the richest people in the world, with a net worth of $17.5 billion. They also made 1,000 of their now 6,000 employees instant millionaires with their IPO. Brin and Page dropped out of their Ph.D. programs in Computer Science at Stanford, in their words, to "'Change the world' through a search engine that organizes every bit of information on the Web for free."[51] (Inspirational Leadership)

When they first met, they found each other obnoxious. They argued constantly about random issues, but this behavior soon turned into an intellectual game with the goal of persuading each other over to their viewpoint. Finally, they discovered common ground when it came to solving one of computing's biggest challenges—how to retrieve relevant information from a massive set of data. Today, they still debate in a shared office where they make most decisions together. They also personally approve the hiring of nearly every new employee.[52]

Brin and Page's vision for the future is: "The perfect search engine would understand exactly what you mean and give back exactly what you want." They agree that it is a far-reaching vision requiring research, development, and innovation. (Inspirational Leadership)

Google is actually a noun, a number followed by 100 zeros spelled "googol," but Brin and Page were confused about the spelling and stuck with "Google." Today, Google is synonymous with the Internet and has quickly become a verb. It is used in over 100 different languages with daily searches numbering over 250 million and indexes over 8 billion Web pages.

Sergey was born in 1973 in Moscow, Russia. His father, Mikhail, has a Ph.D. in Mathematics and teaches at the University of Maryland. His mother is also a mathematician and worked as a civil engineer. The family was forced to flee Russia in 1979 because of anti-Semitism.

Sergey has been interested in computers since he received his first Commodore 64 at age nine. He was known as a "math whiz" and one of his classmates recalled that he was "quite cocky about his intellect," often challenging his teachers. He graduated from the University of Maryland with a B.A. in Mathematics and Computer Science in 1993 at the age of 19 and then earned an M.A. in Computer Science in 1995 from Stanford. Sergey is confident, fit, and outspoken.[53] (Achievement Orientation, Initiative, Confidence)

In response to a question about Google being the highlight of his career, he said, "I think it was the smallest of accomplishments that we hope to make over the next 20 years. But I think if Google is all we create, I don't think I would be very disappointed."[54] (Inspirational Leadership, Achievement Orientation)

"We run Google a little bit like a university. We have lots of projects, about 100 of them. We like to have small groups of people, three or so people, working on projects. . . . The only way you are going to have success is to have lots of failures first."[55] (Teamwork and Collaboration, Building Bonds, Change Catalyst)

"Obviously everyone wants to be successful, but I want to be looked back on as being very innovative, very trusted, and ethical and ultimately making a big difference in the world."[56] (Trustworthiness)

More competencies are revealed about the Google culture by looking at the 10 things Google has found to be true, listed on their website:

1. Focus on the user and all else will follow. (Service Orientation)

2. It's best to do one thing really, really well. Google does search and has applied that unique ability to new products (i.e., Nexus One Smartphone, Chrome Browser, and updated Google Maps). (Conscientiousness)

3. You can make money without doing evil. There are no ads on their search page. (Trustworthiness)

4. The need for information crosses all borders. (Service Orientation)

5. You can be serious without a suit. Brin and Page think work should be challenging and the challenge should be fun. They put their employees first when it comes to their daily life. It is a highly communicative environment with few walls, free food at its cafeteria, subsidized massages and haircuts, and many parties. Each team member is given one day a week to spend on their own pet projects. (Teamwork and Collaboration, Building Bonds, Communication, Developing Others)[57]

Below are the EI competencies for Sergey Brin, shining with stars across all four clusters.

Key Strengths/Competencies

- Confidence
- Initiative
- Inspirational leadership
- Achievement orientation
- Adaptability
- Change catalyst
- Service orientation
- Trustworthiness

- Communication
- Influence
- Building bonds
- Developing others

Derailers

- No major ones noticed (. . . yet!)

EI Ratings: Sergey Brin

	PERSONAL	SOCIAL
Understanding	Self ★	Others ★
Managing	Self ★	Others ★

PETE CARROLL

After establishing the University of Southern California (USC) as the most successful college football program of the 2000s, Pete Carroll took on a new challenge in returning to the NFL as the head coach and executive vice-president of the Seattle Seahawks. In Seattle, Carroll hopes to make a name for himself in the pro ranks, where he was once regarded as a failure. According to the *LA Times,* "He has always thought that he would have won more games in his last NFL go around had he been given personnel control. In his decision to leave USC for the Seahawks, that was a non-negotiable."[58] (Confidence) Carroll is the final word on Seahawks personnel moves. He left USC with an astounding winning record of 97-19 (85.6%). In May 2008, Carroll was named the coach who did the most to define the first 10 years of the BCS (Bowl Championship Series) era.

When Carroll arrived at USC in 2001, they had been 56-39-2 the eight years prior. They were 5 and 7 in 2000, the year before Carroll arrived. His record was a remarkable feat of national reemergence, teamwork, and leadership, attributable to Carroll's unorthodox coaching style, which is rife with EI competencies. He is known as a "player's coach" versus an authoritarian command, control type of coach.

A football coach focuses most of his time on developing the talent of players and their ability to function together as a highly effective team. The best corporate leader may be focusing as much as 50% of his or her time on development, but that is rare indeed. Examining the leadership of Carroll uncovers many valuable examples of successfully applying Emotional Intelligence skills and tools to sports and business.

Carroll was actually the fifth choice of coaches considered suitable to reenergize the USC Trojans. Other coaches such as Dennis Erickson of Oregon State, Sonny Lubick of Colorado State, Mike Belotti of Oregon, and Mike Riley from the San Diego Chargers either were not interested in USC or didn't work out. Although Carroll had spent 16 years in the professional football world and was head coach of the New York Jets and New England Patriots, he had a less than overwhelming 33-31 record; plus, he was fired from each head coach job. USC was concerned about whether he had what it takes to coach in the college ranks, but in his interviews his enthusiasm and concise plan for rebuilding the team were impressive. (Conscientiousness) The assistant athletic director said, "Pete was just so amazingly engaging. His enthusiasm and his energy mixed with his expertise." [59]

Carroll is confident, enthusiastic, always pushing, striving to improve, and not afraid to take risks. These traits were highlighted in his USC years of risk-taking and bold moves in player selection while in Seattle. He said, "The last thing I want to do is sit back and see what happens. I want to get it and make opportunities." [60] (Confidence, Achievement Orientation, Initiative, Inspirational Leadership)

Carroll was a defensive back in college at the University of the Pacific and won all-conference honors as a safety in 1971 and 1972. After an unsuccessful shot at the pros, he returned to graduate school at Pacific. There Carroll learned about the Human Potential movement, sports psychology, and read Tim Gallwey's *Inner Game of Tennis* and Abraham Maslow's *Religions, Values, and Peak Experiences*. These experiences and books resonated with him and opened him up to a new leadership style.

As a young coach, he applied what he learned in the classroom to the practice field. After some tough seasons, he asked his defensive backs who were having problems which coverages they felt most comfortable with and which techniques they wanted to practice more. This approach was rather unconventional compared to the traditional football hierarchy, which would rarely engage players in team or coaching strategies. Carroll recalled that his players were rejuvenated by the meeting. One of his coaches, after hearing what he had done, said, "Wait just a damn minute, boy. Don't you ever ask them what they want. You tell them what they need."[61] Carroll was totally deflated by this.

This didn't last long, though, as he was quickly identified as an up-and-coming coach with special talent. In the pros, he refined his leadership style when dealing with players one-on-one, sometimes cracking the whip and other times talking to them about their life. He certainly was not the authoritarian coach of a Bear Bryant or Bill Parcells. "That can be a great way to teach, but it's not for me. I get more out of you if I connect with you. Instead of knocking you down . . . I'm going to build you up."[62] He tries to understand the player and figures out the best way to inspire them. (Accurate Self-Assessment, Developing Others, Building Bonds)

After three years working with the New England Patriots, Carroll was fired and took a year off from coaching to reflect. He read a book by the late John Wooden, UCLA's legendary basketball coach, and Wooden's concept of "knowing exactly what you want to get done" was inspiring for him. He thought about what felt natural for him as a coach and recognized it was his energy, optimism, and desire to relate directly with his players. "That's who I am." If he believed in himself he figured the players would too.[63] Carroll decided to make only fine adjustments within his leadership style and stay with his strengths. (Emotional Self-Awareness, Accurate Self-Assessment, Trustworthiness, Communication)

The successes Pete Carroll has had at USC are a great example of Emotional Intelligence in action. He stayed with his strengths and made only small micro-initiatives in his leadership that created a macro impact. It is a tribute to the competencies of knowing himself, motivating himself, developing empathy and strong bonds with his players, and creating a strong vision of teamwork and leadership that the players, the university, and the USC community have all embraced and celebrated. Now he will use his EI skills to do the same with the Seattle Seahawks.

Below are the EI competencies for Pete Carroll, shining with stars across all four clusters.

Key Strengths/Competencies

- Confidence
- Initiative
- Accurate self-assessment
- Inspirational leadership
- Achievement orientation
- Adaptability
- Change catalyst
- Empathy
- Trustworthiness
- Communication
- Influence
- Building bonds
- Developing others
- Teamwork and collaboration

Derailers

- Possibly overused confidence and optimism

EI Ratings: Pete Carroll

	PERSONAL	SOCIAL
Understanding	Self ★	Others ★
Managing	Self ★	Others ★

MEG WHITMAN

Meg Whitman resigned as CEO of eBay in 2007. Her leadership skills turned to teaching as she stayed at eBay through 2008 in order to advise the new CEO, John Donahoe. By the end of that year she was officially recognized for her leadership aptitude by being inducted into the U.S. Business Hall of Fame. In her decade at the helm she took eBay from a start-up to an $8 billion global powerhouse, revolutionizing the way goods are bought and sold online. As a matter of fact, eBay has been the "fastest growing company in history, faster than Microsoft, Dell, or any company during the first eight years of its existence."[64] *Fortune* magazine twice named her the most powerful woman in business. Whitman is running to be the first woman governor of California in 2010.[65]

One of the first things that attracted Whitman to eBay, then a two-year-old start-up in 1998, were the company's values that people are basically good, everyone has something to contribute, people should be treated respectfully, and an honest, open environment can bring out the best in people. The second thing she was impressed with, as a business executive, was the growth at 70% per month and costs so low that their profits were 85% of revenue. She saw that eBay is a company of the future, with no factories or inventories, and where the customers do the work.[66] In 2000, when revenues were $431 million, Whitman announced that eBay would reach $3 billion in 2005. (Initiative, Leadership, and Achievement Orientation) "Few investors believed in her, and even her board had doubts."[67]

Whitman was the youngest of three children and grew up in Long Island, New York. She went to Princeton University and majored in Economics and then attended Harvard Business School. She has always been driven and even had the *Wall Street Journal* delivered to her dorm room as an undergraduate. Whitman studied brand management at Proctor and Gamble and strategy at Bain Consulting. She then worked at Disney, Stride Rite, Florist Transworld Delivery (FTD), and Hasbro.

As president and CEO of FTD, Whitman had her first taste of the limelight. In 1995 she rejuvenated the brand and it became a profitable private company. She was attractive to eBay because of her consumer marketing background. Whitman demonstrated her adaptability, leadership, and change management skills numerous times at eBay. She fended off competition, hired a top technology chief at all costs, and survived a 22-hour website crash, which she called a "near death experience." eBay's purchase of PayPal was risky yet successful. Terry Semel, former CEO of Yahoo!, called it "a great acquisition." (Adaptability and Change Catalyst)

eBay's success is built on service orientation. Whitman herself responded to many customer emails. The company responds to emails in 24 hours or less and maintains customer loyalty, and more than half of the eBay referrals are from customers. Listening to customers and providing for their needs had helped Whitman expand the company and maintain the "small-town feel on a global scale." (Service Orientation) Onstage before several thousand customers, she told them, "eBay's success will always be based on your success. eBay reaffirms my faith in humanity. eBay is proof that people are basically good."[68] (Empathy and Leadership)

In her 2010 book, *The Power of Many*, she describes her key leadership values, many of which align with the EI competencies. She writes, "I believe that being willing and able to actively listen is a vital skill for any leader. Not only is listening the right thing to do, an antidote to arrogance, it also leads to all sorts of competitive advantages." She saw the value of "the power of many" in building the eBay community and wants to empower California voters to experience its benefits.[69] (Communication)

Whitman was not flashy or charismatic like other CEOs, but yielded her power in a folksy den mother approach where she is nurturing values. She is non-threatening, easy to talk to, and self-effacing. She called herself "frumpy but I deliver." (Trustworthiness) Terry Semel of Yahoo! says, "Meg is Meg. She is exactly who you meet. She is smart, straightforward, and to the point. She's just really nice to do business with."[70] Clearly Meg Whitman is a Star Performer in all four clusters.

Whitman's net worth is $1.2 billion, and she pledged not to accept a salary if elected to Governor. Her husband is a neurosurgeon at Stanford. She recharges herself by spending time with her family, escaping a few times a year to go fly-fishing at her husband's family farm in Tennessee.

Key Strengths/Competencies

- Confidence
- Initiative
- Leadership
- Achievement orientation
- Adaptability
- Change catalyst
- Service orientation
- Empathy
- Trustworthiness

- Conscientiousness
- Influence
- Organizational awareness
- Communication

Derailers

- Possibly overused confidence

EI Ratings: Meg Whitman

	PERSONAL	SOCIAL
Understanding	Self	Others
	★	★
Managing	Self	Others
	★	★

BILL CLINTON

Bill Clinton, our 42nd president, exemplifies a derailed leader because of his failings on the personal competencies. He was and is extremely socially competent, capable of knowing "how to feel people's pain" and provide social services to the masses. (Empathy and Service Orientation) Clinton was one of our best and most charismatic communicators. As president, he communicated a compelling vision in his re-election campaign, with the potent phrase "cross the bridge with me to the new millennium." (Leadership and Communication) He was excellent at championing change: using his influence and persuasion skills, he built a strong team among his cabinet to react quickly and effectively to political issues. (Influence, Teamwork, and Change Catalyst)

In his first year out of office he made $9.2 million in speaking fees, charging $75,000 to $350,000 per speech. "In cold hard cash it is almost certainly the most ever. The guy still fascinates people," said Stephen Hess, a presidential expert at the Brookings Institution.[71]

In addition, Clinton signed a reported $10 million contract with Alfred A. Knopf, Inc., to write his memoirs, a deal believed to be the biggest ever for a nonfiction book. The book came out in July 2004 and was also the biggest debut for a nonfiction book, with 2.575 million copies printed.

Clinton has started the Global Initiative, which has brought together political and business leaders for humanitarian projects. The Initiative has already raised over $2 billion for more than 200 projects around the world. His post-presidential career is emulating Jimmy Carter's, focusing on human rights. Clinton's work with AIDS is "already saving hundreds of thousands of lives and promises to save millions more."[72] He has partnered with Presidents Barack Obama and George H. W. Bush as one of the faces of the Haiti earthquake relief campaign.

The social competencies are going to keep Clinton in the public eye and continue to make him a fortune. Yet the personal competencies derailed him. (Self Awareness, Accurate Self-Assessment, and Self-Control) He was only the second president to be impeached, when he was charged with perjury and obstruction of justice in regards to his relationship with Monica Lewinsky. The senate acquitted Clinton, but the mistakes in his personal life have forever tarnished his legacy as a president.

Clinton certainly had some blind spots in understanding and managing himself. There were gaps between the awareness of his feelings and understanding the implications of his feelings. He failed to manage his impulses and was unable to publicly admit his mistakes. One would think the charges of his having extramarital affairs during the 1992 Democratic primaries would have forced him into planning ways of exerting more self-control in the future. Why would he risk all that he had worked so hard for to have momentary pleasures? From a cognitive perspective it certainly doesn't make sense, but Clinton's lack of emotional awareness overpowered his rational side and muted all the strengths he portrays in the social competencies.

In his book and interviews he states: "I think I did something for the worst possible reason—just because I could. I think that's just about the most morally indefensible reason that anybody could have for doing anything. When you do something just because you could . . . I've thought about it a lot. And there are lots of more sophisticated explanations, more complicated psychological explanations. But none of them are an excuse . . . Only a fool does not look to explain his mistakes."[73]

Key Strengths and Competencies

- Empathy
- Service orientation
- Leadership
- Communication
- Influence
- Teamwork
- Change catalyst
- Initiative
- Adaptability
- Building bonds
- Organizational awareness

Derailers

- Low self-awareness
- Inaccurate self-assessment
- Low self-control
- Low trustworthiness

This graph illustrates Clinton's undeveloped and Star competencies.

EI Ratings: Bill Clinton

	PERSONAL	SOCIAL
Understanding	Self ☖	Others ★
Managing	Self ☖	Others ★

EARVIN "MAGIC" JOHNSON

Only an elite handful of athletes have ever dominated their sport so thoroughly and with as much flair as Earvin "Magic" Johnson Jr. did throughout his storied basketball career. Magic Johnson is widely recognized as the greatest point guard ever to play the game and has become the standard for excellence at his position. Despite all his endless accolades as a basketball player, however, Johnson is more proud of his post-basketball accomplishments as an entrepreneur and community leader that displays many of the EI competencies. He states in his book *Earvin "Magic" Johnson: 32 Ways to Be a Champion in Business*, "I am grateful for my experiences as an athlete. Yet the rewards of my entrepreneurial endeavors have been even more fulfilling. I've learned that creating jobs and providing goods and services to urban communities beats even five NBA championships." [74] (Service Orientation) Magic Johnson Enterprises encompasses numerous business ventures and is valued at over $700 million, while also investing in the development of at-risk urban communities. Through his strategic partnerships with the likes of Starbucks, 24 Hour Fitness, and T.G.I. Friday's, Johnson has invested $1.5 billion to raise the quality of life in cities such as Atlanta, Baltimore, Chicago, Cleveland, Las Vegas, Los Angeles, Miami, and Washington, D.C.

Johnson was one of nine brothers and sisters growing up in Lansing, Michigan. As a child his basketball heroes were Wilt Chamberlain and Bill Russell. His real role models and mentors, though, were two neighborhood entrepreneurs, Joel Ferguson and Greg Eaton. Their holdings included banks, community developments, apartments, television stations, janitorial services, and car dealerships. Johnson worked for them in high school. They were self-made millionaires who really cared about the community and built affordable housing for low-income and elderly residents. One night Greg Eaton saw the young Magic sitting at his desk and asked him, "What are you doing?" Johnson said, "Just seeing how it feels. One of these days I am going to be a businessman and have my own."[75] (Initiative, Achievement Orientation)

A tremendous basketball talent from the outset, Johnson earned the moniker "Magic" at age 15 after posting an exceedingly rare "triple-double" of 36 points, 18 rebounds, and 16 assists. Johnson led his high-school team to win the Michigan State Championship game. He won the NCAA college championship with Michigan State and was voted the most valuable player, was the first draft pick of the NBA in 1979, and went on to win the NBA championship in his first year as a professional for the Los Angeles Lakers, taking home the finals most valuable player trophy. The Lakers won the championship four more times in Johnson's 14 years as a pro under his leadership and unselfish play. Truly, his real magic was in making his teammates better. He possessed an acute awareness of how his teammates played that allowed him to predict where they would be on the court before they even got there. He enjoyed making assists to his teammates more than his own scoring. (Leadership, Teamwork and Collaboration)

Growing up in a working-class family in Lansing, Michigan, Johnson's entrepreneurial father played a crucial role in developing leadership and interpersonal skills in young Magic. Earvin Sr. didn't care if Magic had starred in a victory on Friday night. He would wake Magic up at 6 A.M. on Saturday to help him with his waste disposal business, often in sub-freezing temperatures. After Magic complained once about the tediousness of the work, Earvin Sr. promptly told his son that his business was not merely about picking up trash; they were taking care of people. Magic carried this focus on people rather than tasks over to his career in both basketball and business. (Service Orientation and Influence)

Though Johnson had early success in his career, he also had to deal with failures and setbacks. In 1989, at the peak of his illustrious career, Magic Johnson revealed to a shocked nation that he had contracted HIV and was retiring from basketball. The sports world seemed to stand still for a moment as fans and passive observers alike were left dumbfounded by the news. This startling end to one of the greatest sports careers ever led many critics to promptly declare that Johnson's life was over. Indeed, it would have been easy for him to slink into the shadows and rest on the laurels of his past successes, but he possessed an uncanny ability to adapt to new situations. This adaptability, coupled with optimism and a passion to serve, propelled him toward success in his life after basketball.

One of Johnson's early business ventures, though, never made it off of the ground, in large part because Johnson overestimated his talents. The venture in question was a sports memorabilia store for which Johnson handpicked the clothing the store would carry. He found out the hard way that his own tastes did not reflect those of his customers. In his book, Johnson credits his tremendous accomplishments in the business world to a willingness to "check my ego at the door." This story provides an apt example of the way that overestimation of one's skills can become a derailer. However, Johnson was able to recognize his own weaknesses and change his business strategy accordingly. (Accurate Self-Assessment, Trustworthiness)

Johnson in his book highlights many of the EI competencies that have made him successful.

- **Vision:** One of his first lessons about vision was from his father's view of his business. Johnson states, "The vision should give your business or career purpose and meaning beyond paying the bills."[76]

- **Emotional Self-Awareness and Emotional Self-Control:** "When fears plant themselves in your mind, they take on more power. We give them power. That's why it is important to recognize what they are. Fears are emotions. They are not real. You can walk right through them if you just make yourself take the first step, and keep going."[77]

- **Hiring and Developing Others:** "I don't hire people to work for my company. I hire them to *be* my company. . . . The quality of people you hire determines how successful your business will be."[78]

- **Focus on Strengths:** "Build on your strengths, and you will overcome your weaknesses." Johnson talks about how Michael Jordan failed at a baseball career and he himself failed as a late-night talk host after eight weeks on Fox. He states, "Rarely can you turn a weakness into a strength. Greatness is achieved by building on strengths and managing your weaknesses so they do not matter."[79]

"What I'm trying to do [is] leave a legacy for . . . minority people," Johnson said. "I've always considered myself more than just a basketball player."

Below are the EI competencies for Magic Johnson, which show stars shining across all four clusters.

Key Strengths/Competencies

- Emotional self-awareness
- Emotional self-control
- Confidence
- Initiative
- Achievement orientation
- Adaptability
- Change catalyst
- Service orientation
- Trustworthiness

- Communication
- Inspirational leadership
- Influence
- Building bonds
- Developing others
- Teamwork and collaboration

Derailers

- No major ones noticed

EI Ratings: Earvin "Magic" Johnson

	PERSONAL	SOCIAL
Understanding	Self ★	Others ★
Managing	Self ★	Others ★

LACK OF SELF-CONTROL AND THE INABILITY TO DELAY GRATIFICATION

It is apparent that lack of impulse control or self-control is a common theme for leaders who have derailed. This weakness is contradictory to our need for someone who is consistent, steady, and grounded. If a leader lacks self-control, he or she becomes unpredictable and untrustworthy. No one knows when or to what the leader may react. In primitive terms, this kind of person becomes unsafe and even dangerous to others and the organization. Today it is more and more apparent how blind spots in the personal competencies of executives' Emotional Intelligence have led to the greed, lying, and manipulations inside major corporations such as Enron, Adelphia, and WorldCom, to name a few. "It feels like almost every

> Today it is more and more apparent how blind spots in the personal competencies of executives' Emotional Intelligence have led to the greed, lying, and manipulations inside some major corporations.

day a politician, sports figure, or celebrity falls from grace.

Many of these former Star Performers who became fallen heroes had the inability to delay gratification. Goleman talks about the "amygdala hijack," a situation where your brain's alarm system overrules executive functioning in the prefrontal lobes.[80]

The amygdala is the brain's alarm center. It houses the ancient emotional brain, which plays a key role in reacting to emergencies. It also is the center of emotional memory and responds to threats with primitive reactions of fight or flight. The prefrontal lobes of the brain dictate executive functioning, including decision-making, planning, comprehension, reasoning, and learning. For most people, their prefrontal lobes organize around executive functioning, bringing rational thought and control to the initial amygdala reaction. But it doesn't always work that way. In Chapter 2 you will learn more about the neuroscience behind the amygdala hijack, how it affects IQ and performance, and about the tools to enhance emotional self-control.

THE MARSHMALLOW STUDY

Four-year-olds at Stanford Pre-school were each given a marshmallow by a researcher. They were told, "You can have this marshmallow now if you want, but if you don't eat it until after I run an errand, you can have two when I return." Some students immediately ate the marshmallow; others contrived all kinds of distractions for themselves to manage the urge to grab and swallow it. This was a longitudinal study and, 14 years later, when the once 4- but now

18-year-olds were evaluated, researchers compared the "grabbers" versus "those who waited." It turns out that the "grabbers" grew into young adults who displayed tendencies to fall apart more easily under stress, pick fights more often, and have less resistance to temptation in the pursuit of their goals than "those who waited."[81]

A surprising finding was that "those who waited" also scored an average of 210 points higher on their SAT tests than the "grabbers" did. The amygdala is the source of emotional impulse and distraction. When mediated by the prefrontal lobes—the source of the working memory, executive function, and the capacity to pay attention to what is on your mind—a performer manifests discipline and the ability to put off urges and stay focused with the task at hand.

The "grabbers" and "those who waited" continued to be studied into their late 20s. The researchers discovered that "those who waited" were more intellectually skilled and attentive, better able to concentrate and develop close relationships, and displayed more self-control, dependability, and responsibility in the face of frustration.[82]

STRETCHING STRENGTHS: GOING FROM GOOD TO GREAT LEADERSHIP

There has been a convergence of thought in the last 10-12 years that the best way to be happy and more successful is to identify what you do well and do more of it, and get others to do what you don't excel at. Below are some of the experts' thoughts on leadership and why focusing on your strengths is so important for your development plan.

First, one definition of "a strength" is: "a pattern of behavior, thoughts, and feelings that produces a high degree of satisfaction and pride; generates both psychic and/or financial reward; and presents measurable progress toward excellence."[83]

In *The Extraordinary Leader,* Zenger and Folkman studied a database of 200,000 questionnaires completed on more than 20,000 leaders who had 360-degree feedback to examine what makes an extraordinary leader. They discovered key findings such as:

- Great leaders make a huge difference when compared to merely good leaders. Leaders in the top 10% produced twice as much revenue to the organization as managers in the 11th through 89th percentiles. Great leaders also have a positive impact on profitability, turnover, employee commitment, and customer satisfaction and retention.

- "The more great leaders an organization develops, the more it will become an outstanding organization."

- There is a significant difference in performance when a leader is in the top 20%. Good leaders in the 40th to 80th percentile are not significantly different from one another in performance.

- The key to developing great leaders is to build strengths.

- If there are "fatal flaws" (derailers), they must be fixed.[84]

Donald O. Clifton and Paula Nelson wrote *Soar with Your Strengths* as a result of research they did with the Gallup consulting firm. Clifton had been pursuing the following question since graduate school, over 50 years before: "What would happen if we studied what was right with people versus what's wrong with people?" Some of their key findings were:

- "Maximum productivity can be gained from focusing on strengths and managing weaknesses."

- Understanding strengths leads to knowing the difference between good and great.

- Stop wasting time working on weaknesses.

- You can make more effective decisions by studying what's right versus what's wrong.

- Strengths develop best when sufficient time is devoted to a single subject or goal.[85]

Martin Seligman, one of the fathers of Positive Psychology and the author of *Authentic Happiness*, found that the "highest success in living and deepest emotional satisfaction comes from building and using your signature strengths." His research shows that the happiest people are the ones who are using their strengths the most. "Signature strengths" are defined as strengths that are deeply characteristic of you. Seligman defines the "good life" as "using your signature strengths to obtain abundant gratification in the main realms of your life." A "meaningful life" he defines as "using your signature strengths and virtues in service of something much larger than yourself."

> ... the best way to be happy and more successful is to identify what you do well and do more of it . . .

Mihaly Csikszentmihalyi is the author of *Good Business* and creator of the term *flow* used in sports and other performances. He states that in "creating oneself, it makes sense to build on one's strength." People who are blessed with a particular gift will typically pursue what comes easily to them.

Dan Sullivan coaches thousands of executives to focus on their "unique abilities" and delegate as much as possible the areas they are not good at.

Finally, Marcus Buckingham, who for years worked at Gallup, describes in his new book, *The One Thing You Need to Know*, the difference between good and great management. "Great managers turn a person's talent into performance." He states that the three things you must know about a person to manage him or her effectively are strengths and weaknesses, triggers, and his or her unique style of learning. Buckingham sums it up well:

> I've found that while there are many styles of managers, there is one quality that sets truly great managers apart from the rest: They discover what is unique about each

person and then capitalize on it. Average managers play checkers, while great managers play chess. The difference? In checkers, all the pieces are uniform and move in the same way; they are interchangeable. You need to plan and coordinate their movements, certainly, but they all move at the same pace, on parallel paths. In chess, each type of piece moves in a different way, and you can't play if you don't know how each piece moves. More important, you won't win if you don't think carefully about how you move the pieces. Great managers know and value the unique abilities and even the eccentricities of their employees, and they learn how best to integrate them into a coordinated plan of attack . . . Average managers treat all their employees the same. Great managers discover each individual's unique talents and bring these to the surface so everyone wins.[86]

Identifying your strengths and the strengths of the people you are developing is the *first step* in improving Emotional Intelligence. The *second step* is developing your plan. In your plan the first action is to determine how can you stretch, redeploy, or build on your strengths. The next step is to identify "fatal flaws" that could derail you if not attended to.

Average managers play checkers, while great managers play chess.

The EI Star Profile can be used to clarify these strengths and to develop a plan to focus more on your strengths. Using 360-degree feedback, which many organizations do, can also help you identify your strengths so that you can understand how others perceive you. Aside from the ECI administered by the Hay Group, www.haygroup.com, you can use the Emotional Quotient Inventory (EQi) and the EQi 360 from Mental Health Systems, www.mhs.com, or the Emotional Intelligence Appraisal from TalentSmart at www.talent smart.com to identify your Emotional Intelligence skills.

See the Additional Resources section for more information about these programs and other resources available to help raise Emotional Intelligence. Also, the website www.truenorthleadership. com has *free* EI assessment articles and tools.

MICRO-INITIATIVES: D.O.D. OF GREAT LEADERSHIP

Discovering the "degree of difference" (D.O.D.) between good and great leadership has been the focus of many writers. Goleman, Boyatzis, and the Hay Group use the term *tipping point* to describe the behaviors that tip or move a performer into the top 10%. Using your strengths more in a disciplined fashion is the first strategy to improve performance.

In working with organizations and executives, I have found the D.O.D. is made up of doing many small things regularly. I call these "micro-initiatives." They don't take a lot of time but are crucial habits for great leaders. The average or good leaders could do them but don't, as they are often neglected and given lower priority. Zenger and Folkman found that doing five things really well put a leader in the top 10%.[87] Micro-initiatives make a macro impact. Or:

$$MI = MI$$

In cycling races or track meets the difference between the winners and the placers can be fractions of a second. Great leaders have a series of actions that separate them from the pack that take as little as 10 seconds and as long as 45 minutes to a few hours. They make the time to do these "micro-initiatives" to foster development for themselves and others. When I coach executives, I often talk about just how long these actions take because the first response of a busy leader is "I just don't have time." When we are talking about just how little time it actually

> Great leaders have a series of actions that separate them from the pack . . .

takes to do these micro-initiatives, they usually agree that time isn't the real issue. What is required is commitment and discipline.

Below are a few examples of the "degree of difference" in time and action that separates the great leader from the good leader:

Average to good leader gives feedback:

"Mary, thanks for getting the report to me."

Time = 3 seconds

Great leader gives feedback:

"Mary, terrific job on the report BECAUSE it was well-written. I appreciate you checking in with me during the process. I liked how you collaborated with others on it. It will make us and you look great in the customers' eyes, thanks."

Time = 12 seconds

Average to good leader on relationships:

Works in his or her office on a project and then takes a break. On the way to the bathroom, nods at a few people and walks past some without even looking. Heads right back to the computer.

Time = 2 minutes each time

Great leader on relationships:

Takes a break and stops at several people's cubicles to check on how they are doing. Asks about the projects they are working on and inquires about any issues or challenges they are having. The leader then asks, using the person's name, how his or her sick spouse is doing and thanks the person for volunteering for a new task. At other times during the day the leader connects in a similar way.

Time = 5 minutes each time

Average to good leader with a poor performance issue:

John is not performing as I would like him to. "John, let's make sure you do everything to get this right."

Time = 2 seconds

Great leader with a poor performance issue:

John is not performing as I would like him to. "John, let's spend time going over the next assignment together. You haven't been performing like I know you can and I want to help. You have always met expectations, so tell me what is going on here. I'm sure we can come up with a plan that will make a difference to you. When can we meet?"

Time = 18 seconds

Average to good leader on self-management:

Thinking to self: "I'd better work through lunch because I am behind and can catch up if I eat at my computer."

 Time recharging = 4 minutes

Great leader on self-management:

Thinking to self: "I am feeling tired and need to recharge. Going to lunch will help keep things in perspective and I will come back refreshed and better able to deal with these next challenges."

Time recharging = 45-60 minutes

Average to good leader on managing up with the boss:

Thinking to self: "I am not sure what she thinks of me or how I am doing. I know she is very busy and probably doesn't need another interruption. I'll stay away unless she needs something from me."

Time with boss = 15 minutes informally through the week

Great leader on managing up with the boss:

Thinking to self: "I am not sure what she thinks of me or how I am doing. I will schedule some time with her and clarify expectations and make sure I am doing what she wants. It will also give me some visibility on my projects. Scheduling a weekly check-in is something that will help me. I will take the initiative to create the agenda and keep the meeting focused. I will also update her on my projects with an email status if that will help her."

Time with boss = 30 minutes weekly

Time creating email summary = 25 minutes

If you are not doing these micro-initiatives, these examples can help get you started. Add actions that will move you closer to your goals. As you can see, none of these actions are especially demanding or challenging. When done as a part of an overall leadership strategy, these micro-initiatives add up to a winning difference. Stars make a habit of doing what the average performer is uncomfortable doing.

> Stars make a habit of doing what the average performer is uncomfortable doing.

For many leaders a few actions will be the "degree of difference" that transforms them into Stars. I like to tell leaders that they are more than likely 85% there already. We are looking for these few actions that will push them into the 90th and above percentile. Knowing these small but crucial moves are a mere 5-7% change of habit that will put them in the top 10% makes the process seem easier and builds motivation to act and incorporate these micro-initiatives into their lives.

As you assess your Emotional Intelligence, determine what micro-initiatives you can implement to help move you into the top 10%. Choose one or two actions from the Star Profile and *Coach's Corner* to incorporate and leap from average to Star Performance.

COACH'S CORNER ON ASSESSMENTS

This is an opportunity to rate yourself on the key characteristics of being a Star and also to see if there is any evidence of derailers. We all want to know how we measure up on key aspects of success, but you may be apprehensive about assessing yourself. Benjamin Franklin said, "There are three things extremely hard: steel, a diamond, and to know one's self." A few tips on taking these assessments:

- These assessments are strictly for your development a you don't have to share the results with anyone. The goal i to identify a few actions that will help in your development. This may mean doing even more of what you do well.

- Be honest with yourself and try not to censor your answers. "There is always a trade-off between how you want to feel and what you want to know."[88]

- Give yourself credit for what you are good at it. Sometimes people under-evaluate themselves on items.

- In filling out these assessments on direct reports, again, be as honest and accurate as you can. This will give you specific information on ways that can assist them on their development.

TAKING THE EI STAR PROFILE ASSESSMENT

This assessment gives you many options to assess your Emotional Intelligence and/or that of your direct reports. It can allow you to see if your top competencies align with what your direct reports see as most important for you and to see how you are doing on these competencies.

There is a tendency to overestimate oneself on the EI Star Profile. Really think about how often you do these behaviors. To do some of these behaviors 50% of the time is challenging and would be a 5. To do something 80% of time or an 8 truly means you have mastered that behavior and are very consistent in doing it.

A good metaphor for the frequency of these behaviors and determining whether you are average or a Star is an exercise regimen. Think of how often an exerciser who is a top 10% performer and is highly effective or exceeds expectations would exercise. Most people would say more than five times a week, where an average or "meets expectations" exerciser does it about three times week. Both performers exercise, but with different frequency. In the same way, you may do the following behaviors, but how regular and consistent are you?

67

⎯0 competencies are the most important for your
⎯e would be ranked with a 1.

⎯lf on each competency, keeping in mind how fre-
⎯⎯ do each behavior. Remember that if you only do it
50% of the time, that is a 5, and 80% of the time is an 8.

RANK YOUR DIRECT REPORTS

- Select which 10 competencies are the most important for your direct reports' positions; those would be ranked with a 1.
- Rank your direct reports on each competency, keeping in mind how frequently they do this behavior. Remember, if they only do it 50% of the time, that is a 5, and 80% of the time is an 8.

ADDITIONAL OPTIONS

- Use the EI Star Profile to get 360-degree feedback. Copy the assessment and have your direct reports, boss, peers, family members, or others rank you on the competencies using the "DR" column.
- Have your boss and direct reports pick the top 10 competencies they think are most important for your position. Compare and discuss their alignment with what you have listed as the top 10.

This assessment is also available at www.leadingwithei.com.

COMPETENCY	IMPORTANCE	SELF	DR
SELF-AWARENESS	SELF / DR	1-10	1-10
1. Emotional Self-Awareness: Recognizes feelings and how feelings affect him-/herself and his/her job performance		8	
2. Accurate Self-Assessment: Recognizes strengths and shortcomings and focuses on how to improve		8	
3. Confidence: Presents in an assured, forceful, impressive, and unhesitating manner	1	5	
SELF-MANAGEMENT			
4. Emotional Self-Control: Stays calm, unflappable, and clear-headed in high-stress situations	1	6-7	
5. Trustworthiness: Openly admits faults or mistakes and confronts unethical behavior	1	8-9	
6. Adaptability: Is comfortable with ambiguities and adapts to new challenges	1	8-9	
7. Conscientiousness: Takes personal responsibility to make sure that tasks are completed		8-9	
8. Achievement Orientation: Works through obstacles and takes risks to meet his/her challenging goals to continually improve	1	8-9	
9. Initiative: Seizes or creates opportunities for the future		8-9	

COMPETENCY	IMPORTANCE	SELF	DR
SOCIAL AWARENESS	SELF / DR	1-10	1-10
10. Empathy: Understands others' perspectives; and says is open to diversity		6-7	
11. Organizational Awareness: Understands the political forces and unspoken rules at work	1	7	
12. Service Orientation: Is proactive about customer satisfaction and addresses underlying needs			
RELATIONSHIP MANAGEMENT			
13. Developing Others: Gives timely and constructive feedback; mentors	1	8	
14. Inspirational Leadership: Communicates a compelling vision; inspires others to follow		6-7	
15. Influence: Finds the right appeal to build buy-in; develops a network of influential parties	1		
16. Change Catalyst: Leads change efforts and champions new initiatives	1	8	
17. Communication: Effective give-and-take with others; continually fine tunes his/her delivery		8	
18. Building Bonds: Builds strong networks and uses them for answers and support		8	
19. Conflict Management: Understands all sides and finds common ideals to endorse		8	
20. Teamwork and Collaboration: Is encouraging and draws others into an active commitment for the collective effort		8	

NUMBER OF STARS RATED "8" AND OVER

CLUSTER	SELF	DR
Self-Awareness	*2*	
Self-Management	*5*	
Social Awareness		
Relationship Management		
TOTAL		

Adapted from Goleman, D., Boyatzis, R., and McKee, A. (2002) *Primal Leadership: Realizing the Power of Emotional Intelligence.* Boston, MA: Harvard Business School Press. Reprinted with permission.

ARE YOU OR YOUR BOSS DEBILITATING?

Unless you are the CEO, you have a boss. Even CEOs have a board to report to. What kind of boss are you to your direct reports? Would anyone call you Debilitating? In learning how to be a great leader, it helps to know what bad leaders do so you can avoid those behaviors. The Derailer Detector assessment follows this section so you can determine if any Debilitating behavior plagues you or someone you know.

James is an Information Technology consultant. His boss is a poor communicator. When James's boss gives James a task, he rarely expresses his expectations. At the end of a project, the boss would inevitably announce that the work was not up to par and would be overly critical. Then he'd demand that James put in extra time to fix the problem. James, of course, was rarely aware of what the problem actually was. This kind of crazy-making leadership has profound and negative impacts. Not surprisingly, James: 1) was angry with his boss and had lost all respect he might once have had for him, 2) had lost valuable personal time and resented that kind of abuse, and 3) didn't want to do his best work for his boss because he figured he would be criticized no matter what he did. James was zapped of his productive energy and emotionally deflated in his job because of the behavior of his Debilitating Boss.

WHAT IS A DEBILITATING BOSS?

A Debilitating Boss is a boss who makes his or her employees feel ineffective, inadequate, weak, lacking confidence, confused, and generally under-performing. Often unknowingly, these bosses suck the passion, soul, and energy right out of you by being negative, critical, and confusing. Instead of using your creativity and effort for superior performance, you ruminate about the injustices and unfair treatment at the hands of your boss. These stories of grievances, inequity, and negative emotions spread, expand, and lead to a toxic environment. Any commitment, dedication, or loyalty is wiped out by the Debilitating Boss.

In a study, 40% of employees who rated their bosses as poor said they were likely to leave.[89] Clearly, Debilitating Bosses leave a trail of disheartened, disgruntled, and disengaged workers behind them.

DISENGAGED WORKERS AND THEIR COSTS

The number one reason most Americans leave their jobs is they don't feel appreciated at work, predominantly by their bosses. The Saratoga Institute reports that 50% of work-life satisfaction is determined by the relationships workers have with their bosses.[90] In a survey of 4 million workers, the Gallup Poll found that 65% of Americans received absolutely no recognition for good work in their last year. The poll also found that 55% are not engaged (i.e., are just putting in time) and 19% of workers are actively disengaged (i.e., unhappy and spreading their discontent or being Debilitating to others). That totals approximately 22 million workers who are: 1) less productive and loyal, 2) more stressed-out, 3) missing more days of work, and 4) less satisfied with their personal lives. The cost to the United States is about $370 billion annually in economic performance.[91] This is an underestimation because it doesn't take into account absences, illness, and other problems that result from disengagement and bad leadership.[92]

WHAT EMPLOYEES WANT

Beverly Kaye and Sharon Jordan-Evans in their recent Retention and Engagement Drivers Report had 7,665 respondents. They found the top reasons people stay on the job were:

- Exciting work and challenge = 48.4% of respondents
- Career growth, learning, and development = 42.6% of respondents
- Working with great people and relationships = 41.8% of respondents

POWER OF LEADERSHIP

The Philadelphia-based Hay Group has studied leadership and its effect on the work climate. They evaluated a number of components:

- How clear is the vision of the leadership?
- What are their standards?
- What is expected of the team?
- What is the type and amount of responsibility employees can handle?
- How flexible are they in getting things done?
- What kind of teamwork, pride, and collaboration do they have?

They found that:

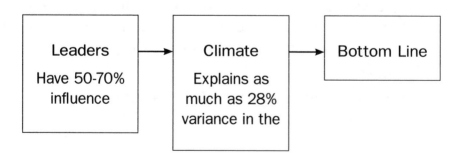

Leaders	Climate	Bottom Line
Have 50-70% influence	Explains as much as 28% variance in the	

In some cases, where the team is small or the leader is very influential, the leader may have a 90% influence over the climate of the team or organization. That is why your relationship with your boss is one of the biggest factors in whether you leave your job or get a promotion.

Good bosses raise the "discretionary effort" of the team. Discretionary effort is the dedication, loyalty, and amount of effort put into a project or assignment.[93] Most employees fail to put in 100% on everything. But if you have a good boss, you usually want to please and do a good job for him or her, and usually you will put more into your assignment. You will check your work more often, ask the advice of others, and think about ways to work smarter. If the effort is discretionary, you put more into it than an employee with a bad or average boss. Small increases in discretionary effort, even 5-10%, can increase productivity and change good performers into great performers.

THE SOLUTION: IF YOU OR YOUR BOSS ARE DEBILITATING

There is an inoculation that can protect you from the contagion of the Debilitating Boss. You have your Emotional Intelligence competencies to build up, strengthen, and repel their impact on you, such as:

- Managing your impulses and inoculating yourself from your boss

- Communication and conflict resolution skills to interact with your boss in an effective way, to attenuate his or her impact on you, and to feel you stood up for yourself

- Confidence to prevent your boss from getting under your skin

- Achievement orientation to find ways to get your goals accomplished in spite of a Debilitating Boss

- Teamwork and building bonds skills to get others to support you and help in achieving the completion of projects
- Initiative to find yourself another job if you are unable to find your desire and motivation again in this problematic relationship
- If you are a Debilitating Boss, read on; *Leading with Emotional Intelligence* will equip you with some of the basic tools to counter the dark side.

TAKING THE DERAILER DETECTOR

This assessment gives you four options to assess career "derailers" for yourself and your direct reports. Each organization has a different climate, and some may tolerate these derailers more than others, so the risk factors can vary.

RANK YOURSELF

Rank yourself on each derailer, keeping in mind how frequent you do this behavior, 1 = almost never, 2 = once every three months, 3 = once a month.

RANK YOUR DIRECT REPORT

Rank your direct report (DR) on each derailer, keeping in mind how frequent they do this behavior, 1 = almost never, 2 = once every three months, 3 = once a month.

ADDITIONAL OPTIONS

- Use the Derailer Detector to get 360-degree feedback. Copy the assessment and have your direct reports, boss, peers, family members, or others rank you on the derailers using the "DR" column. Compare and discuss the alignment with what you have.

SCORING

Ideally have someone else score the assessments and average all the scores together so you get an average on each question. You could have your assistant, human resource professional, coach, or a co-worker do that. If not possible you can average the scores yourself.

AFTER YOU RECEIVE THE ASSESSMENT RESULTS

- Use the Star Performer Action Plan to respond to the questions to develop your plan for building on your strengths, preventing your derailers, and creating support for your changes.
- Look for themes that you see in the results, such as overusing your strengths or not taking enough initiative.
- Discuss the results with your boss or coach.

This assessment is also available at www.leadingwithei.com.

YOU		DR
	1. **"Smartest person in the room" syndrome:** Has to be right all the time, married to own ideas, and not open to or distrusting of new ideas	
	2. **Lack of impulse control:** Emotionally reactive, volatile, abrasive, and follows urges to an unhealthy extreme	
	3. **Drives others too hard:** Micromanages and takes over rather than delegates	
	4. **Perfectionism:** Sets unrealistic goals; rejects criticism	
	5. **Defensive:** Blames others; is inflexible and argumentative	
	6. **Risk averse:** Lacks courage to take risks	

7. **Failure to learn from mistakes:** Same kind of mistakes show up

8. **Lacks insight into others:** Can't read others' emotions or reactions

9. **Doesn't ask for feedback:** Misses opportunities to include others for better decisions

10. **Self-promotion:** Is attention-seeking; overlooks others' accomplishments for own recognition

11. **Lack of integrity:** "Unhonest" with self and then others; omits and minimizes

12. **Failure to adapt to cultural differences:** Does not change leadership style appropriately

13. **Indirect with others:** Does not give the hard feedback or make the difficult decisions about people

14. **Approval dependent:** Needs too much approval before making decisions

15. **Eccentricity:** Unpredictable and odd in behavior

16. **Mistreats others:** Callous, demeaning, or discounting to others and their needs

17. **Self-interest:** Acts in self-interest instead of the interest of the whole organization or larger group

18. **Insular:** Disregards health and welfare of group outside the responsibility of own organization or team

Count up your number of 2's and 3's

SELF   DIRECT REPORT

2's = | 2's =

3's =   3's =

Three or more 2's = Warning signs for derailers

Two or more 3's = At risk to you and the organization!

Now what? If you score or your direct report scores in the "warning" or "at-risk" level, make sure you read and study the next sections. Many suggestions and practices will be helpful in keeping you or your employee on track and more effective.

*Adapted from Leslie and Van Velsor, *A Look at Derailment Today: North America and Europe* (1996); Byram, Smith and Paese, *Grow Your Own Leaders* (2002); Kaplan, *Beyond Ambition* (1991); Dotlich and Cairo, *Why CEOs Fail* (2002); Kellerman, *Bad Leadership* (2004); and Lipman-Blumen, *The Allure of Toxic Leadership* (2005).

STRATEGIC USE OF STRENGTHS

How can you use your strengths more strategically? First, look to see if there are some obvious ways your strengths can be used or applied to help beef up some important competencies. Zenger and Folkman use the term *competency companions* to describe how one competency can enhance another.[94]

Leaders who scored in the top 10% on the differentiating behavior also tended to score very high on these supportive behaviors. We have called these supporting behaviors 'competency companions' or . . . 'behavioral buddies.' [95]

They list mechanisms that best explain the competency companion phenomenon:

1. Competency companions facilitate the expression of their competencies.

2. Achieving excellence in one behavior helps develop a related behavior.

3. One competency is a building block or main element for another competency.

4. Developing a competency companion can change the skill level of a leader.[96]

Following are a few examples of how you can utilize your strengths to support other areas. I've often seen leaders who have great skills in one area but are blind to using the same skills in a new arena. These examples will help you think about how to stretch your strengths. These groupings have not been statistically established. Each position in an organization may require mastery in some competencies over other ones. You will still need to be skilled in what tools to use in these situations, and *Leading with Emotional Intelligence* will provide you with the answers.

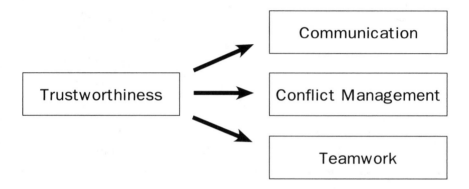

Having high trust from others gives you the equity to communicate more directly with others, especially if there is conflict. There is an effective give-and-take. You will be given the "benefit of the doubt." Your team will better follow your leadership when they trust you.

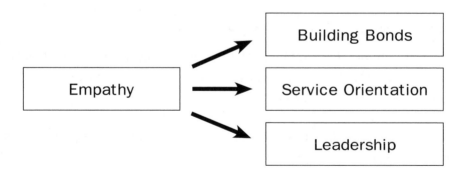

Empathy skills will help in building relationships, whether it is with internal or external customers or with peers or stakeholders. When people feel you understand and care for them as individuals they will also become more committed to you and your vision as a person or leader.

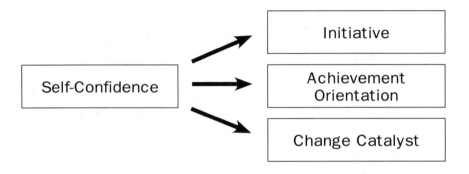

Self-confidence is important for going after and achieving your goals. Taking risks and actions for the future, anticipating obstacles, and personally leading change are all enhanced when you are confident. Self-efficacy is a strong predictor of your ability to set high goals, persist in the face of obstacles, be resistant to setbacks, and achieve the goals you set.[97]

STAR PERFORMER ACTION PLAN

Read through the EI Star Profile, the Derailer Detector, and Strategic Use of Strengths and answer the following questions to help you develop your Star Performer Action Plan.

Remember, you only need to do a few things better to go from good to great. Start with what you are already good at. Micro-initiatives can make a macro impact.

Which competencies do you currently perform as a Star Performer that you would like to improve even more?

1. _Developing others_
2. _Teamwork & collaboration_
3. _Change Catalyst_

Are there any critical derailers you identified? If so, what are they?

1. _None critical, but would like to work_
2. _on being more Direct to others._
3. _____

How would you bring these strengths into your development areas?

1. _____
2. _____
3. _____

What resources do you need to make this happen (e.g., training, feedback from your boss or direct reports, etc.)?

1. _Feedback from AS. DON + TLs_
2. _____
3. _____

Who can support you and hold you accountable?

1. _AS. DON + TLs_
2. _____
3. _____

What can they do to support you (i.e., specific actions)?

1. _Provide Regular open + honest feedback._
2. _At times Be a "sounding board"_
3. _____

How might you sabotage your efforts and best intentions?

1. _By becoming discouraged R/t lack of_
2. _letting emotions rule delay in by organizate_
3. _____ / and r Directors._

What will be your first steps in this plan?

1. Discuss ē the group As DIN/TLs _____

2. _____

3. _____

Share this plan with your support people. Good luck!

CHAPTER TWO

EMOTIONAL SELF-CONTROL
TOOLS AND STRATEGIES

*Mindfulness isn't difficult. What is difficult
is to remember to be mindful.*

—John Teasdale

Mindfulness is the opposite of mindlessness.

—Dan Siegel

This section provides the tools and strategies to help you become a Star Performer in Emotional Self-Control. A definition of Emotional Self-Control is provided and illustrated by examples of "Fallen Stars"—those who suffered career derailment because they were unable to control their impulses. Of all the derailers, this one seems to bring down Stars the fastest, and it seems to be the most common. Other chapters start with a Star Secret success story rather than Fallen Stars stories.

The *Coach's Corner* identifies tools you or your direct reports can use to manage your impulses and emotions. In the corporate world, a four-second outburst can tarnish a leader's career because it is what becomes chiseled in others' minds about you. What causes this unintended outcome, and what can we do to prevent this loss of rational thought and reputation? Tools to gain more cognitive control will be presented and explained in this chapter.

WHAT IS THE EMOTIONAL SELF-CONTROL COMPETENCY?

Emotional Self-Control is demonstrated by a leader being able to manage impulsive and/or distressing feelings. Leaders who are competent in Emotional Self-Control are able to stay composed, calm, and unflappable in stressful situations, regardless of the environment. They have control of their emotions versus their emotions controlling them. Leaders with Emotional Self-Control think clearly while under pressure.[1] Their IQ and executive functioning stay intact. One reason why Emotional Self-Control is so critical to focus on is that it is fragile and thus can be lost in a second with devastating effects.

EMOTIONAL INTELLIGENCE RESEARCH EXAMPLES

Case studies of wrecked careers were examined by a consulting firm in the course of testing 4,265 people from all levels in the organizations studied. These employees all had lack of impulse control, with little ability to delay gratification.[2] In a study of 700 professional football players in the NFL, including draft choices and college players, those with higher levels of restraint were rated by their coaches as having greater ability, being more motivated, being stronger leaders, and as easier to coach.[3] Store managers who are best able to manage their stress and stay unemotional have the most profitable stores in a national retail chain.[4]

STRESS, EQ, AND IQ

Henry Thompson has been studying the effects of stress on EQ and IQ since the early 1980s. In one study he exposed people to the stress of a baby crying and found that the higher the stress the less emotionally intelligent participants behaved.[5] Thompson did another study with 62 participants taking the EQi under normal and simulated "stressed-out" mindset conditions. He found the stressed-out mindset participants scored 20 points below the normal participants. This was one standard deviation less than the norm. These results suggest that "Stress may reduce the leader's access to his or her full EI ability."[6] Thompson had similar findings when using the MSCEIT assessment: the "stressed-out" mindset had an average total score again almost one standard deviation (13 points) below the normal group.

When stress is high, as it is in most organizations, it is critical that the leader be able to manage his or her stress as well as the teams'. Leaders who are unable to manage their stress fall into the EQ, IQ Brain Drain Loop discussed in the Introduction. When their EQ goes down it affects their IQ and their cognitive decision-making abilities. Thompson has stated that a "high stress environment would be expected to restrict leaders' access to their full EQ and IQ potential."[7] This is exactly what I have witnessed time and time again with the business simulation we conduct with organizations.

Are you a Star Performer in emotional self-control or just average? Do you regularly, consistently (at least 80% of the time) stay calm, unflappable, and clearheaded in high-stress situations?

WHERE DID MY IQ GO?

We have all had the experience of doing something in the heat of the moment that we regretted later. Our reaction flew out of the gate before we could catch it. It's as if our rational mind stopped and what came out not only surprised us, but everyone around us too. We ended up saying, "How could I do that? What could I have possibly been thinking?" Well, in reality, we weren't thinking clearly, we were overwhelmed with an emotional reaction. We were *hijacked*.

The *amygdala hijack* is a term coined in Daniel Goleman's *Emotional Intelligence*, his first book on the subject. The amygdala is the emotional part of the brain that regulates the fight, flight, or freeze response. When threatened, it can respond irrationally. A rush of stress hormones floods the body before the prefrontal cortex (PFC) can mediate this reaction. The prefrontal cortex regulates executive functioning, which includes understanding, deciding, recalling, memorizing, and inhibiting emotions. It is essential for thinking things through versus being on "autopilot."[8] The PFC is relatively slow in making decisions (100 milliseconds), while the amygdala is quick (15 milliseconds).[9] This means we feel before we think! The amygdala can override the prefrontal cortex with uncontrolled automatic responses.

Over the last few years we have gained a more user-friendly knowledge base about the brain and leadership from David Rock, who created the field of NeuroLeadership and has integrated the works of many neuroscientists in annual conferences and in his recent books *Your Brain at Work* and *Coaching with the Brain in Mind*. Rock presents the work of Amy Arnsten, a professor of neurobiology at Yale Medical School. She has devoted her career to the mysteries of the prefrontal cortex. Arnsten reports that the PFC holds the contents of the mind, especially those which we generate ourselves internally. It has limitations, though, as it can only hold so many thoughts. "It has to have everything just right or it doesn't function well."[10] Deciding and holding what you want to see happen while inhibiting the plethora of emotions and stresses drains your prefrontal capacity and creates the foundation for an amygdala hijack.

BRAIN NEUROSCIENCE: UNDERSTANDING HOW THE HIJACK HAPPENS

We now know there are two minds—one that thinks and one that feels. Research by Joseph Le Doux reported by Goleman states, "The architecture of the brain gives the amygdala a privileged position as the emotional sentinel, able to hijack the brain."[11]

The stimulus comes in from the eyes or ears and goes immediately to the thalamus and then directly to the amygdala before a signal reaches the neocortex. This survival mechanism lets us react to things before the rational brain has time to mull over the situation. Unfortunately, the hair-trigger amygdala can be sloppy and distort things in this quick reaction, as the following examples of Fallen Stars show.

It has been found that the amygdala in animals can respond to a perception in as little as 12 thousandths of a second (.012). The antennae are up in the amygdala to constantly scan the environment for anything that may hurt us or that we should fear. Any strong emotion, anxiety, anger, joy, or experience of betrayal trips off the amygdala and impairs the prefrontal cortex's working memory. The power of emotions overwhelms rationality. That is why when we are emotionally upset or stressed we can't think straight.

Matthew Lieberman, a neuroscientist, has found an inverse relationship between the amygdala and the prefrontal cortex, the brain's executive function where rational thought and judgment sit. When the amygdala is active with blood and oxygen, there is less activation in the prefrontal cortex. When this occurs our thinking power is disrupted and there are deficits in our problem solving because the blood and oxygen are in the amygdala rather than the prefrontal cortex. It is like losing 10 to 15 IQ points temporarily, which explains the "What was I thinking?" experience. In this situation we are thinking, but with less capacity and brainpower.

In today's economy most people are walking around with greater than normal stress, apprehension, and fear of the future. You could say that every organization is suffering at some level from emotional hijacks, and thus organizations may be operating in a "dumbed-down" fashion because too much stress turns off the prefrontal cortex. This is at a time when we need all our IQ points and more resources, not less.

Emotions are contagious, so if one person is emotionally hijacked on your team or in your organization, most likely others will catch it, like the flu. Thus, your team can quickly lose IQ points, thereby jeopardizing executive decisions and deteriorating teamwork and collaboration.

Leaders' ability to manage their emotions then is paramount as they are the "emotional thermostat" for the team and can influence the team's mood and productivity. Their emotions of the leader are the most contagious. The Hay Group has found that the leader has a 50% to 70% influence over the climate of the team. Freedman and Everett state that 70% of the top issues in the workplace are tied to leadership. So leaders and their level of emotional intelligence have an enormous influence on the team.[12]

STRESS ⇧   EQ ⇩   IQ ⇩

Thompson has hypothesized that the lower one's EQ, the faster one may get hijacked, and the lower one's starting EQ, the less stress it will take to get hijacked.[13] This is a powerful rationale for raising the organization's EQ with resulting higher IQ, better decisions, and overall increased performance.

FAMOUS FALLEN STAR HIJACKS

Let's look at some famous amygdala hijacks and the results for these Fallen Stars. What themes do you see? Although we may not be famous, what can we learn from these stories about ourselves and the managing and integration of our relationships, brain, and mind?

ZINEDINE ZIDANE'S HEAD-BUTT

In front of 28.8 million viewers in 213 countries, Zinedine Zidane, a worldwide soccer role model, lost his self-control and head-butted Marco Materazzi in the 2006 World Cup soccer finals. Zidane was kicked out of the game. France lost the World Cup to Italy, and Zidane's career ended in disgrace. The viewers might have wondered, "What was he thinking?" Again, he wasn't.

Zidane's surprising and aggressive response demonstrates the three signs of the amygdala hijack: 1) strong emotional reaction, 2) sudden onset, and 3) regret for your actions when you reflect later.

Zidane apologized to the worldwide children and fans for his actions, but he remained unrepentant to Materazzi and rationalized that Materazzi's statements provoked him. Zidane's comments demonstrate the seriousness of his high-profile hijack. His logic was suppressed by the powerful tunnel vision survival reaction of the amygdala. No one else can *make* you do something against your better judgment, but the amygdala always can.

Zidane rationalized later that he knew there were only minutes left in his last career game and Materazzi's remarks demanded retaliation. He was not thinking logically at that time, and his response in explaining his behavior afterward characterizes what we call cognitive dissonance. In other words, he sought to explain his action by arguing that there must have been a good reason to do something so stupid in front of 28.8 million viewers.

TIGER WOODS'S SEX SCANDAL

The world's best golfer is suddenly discovered to have had multiple affairs or flings outside of his marriage. He is known as a private person who calls himself and his wife Elin "boring people." We further learn that he backed out of his driveway in the morning and hit a fire hydrant, damaging his car, and got banged up himself. Then after attempts to deal with the matter privately he admits to numerous transgressions—as many as 14 different women over many years—and enters a sex addiction clinic. What happened to his self-assessment and insight into himself? How could he think no one would find out? Where did his IQ go? What prevented him from managing these impulses? Will he ever be able to get back his career without distractions? How many millions of dollars will he continue lose as a Fallen Star? These questions will be answered in the months and years to come. What was he thinking? Again, he wasn't.

In his apology, Tiger Woods stated, "I convinced myself normal rules didn't apply to me. . . . I thought I could get away with whatever I wanted. I felt entitled thanks to money and fame. I don't get to play by different rules. How could I be so selfish and self-centered? Failure has helped me look at myself in a way I never have before."

JOE WILSON'S "YOU LIE!" OUTBURST

Representative Joe Wilson, the GOP congressman from South Carolina, shocked many observers when he shouted, "You lie!" after the president denied that health care legislation would provide free coverage for illegal immigrants in a 2009 speech. Wilson said he was referring to two amendments on one version of the proposed health care legislation that he said would have provided for verification of citizenship, but were defeated.

Wilson's outburst was criticized by members of both parties. After the speech, Senator John McCain of Arizona, the Republican presidential candidate in 2008, called Wilson's outburst "totally disrespectful" and told CNN's "Larry King Live" that there was "no place for it in that setting or any other."[14]

Other Republicans also criticized Wilson, along with the expected Democratic condemnation. "It was crude and disrespectful," said Senate Majority Whip Dick Durbin, D-Illinois. "I think the person who said it will pay a price."

CNN reported that shortly after Obama's speech, Wilson called the White House and issued a statement apologizing for his "inappropriate and regrettable" comments. According to Wilson, administration officials said they appreciated his call and emphasized the need for "a civil discussion." "I certainly agree with that," Wilson said. Wilson said his outburst wasn't planned—in other words, it was a hijack that he wasn't able to manage.

"It was spontaneous. It was when he stated, as he did, about not covering illegal aliens, when I knew we had those two amendments, and I say that respectfully," Wilson said.

Wilson is expected to have tough time against his Democratic challenger in his next election as result of his outburst. Those few seconds of lack of emotional self-control and not thinking have defined his career and possibly arrested it.

SERENA WILLIAMS'S OUTBURST

Serena Williams screamed obscenities to the line judge in her 2009 U.S. Open tennis match final with Kim Clijsters.

She was serving at 5-6, 15-30 in the second set and faulted on her first serve. She had already lost the first set. On the second serve, a line judge called a foot fault, making it a double fault, which made the score 15-40 and just about gave Kim Clijsters the victory with one more point. Williams "lost it" by yelling, cursing, and threatening the line judge. The judge then assessed a point penalty for a code violation of unsportsmanlike conduct, which meant Williams not only lost her cool but also the match.

Williams subsequently was fined a record amount of $82,500 and was put on probation for the next four Grand Slam events. During the probation period, Serena had to remain calm and play her game or she would get barred from the next U.S. Open and have to pay an extra $175,000.

One interesting aspect about this outburst was that Williams was so emotional she didn't remember what she had said. Her prefrontal cortex was so overwhelmed by the amygdala's reaction that she had no cognitive recall.

In talking about the outburst in her post-match news conference, Williams said, "I used to have a real temper, and I've gotten a lot better, so I know you don't believe me, but I used to be worse. Yes, yes, indeed. . . . I didn't threaten [her]. I don't remember anymore [what I said], to be honest. I was in the moment. And, you know, everyone's fighting for every point. It was a really crucial point."

Williams has been criticized for her arrogant response and for not seeming repentant, as she stated, "Players, athletes get frustrated."

OTHER FAMOUS HIJACKS

You may be familiar with other celebrity hijacks, such as Mike Tyson biting Evander Holyfield's ear in their 1993 title boxing match. His hijack cost him $3 million and lost his boxing license. Enron's executives appear to have experienced numerous hijacks over their tenure, which ended with many in jail, with plenty of time for clearer thinking.

THE COACH'S CORNER: 8 STRATEGIES FOR EMOTIONAL SELF-CONTROL

The good news is that this loss of IQ points is temporary. Self-Control and Self-Management are a leaders' ability to be aware of what they are experiencing as another data set of information and be able to accept, manage, and adjust to their emotions. These emotions are just as important as our thoughts, if not more, given their power to overwhelm us.

Below are strategies and actions to use to gain better Emotional Self-Control and help yourself or others to become Star Performers. As you read through the section, be aware of what you are already doing and which actions you could do more of.

Read through the strategies, and actions applications and pick one or two to try out.

1. SELF-AWARENESS: ARE YOU PREDICTABLE?

The first strategy for increasing Emotional Self-Control is to practice self-awareness.

The *Harvard Business Review* reminds us of the importance of self-awareness: "Executives who fail to develop self-awareness risk falling into an emotionally deadening routine that threatens their true selves. Indeed a reluctance to explore your inner landscape not only weakens your own motivation but can also corrode your ability to inspire others."[15]

"Awareness equals responsibility." This statement was made famous with the Gestalt Therapists. It means that being aware helps you have to the "ability to respond" or be "responsible." In the EI model awareness of yourself is the starting point—awareness of your strengths and weaknesses, your mood, your varying feelings, your behavior, your impact on others, your patterns, and your personal story. Once aware you are better able to manage, monitor, regulate, and control your reactions to situations. One useful awareness is evaluating your predictability.

A common issue with many executives is they may appear unpredictable to their followers. Unpredictability easily leads to feelings of distrust or a threat. Followers don't know if they can trust what the leader says or may do, as the leader may be impulsive and constantly changing their thoughts. If the leader is aware of their emotions, moods, strengths, and patterns they become more predictable and easier to trust. Predictability is more "brain friendly" than unpredictability. The brain and mind are free to pursue creative endeavors rather than be on the look-out for the next unpredictable event.

When dealing with trust issues, I often try to identify what is the core component of the lack of trust. I ask the leader to either rate themselves or one of their direct reports on a 1-10 rating, where 10 is high, on the following three areas:

1. Competency: Knowing their job, are they good at their technical skill?

2. Predictability: Are they consistent and do what they say would do?

3. Dependability: In a crisis or crunch can they be counted on being there and doing what it takes to get the job done?

Usually the lowest score is predictability, the person is not consistent thus it is hard to trust them. It usually comes down to the person not doing what was expected and not communicating about it. The unpredictability becomes the intermittent reinforcer or here the intermittent negative event that the receivers are cautiously watching out for. It is the same psychological factor that happens in gambling. People are poised to win the next time on a slot machine, either the 5th, 50th, or 500th time. Because it is intermittent or unpredictable, the whole time they are focused and ready to win at any moment. With an unpredictable outburst, dropped task, or uncommunicated mistake, the followers can be poised or looking for the next possible mishap versus looking for opportunities for growth or innovation.

This awareness of which trust component is causing the mistrust helps the leader or direct reports have a target on what to correct or monitor. Often it is the old adage of under promise and over deliver.

QUESTIONS AND ACTION APPLICATIONS

- Rate yourself on the three trust components, 1-10 where 10 is high.
- Which ones do you need to focus on the most?
- Ask your boss, co-workers, and significant others to rate you on the three.
- Where do you see commonality and where do you see differences?
- What are your next steps to improve here?

2. AFFECT LABELING

For decades, psychologists, counselors, priests, and educators have been helping people identify or label their feelings. For example, a counselor might say, "You must be very sad about your loss." Now we know from new research using the functional MRI that labeling these feelings helps reduce their intensity and return some of the activity back to the prefrontal cortex, resulting in more cognitive control. This identification can help the individual accept and normalize what he or she is feeling. The feelings are cognitively reappraised or reframed and thus less aroused. This is called affect labeling.

Dr. Matt Lieberman and colleagues scanned the brains of 30 people—18 women and 12 men between the ages of 18 and 36—who were shown pictures of faces expressing strong emotions. What they found is that when people attached a word like *angry* to an angry-looking face, the response in the amygdala portion of the brain that handles fear, panic, and other strong emotions decreased. Lieberman states, "This seems to dampen down the response in these basic emotional circuits in the brain. What lights up instead is the right ventrolateral prefrontal cortex, part of the brain that controls impulses."[16]

So, one way to gain back your lost IQ points is to label your feelings. We tell clients they need to name the feeling, normalize it, and nurture a new direction or action. In Alcoholics Anonymous they help people manage their emotions with the statement "you have to name it to tame it." Neuroscientists tell us the brain changes with attention and focus as these can change what parts of the brain are being activated. Chapter 6 offers tools to practice affect labeling and listen with empathy.

QUESTIONS AND ACTION APPLICATIONS

- Try naming your emotions many times in the day to develop a refined language of your feelings. There are many feeling word lists that help you get beyond the preliminary level of bad, mad, sad, and glad. *—paraphrase, feelingident.*
- Practice the Level 3 Listening in Chapter 6.
- Notice what patterns you see in the most common feelings you experience.
- Which range of feelings don't you experience often?

3. THE EMOTIONAL AUDIT

A leadership tool that can help with both self-awareness and self-management is called the Emotional Audit. It is designed to ask strategic questions that can change the focus when a person is emotionally charged or about to get hijacked. When you are counting to 10 to calm down, ask these questions to better direct your brain's thinking.

This audit is helpful, especially if you are feeling "triggered" by someone or something. Wait five seconds until you get an answer to each question. To build your self-awareness and self-management, use the audit numerous times during the day. You may notice certain patterns in what triggers you, how you are feeling, and how you get in your own way as a result of unmanaged emotions.

Below are the strategic Emotional Audit questions along with explanations of the hypothesized brain components that may be accessed by asking yourself these questions. The goal is to refocus activity away from the amygdala and "light up" other areas of the brain to gain more cognitive control and give you constructive options and direction. The first two questions access and label your thoughts and emotions. The third question makes your intentions conscious. The fourth question evaluates your actions in line with your intentions. Patterns of how you get in your own way may emerge. The last question takes in all this new conscious data and allows you to better direct your brain and actions toward the goals you want to achieve.

The more you practice the Emotional Audit the easier it will become, and you will see patterns emerging. I imagine you will get the same two or three answers to the first four questions each time you ask them. This acute awareness will give you more information, control, and self-management to generate better solutions with the fifth question, "What do I need to do differently now?" Making a few subtle changes can move you into the top 10% of performance.

As Dan Siegel explains it, "Our ability to pause before we react gives us the space of mind in which we can consider various options and then choose the appropriate ones."[17]

EMOTIONAL AUDIT

What am I thinking? (Accesses the basal ganglia, which integrate feelings, thoughts, and movements.)

What am I feeling? (Accesses the basal ganglia, which integrate feelings, thoughts, and movements, and the temporal lobes, which regulate emotional stability, by labeling affect or emotion, which allows you to "name it to tame it.")

What do I want now? (Accesses the cerebellum, which carries out executive functions and connects to the prefrontal cortex, where cognitive integration takes place.)

How am I getting in my own way? (Accesses the prefrontal cortex, which allows you to learn from mistakes.)

What do I need to do differently now? (Accesses the prefrontal cortex, which handles the "boss" supervision of life including executive functioning, planning, goal setting, and insight, as well as the anterior cingulate gyrus, the brain's "gear shifter" that sees options and goes from idea to idea to choose the best option.)

ANATOMY OF A HIJACK USING THE EMOTIONAL AUDIT

John was a leader who was known to have a hot temper. He was aware of it, and his supervisor had noted it as a part of his performance review. John was presenting at an internal national sales meeting when he "lost it" by yelling at some of his team members during the presentation to put their computers away. There was a hush and awkwardness as he continued his presentation. This was very embarrassing for him, cemented his "hothead" image, and limited his promotion potential.

What happened? John felt extreme pressure to do a good job. He prepared well and delivered the whole presentation himself. He did not delegate any of the preparation or delivery to his team members. Before the presentation, a few people came to him and said they were not going to attend his presentation because they were going to play golf with some of the executives. This was very irritating to him. John also was trying to stay on schedule because his time had been shortened and he was trying to squeeze a lot in. The presentation was also at the end of the day, a time when John's energies and his audience were dissipating. His executive functioning brain capacity to manage or regulate his emotions was spent or used up by this time. At the beginning of his presentation, some members of his team were answering e-mails on their computers in the back of the room. This upset him because he thought it was unprofessional of them, as well as embarrassing, because it was his team, and he asked them to put their computers away. He was also resentful that he was doing everything himself, even though it was his own decision. When John saw his team members later in the presentation again with their computers open answering e-mails, his amygdala saw this as a major violation. All the stress mounted into an emotional reaction, and he "lost it" and yelled at them.

As John was getting triggered with the second e-mail violation and he felt his tension building, an Emotional Audit could have revealed the following:

- **What am I thinking:** What are they doing? I already told them to put the computers away!
- **What am I feeling:** I am so frustrated with them—I can't believe this!
- **What do I want:** I want them to put the computers away and support me here.
- **How am I getting in my own way:** I am fuming and not calming myself down. I am ready to pounce on them.

- **What do I need to do differently:** I need to take a breath and walk over there and quietly say something to them.

We all get hijacked at times, but great leaders know themselves well, anticipate situations that may be stressful for them, and take preventative measures before the emotional build up or explosion. In the stressful moment, they know what they are feeling *and* what they are thinking. They then have multiple constructive solutions to prevent an amygdala hijack and maintain their top performance.

QUESTIONS AND ACTION APPLICATIONS

- Write down a time you got hijacked and answer the five questions to better understand what was happening to you.
- To enhance your emotional self-awarenesss and emotional self-control practice doing the audit four times a day and see what patterns you recognize.
- Teach the audit to someone in your office or at work or home to help ingrain the questions.

4. PUTTING ON THE BRAKES

Why is it so hard to prevent these hijacks, especially after one begins? David Rock, in *Your Brain at Work*, examines the inhibitory or braking system for impulses that can lead to a hijack. The region within the prefrontal cortex that "lights up" when someone is inhibiting an impulse, cognition, or emotion is called the ventrolateral prefrontal cortex (VLPFC) and sits behind the right and left temples. This area appears to be central to the braking system. The better you can use this braking system the better you are at focusing and eliminating distractions.

This braking system is "part of the most fragile, temperamental and energy-hungry region of the brain, so stopping yourself from acting on an urge is something you can do sometimes but is often not that easy," Rock writes.[18] An important finding is that your capacity to put your brakes on decreases each time you do so. It is like the brake pads of your car getting eaten up each time you apply the brakes. Each time you stop yourself from doing something, the next impulse is harder to stop. Roy Baumeister of Florida University found that "Self-Control is a limited resource." This explains many of the hijacks in the examples. For example Serena Williams, Joe Wilson, and John above all used up their brain energy inhibiting previous impulses and urges before their outbursts.

In explaining their sexual scandals, Tiger Woods and other high-profile males like John Edwards and Eliot Spitzer, past governor of New York, may have used cognitive dissonance to rationalize their behavior: "I give so much to others I deserve this," or "I am entitled to this behavior, therefore I am not a bad person." Once they started this behavior and rationalized it their ability to control it was severely compromised.

Rock quotes the work of Libet on "free will" in the brain. Researchers found there are two-tenths of a second after we are aware of an impulse when we have "free will" or a chance to inhibit it. "Free won't" is a term coined by Dr. Jeffrey Schwartz to describe how we can circumvent or prevent urges—however, we have only this small window of time in which to say no to an urge.[19]

So to summarize, if we want to inhibit an impulse or urge we must consider the following:

1. We use up mental capacity each time we inhibit an emotion.
2. Once we are aware of the impulse, the window of time is quite small when we can exercise self-control and redirect our actions.
3. Each time we redirect our action, that pathway gets stronger.
4. Awareness or mindfulness can help increase our choices or solutions.

QUESTIONS AND ACTION APPLICATIONS

- Notice and write down what works when you put your emotional brakes on. What did you do and say that helped regulate you?

- Watch others to decipher what they are employing to manage their emotions.

- What are your cues that your emotions are getting triggered or you are getting overwhelmed? Try to be aware and catch and redirect yourself early before the buildup. For me, I notice I exchange or fumble over words more while talking. This tells me to slow down and do something to relax.

- What activities work the best for you to drain your emotional intensity, like taking a walk, talking to a friend, exercising, stretching or yoga, starting a different task, deep breathing, or relaxation.

- What activities recharge you the most and give you more energy during the day? Are you doing them regularly?

5. MINDFULNESS

Dan Siegel writes, "Being mindful, having mindful awareness is often defined as a way of intentionally paying attention to the present moment without being swept away with judgments."[20]

Mindfulness has been practiced in the East and West from ancient times to the present. Although it is practiced in many religions, mindfulness is not necessarily religious. It is a focusing of our attention that promotes health and can be seen as a brain hygiene.[21] It is a form of mental activity that trains the mind to become aware of its awareness and its own intentions. Also it promotes health, resilience, flexibility, calmness, and focus. These are key components for being a Star Performer, maintaining your IQ points, and being in the top 10%.

Neuroplasticity is the term used to describe the capacity for creating new neural connections and growing new neurons in response to an experience we have.[22] We now know that neuroplasticity occurs for a lifetime. We are always making new neural pathways, and it happens with our focus and attention.

What we focus on grows connections in our brain. Siegel writes, "The brain changes physically in response to experience, and new mental skills can be acquired with intentional effort, with focused awareness and concentration." Or easier to remember is the saying "Neurons that fire together wire together."

Research evidence that supports this indicates that animals rewarded for noticing sounds have growth in their auditory centers. Similarly, animals rewarded for attending to sights have growth in the visual areas in their brains. Researchers also report that the hippocampus, which is vital for visual memory, is enlarged in taxi drivers.[23]

Mindfulness practice can take many forms likes yoga, meditation, breathing awareness, Tai Chi, washing the dishes, and walking and being aware of all your surroundings. One executive stops at a golf driving range for 20-30 minutes before he goes home. He focuses on his swing movement, form, breathing, and hitting the ball without being judgmental about the results. The result is that he has discharged the day's stress and is ready to enjoy his family when he gets home.

Your mindfulness practice helps you be attuned to yourself, which helps you attune to others. The results can be more self-acceptance and compassion or empathy for others. Practicing mindfulness for 5 to 10 minutes a day can be what separates you from the good to be great.

QUESTIONS AND ACTION APPLICATIONS

- Try this as you read through this mindfulness exercise. You can do this breathing awareness exercise with your eyes either open or closed. Spend five minutes focusing on your breathing, feeling the air going through your nostrils. Feel your chest filling up with air; notice the sensation of the air leaving your body during exhaling. Hear the sounds around you. Bring your attention to how your stomach is moving up and down with each breath. Be aware of what you may be saying about yourself and stay nonjudgmental, just pay attention to it. Continue to focus on your breathing and stomach rising. Now pay attention to your feet on the floor, what parts are touching? Notice how your back feels against the chair and stay focused on your breath, your feet, and any stories you are telling about yourself. Continue this process of being aware of your surroundings and breathing. Notice the subtle lines and shadows in your room as you breathe until at least five minutes go by. It is OK to do longer than five minutes. If your mind wanders just gently bring back your awareness to your breath. Just observe your thoughts as if you were in a movie theater and your thoughts or memories are passing on the screen. View them in a nonjudgmental way, being open to what emerges. Congratulations—you did your first mindful exercise, if you haven't done this in the past.
- How did you feel after the mindfulness exercise?
- What differences in attention or energy did you notice?
- What patterns emerged for you?
- What do you need to do to make this a regular daily practice?

6. SHUTTLING EXERCISE: INTERNAL AND EXTERNAL AWARENESS

An exercise that can enhance mindfulness is to be purposefully aware of your external surroundings and then your internal sensations. Shuttling between them focuses you on your here-and-now experience in the moment. For example, I am aware of the following as I write this chapter:

- I am aware of the music I am listening to.
- I am aware of my breath.
- I am aware of the clicking of the keys as I type.
- I am aware of my feet crossed underneath me.
- I am aware of the flashing light of the memory stick.
- I am aware of rocking back in the chair.

This exercise can bring you right back into the moment and center you. You can also be aware of your tendency to drift off into thoughts or your internal narrative as you do this exercise, with such thoughts as, "This is hard. How long do I have to keep doing this? Will this really work for me?"

Again be your best friend here without criticizing yourself how you are doing this exercise.

QUESTIONS AND ACTION APPLICATIONS

- Which focus was easier for you—internal or external?
- Did you feel more grounded or centered after you did it?
- Did you experience any difference in energy shift by doing it?
- What did you notice about your narrative interrupting?
- Was there a common theme you noticed?
- Was it hard to be self-accepting about your results?
- What do you need to say to yourself to be kinder about your process and results?

7. IDENTIFYING TRIGGERS

Another exercise that can help with Self-Awareness and Emotional Self-Control is to identify your main triggers. A trigger is something that gets you upset, irritated, or impatient. Make a list of your main triggers that could get your amygdala aroused. Triggers usually are things that others do that irritate you and, less frequently, can be something about yourself. Another way to look at it is to ask, "What are the things that not only irritate me but also drain my mental capacity?"

Some examples include the following:

- People interrupting you
- Someone not honoring your values
- People who seem incompetent
- Someone who talks too much *or asks too many ?'s*
- People being angry or irritated with you *uses too many words to get a point across*
- Rude people
- Lateness
- Clutter
- People who are arrogant or who seem to think they are "the smartest person in the room"
- Too much noise

QUESTIONS AND ACTION APPLICATIONS

- What are your top triggers?
- Which ones are most frequent for you? *too much talking*
- Which ones are most intense for you?
- Which ones do you have the least patience for?
- Which trigger drains you the most?

8. REAPPRAISAL

Reappraisal is a technique drawn from psychotherapy and cognitive restructuring where you give an experience or situation a new, different, and more constructive meaning. This helps bring in the prefrontal cortex functions and releases the grip of the amygdala hijack. The questioning process "lights up" executive functioning like the questions of the Emotional Audit. If you find yourself with distressing emotions, you can ask yourself questions like the following:

- What can I learn from this?
- How can I turn this into a meaningful experience for me?
- What would I tell someone else to do in this situation?
- Is what I am telling myself about this really true?
- What evidence is there to support my interpretation of this event?
- What are two or three other interpretations that could be more accurate?
- What is the best thing for me to do right now?

QUESTIONS AND ACTION APPLICATIONS

- Which questions work the best for you to help change the situation?
- What patterns do you see emerging with your emotions?
- What is your most common emotion?
- Do your interpretations of situations get better after the initial one?

STAR PERFORMER ACTION PLAN

Read through the Fallen Stars examples and *Coach's Corner* to develop your Emotional Self-Control skills. Now, answer the following questions to help you make your plan. Remember, micro-initiatives can make a macro impact.

Which competencies or practices do you already do that you want to continue?

1. _Naming emotions_

2. _____

3. _____

Which new practices do you want to incorporate?

1. _____

2. _____

3. _____

What resources do you need to make this happen?

1. _____

2. _____

3. _____

Who can support you and hold you accountable?

1. _____

2. _____

3. _____

What will be your first steps in this plan?

1. _____

2. _____

3. _____

How might you sabotage your efforts and best intentions?

1. _____

2. _____

3. _____

Share this plan with your support people. Good luck!

CHAPTER THREE

SELF-CONFIDENCE
TOOLS AND STRATEGIES

Confidence is the fuel that ignites other actions.

This section provides the tools and strategies to help you become a Star Performer in the area of confidence. *Self-confidence* is a building block for success throughout one's career and a key competency in the self-awareness cluster. A definition of *confidence* is illustrated with a research example about confidence-building, followed by a Star Profile of Henrik Fisker, one of the world's leading car designers. Fisker shares *10 Secrets & Current Practices* that help him shine as a confident Star Performer. He also describes some of the pitfalls he encounters from actually being overly confident!

The *Coach's Corner* adds to what you've just learned with a selection of 10 powerful proven strategies used by a cross section of top-notch executives and leaders for the development of confidence. Included are practical tools and a Star Performer Action Plan that will help you transform general ideas and concepts into tangible applications for guaranteed performance as a confident Star Performer.

WHAT IS THE SELF-CONFIDENCE COMPETENCY?

Confidence is knowing one's own abilities and having enough faith in them to make sound decisions in the face of uncertainty and pressure. A confident leader exudes a strong self-presentation and expresses him- or herself in an assured, impressive, and unhesitating manner. The confident leader will take on new challenges and hold on to his or her view, even if others disagree.[1]

EMOTIONAL INTELLIGENCE RESEARCH EXAMPLES

A variety of studies have demonstrated the positive impact of confidence on performance. A high degree of self-confidence distinguishes the best from the average performers as supervisors, managers, and executives.[2] Self-efficacy is a form of self-confidence; it is a belief in one's own abilities to take on a difficult challenge.

In a study of 112 entry-level accountants, those with the highest level of self-efficacy at the time of hiring were rated as having superior job performance by their supervisors 10 months later, showing that self-confidence is a higher predictor of performance than is skill level or previous training.[3] In another study, where more than 1,000 high-IQ men and women were tracked over 60 years, from childhood to retirement, those who possessed self-confidence during their early years were most successful in their later careers.[4] In a longitudinal study of managers at AT&T, the expression of self-confidence early in one's career also predicted promotions and success in higher management years later.[5]

Are you a star performer in self-confidence or just average? Do you regularly, consistently (at least 80% of the time) present in an assured, forceful, impressive, and unhesitating manner?

STAR PROFILE: HENRIK FISKER, CEO
FISKER COACHBUILD, LLC

Henrik Fisker is the CEO of the new luxury car company Fisker Coachbuild, LLC. After a successful career designing cars for major car manufacturers, he chose to start his own company, with a focus on designing and producing exclusive, high-end sports cars.

Aside from award-winning designs, Fisker received $528.7 million in federal loans to develop electric and fuel-efficient vehicles. The "Karma" will be an $87,900 plug-in sedan. He is also manufacturing the "Nina," a $47,400 plug-in car, and hopes to sell 75,000 to 100,000 Ninas per year.

Fisker was Director of Ford's Global Design Studio in Irvine, California. He also served as Director of Design for the Aston Martin division at Ford Motors Company and, from September 2001 to August 2003, as Creative Director of Ingeni Design Company. Ingeni is a design studio in London that designs the merchandizing products for Land Rover, Jaguar, Aston Martin, Volvo, Mazda, Lincoln, and Mercury. In the first six months, Fisker took Ingeni from a start-up business to millions in revenue, working with employees from 15 different cultures. He was also responsible for the design and success of the $155,000 Aston Martin DB-9, the car that won the Robb Report "Best of the Best" award in 2005. Fisker also designed the show car and upcoming production car of the long-awaited Aston Martin AM-V8 Vantage.

Before being recruited by Ford, Fisker served as the president of Designworks USA, a division of BMW, where he achieved a 400% profit increase in his first year. He was the designer of BMW's limited edition Z-8 (only 400 were produced), one of the world's most sought-after vehicles that retailed close to $200,000. The car was featured in the James Bond movie *The World Is Not Enough,* was named "Car of the Year" in 2000 by the Robb Report, and won the prestigious Red Dot Award in Germany.

FISKER WAS ASKED

- How did he learn this confidence competency?
- What does he do to be such an effective leader?
- What are his daily practices?
- What are the pitfalls he needs to be aware of?

EARLY LEARNING EXPERIENCES

Fisker stated, "I have always been good at leading people." He recalled a learning experience when he was 13 and engaged in an orienteering course to find a treasure: A group of boys were walking in the forest, and after looking at the map Fisker decided they needed to go to the right. The assigned leader and all the other boys said, no, they had to go left. Eighteen boys went to the left, whereas Fisker and one other boy went to the right and ended up finding the treasure. However, because they had split up his group didn't win, and Fisker got in trouble for leaving his team. One insight Fisker learned from this experience was to follow his convictions in spite of opposition from others. Another powerful result was learning that leaders can be decisive, but they need followers in order to be truly successful.

In his first four months as a designer at BMW, Fisker was working on a car interior with a senior designer, who asked him, "Do you want to take over this project?" Fisker had a feeling he could do it and said, "Yes," confidently, even though he didn't have a lot of experience. He saw that each time he took a risk it added to his confidence.

A role model for Fisker early in his career was Dr. Reitzle, the Development Chief of BMW, who made big decisions for the direction of the company in a very firm manner. "I saw a leader make a firm decision and the domino effect was positive. There was a wave of optimism transmitted down throughout the company." He saw that being decisive was a trait that was admired and was something he emulated.

10 SECRETS & CURRENT PRACTICES OF HENRIK FISKER—STAR PERFORMER

Read through the strategies and pick one or two to try out.

1. TAKE PRIVATE TIME

Fisker takes an hour and a half at lunchtime to work out and think through problems. He states that this dedicated period is "a hundred times more valuable than staying at work" where interruptions are the norm. He plays things over and over in his mind and explores many different scenarios and solutions. This is when Fisker gets a "feeling" for what he wants to do.

2. GET THIRD OPINIONS

Fisker believes in getting different opinions in order to have more information on certain issues. He knows what he thinks, but listens to other people's viewpoints for opinions and perspectives on the issue at hand. Fisker uses his networking skills to acquire multiple perspectives from many different sources.

3. EVALUATE CAPACITIES

Fisker evaluates the strengths and weaknesses of his team during his private time and gets a good feeling for what they can and cannot do. This allows him to gauge their window of capacity, builds trust, and helps him determine what challenges and risks he wants to present and to whom. When his team comes to him for a decision, Fisker has already evaluated what sorts of capabilities they possess and ultimately empowers them as he assigns his tasks.

4. SHOOT FROM THE HIP

Fisker prefers quick, firm, and empowering decisions. He also understands that most people don't like being managed and wants them to feel they are following their own motivation. The perception is that he makes these decisions because of blind trust. The person feels the motivation to work hard in order to demonstrate that he or she deserves that trust. Fisker captures the drama of the moment by seizing the decision-making power rather than waiting and thinking it over, which becomes anticlimactic and less empowering.

He likes to say, "Yes, go make it happen," knowing full well the positive effect this kind of response delivers. While his decisions may appear as "shooting from the hip," this is actually not the case at all. It is a much more calculated system, because of the time Fisker dedicates to Secrets #1, #2, and #3. His quick decisions are well-timed and create an optimum of emotional energy for his team.

5. GO WITH THAT GUT FEELING

Fisker takes pride in "going with his gut." For a designer, the look and feel of a car are more emotional than logical and, many times, beyond what we can put into words. Throughout his career he has depended on developing this visceral skill. Like many executives, Fisker has refined this ability, which allows him to make quick decisions when he needs to.

Cars make us feel a certain way, and this feeling comes from the amygdala, that small walnut-shaped area in the center of the brain. "Every experience we have an emotional reaction to, no matter how subtle, seems to be encoded in the amygdala."[6] There are nerve pathways that run from the amygdala to the internal organs, and thus the "gut feeling" comes from the brain.

6. TAKE INITIATIVE

Fisker believes in putting his "gut feeling" into practice and making decisions from it. After getting the "gut feeling," he assesses the risks and goes for it if appropriate. He feels this is an important part of being a leader. Fisker actualizes what leadership guru Warren Bennis, in his portrait of leadership traits, called "a bias toward action."[7] Fisker wants to take action and likes that quality in his direct reports. Taking initiative is the hallmark of a Star Performer in the confidence competency.

7. IDENTIFY YOUR STRENGTHS AND WEAKNESSES

Fisker believes that leaders should be aware of their "weak side." He defines this as "things you could do, but don't like to do." Preferring to generate power from his strengths, he chooses to have others assume the tasks he likes the least so that he can focus on what he is good at. He knows that when he does what he likes, he remains energized, creative, and competent.

8. TAKE RESPONSIBILITY FOR YOUR MISTAKES

Fisker believes you have to be honest with yourself and admit mistakes, so you can learn and move on. He tells the story of getting a ticket for going 112 mph in London, where any speed over 70 mph means the loss of your license. Aston Martin wanted to hire a lawyer for him, but Fisker decided to represent himself before the judge. Fisker admitted he had made a mistake and confessed that he was speeding because he was simply too busy. He added that he had already altered his schedule to fewer appointments as a way to admit his initiative to change. He took responsibility for the ticket, stated what he had learned, and was allowed to keep his license after paying a small fine.

9. REINFORCE PEOPLE

Fisker believes it is important to read your people and keep them motivated. He does this by being genuinely engaging with them, by asking questions to find out more about how they think and what they do. Fisker then acknowledges and supports their efforts.

10. BE WILLING TO MAKE DECISIONS THAT ARE EXCEPTIONS TO THE RULE

Fisker states that a leader needs to identify the consequences of a decision, decide if it is worth it, and then act on it. Many of his examples focus on paying less attention to time-consuming bureaucratic procedures. If he feels it is the right decision and that he can cope with the consequences, he goes ahead without all of the red tape. Fisker counts on being successful and believes that not following procedures all of the time is minor compared to the potential successes of his decisions to take action.

PITFALLS: WHAT FISKER NEEDS TO BE AWARE OF

- For Fisker, there is the danger of overusing his self-confidence. Fisker admits he can overpower people with it and adds, "You have to use your confidence appropriately and be able to back off strategically where there is the least impact and let things go." He is sensitive to not overruling people if at all possible.

- It is important for Fisker to know his audience and encourage them to have their area of expertise. It is also important that he invite his team to openly ask questions.

- Fisker needs to remember to pace his decisions and actions, never assuming that he is on the same mindset or wavelength as others. He admits that he "wants to keep people in sight" and not leave them behind.

- If Fisker feels he is putting out a lot of fires, he knows he is losing touch with the organization. There needs to be an infrastructure through which he can quickly get information and slow down his speed if necessary. Feedback from the management team is crucial.

ACTIONS: REVIEW FISKER'S CURRENT PRACTICES

What practices can you glean from Fisker's story and employ in order to be a Star Performer in Confidence? Which ones do you want to add to your Star Performer Action Plan?

1. _evaluate capacities of others_
2. _shoot from the hip_
3. _____

THE COACH'S CORNER: 10 STRATEGIES FOR SELF-CONFIDENCE

Below are 10 proven strategies you can use to improve your confidence. Confidence is the fuel to take risks, try new things, and make the micro-initiatives necessary to become a Star. As you read through the list, be aware of what you are already doing and what actions you could do more of.

Read through the strategies and pick one or two to try out.

1. BEING ON YOUR CASE VS. BEING ON YOUR SIDE *NO*

Many leaders have "faulty evaluation systems." They are rarely satisfied when successful and are overly critical of their performance even if they win and win big. This can become a rigid pattern. In the past it may have driven them to great successes, but over time it can become a burden. They tend to continually try harder and often fall short in their own eyes, often sense that they are torturing themselves, and still fall short in their own eyes. These leaders will readily admit that they are hard on themselves, but they believe it is the only way to push themselves to their best performances. It is as if they have a calculator that is defective, but they do not realize it is always off one digit. When evaluating themselves, the calculator should read 1,000, but instead it reads 100. They get upset about the reading, but don't realize their evaluation system is faulty or broken.

> . . . they have a calculator that is defective, but they do not realize it is always off one digit.

There are three major unintended consequences of Being on Your Case rather than Being on Your Side:

- These leaders are never satisfied with their performance, and their self-confidence is affected.

- Because everything seems to be less than they had hoped, they are miserable, tense, and unhappy.

- Unconsciously they treat others the same way they treat themselves—overly critical, picky, negative, and never satisfied.

Most leaders who are hard on themselves are blinded to the problems inherent in their leadership style. Sometimes they require strong language (!) to alert them to the serious impact this kind of pattern has on their ultimate performance and well-being. If you recognize yourself in the above profile, answer a simple question: What percentage of the time are you on your case instead of on your side? Use a scale of 1-100. You can tell if you or others have a faulty evaluation system if after every performance you establish that you should have had:

- Better effort

- Higher quality

- Faster delivery

The manifestation of this kind of attitude is typically feeling scolded by yourself for failing to live up to your abilities. It's almost like you take out your whip and begin snapping yourself into shape. You may even say or think: "How could I be so stupid? When am I going to finally learn? What is wrong with me?" More, better, faster, more, better, faster . . . becomes an automatic negative self-evaluation system.

ANDREA'S STORY

Andrea was an executive in an agency and constantly felt she was behind in everything she was doing—emails went unanswered, voicemails were not returned, one-on-ones with staff were cancelled or rescheduled. Her evaluation system was harsh and unforgiving in spite of many of the positive things she was initiating at the agency. Andrea often spent her first moments with an employee apologizing for something she had failed to get around to. Her confidence was affected and her negative self-evaluation started to influence others. Perhaps she wasn't as competent as they had thought she was?

In one of our coaching sessions, Andrea achieved a breakthrough when I pointed out that she had apologized three times in 30 minutes. It was obvious she was overly critical of herself. She became painfully aware of how automatic this evaluation system was and, more importantly, recognized that it was quite possibly inaccurate. Andrea also became aware of how pervasive this pattern was in all of her interactions and that it undermined her leadership abilities as well.

> Changing our self-evaluation greatly improves how confident we feel and allows us greater awareness of how we evaluate others.

Andrea started out saying she was on her own case 80% of the time. Through talking about this pattern's impact and building awareness, she was able to get it down to about 40%. It was important for her to understand that she was not trying to eliminate Being on Her Case, but rather reframing it into Being on Her Side. With some real commitment and practice, she developed the ability to catch the pattern faster and redirect it from Being on Her Case to Being on Her Side.

Andrea became more On Her Side and, as a result, was less demanding of her staff and more on their side as well. She even encouraged her staff to be more realistic about the amount of tasks they were handling and to cut back on their commitments. In order to help her track this pattern, in each successive meeting I would ask what percentage of the time she was Being on Her Case versus Being on Her Side.

Changing our self-evaluation greatly improves how confident we feel and allows us greater awareness of how we evaluate others.

REDIRECTING QUESTIONS

The best way to change from Being on Your Case to Being on Your Side is first to notice how you behave and then turn the evaluation into a learning and action plan. Following are some examples of whipping statements and statements that will help you redirect yourself to Being on Your Side.

"On Your Case" Whipping

- How could I be so lame?
- Don't I know better than this?
- I'm an idiot for doing this!
- Why didn't I start this sooner?
- I could have done a much better job!
- What is wrong with me?
- I should have known better!

"On Your Side" (Phrases That Redirect Your Habit)

- Which parts of this performance went well?
- What didn't turn out the way I wanted it to?
- What exactly didn't work out here?
- Which part is under my influence?
- Is there anything I could have done differently?
- What will I have to do to accept this performance and not beat myself up?
- What can I learn from this performance?
- What will I have to improve next time?
- Is there any learning, training, or help I need to improve my performance?
- What will be my next step?
- How will I make sure I stay on track?

Notice the quality of the statements above and their effect on you. It is important to first acknowledge what went well, in order to establish the proper perspective in your evaluation and curtail the "more, better, faster" pattern.

The following chart shows the difference between the two types of self-evaluations.

Circle the terms you experienced as a result of your self-evaluation.

	ON YOUR CASE	ON YOUR SIDE
Quality	Demanding	Respectful
	Damaging	Constructive
	Irrational	Rational
	Over-generalized	Realistic
Results	Dissatisfied	Encouraged
	Less confident	Action plan for future
	Overwhelmed	Energized

QUESTIONS AND ACTION APPLICATIONS

- How accurate is your evaluation system?
- On a scale of 1-100, what percentage of the time are you on your case?
- How do you feel after you've been on your case?
- What are the consequences for you and others for being on your case?
- Do you treat others as harshly as you do yourself?
- Is this an effective pattern for you to continue with?
- If you don't change this, what do you stand to lose or miss out on?

- Keep track of the times you have stopped being on your case and then redirected yourself to being on your side.
- What is most difficult about being on your side?
- What helps you to be on your side?
- Keep track in your planner of the percentage of time you are on your side each day, 1-100.

2. REFLECTIONS ON THINKING

When we reflect on our thinking, we usually ask ourselves a series of questions, such as: What am I going to do about this project? Why is my co-worker so uncooperative? Why did I get passed over at the last promotion?

This is an unconscious process that stimulates the answers. The brain has been compared to a computer, even though it is far more complex. When we ask ourselves a question, our brain runs through its files to bring up an answer on our screen of awareness. We take this answer as a fact and move forward without questioning the process. If we ask ourselves poor or unconstructive questions, we will get answers that are negative and not helpful or proactive.

Part of being more confident is to be awake and aware when you ask yourself internal questions. When you pay more attention, you may notice that the questions often catalyze a cascade of negative responses and a familiar pattern of Being on Your Case. Your questions can "lead the witness" with inferences that a judge wouldn't allow in a court of law. The famous "When did you stop beating your wife?" is an example of getting stuck in a nasty loop. Unfortunately, when we ask ourselves self-deprecating questions we rarely come back with an "objection" to the kind of negative answer that comes up. Nor do we consider the fact that this knee-jerk answer may not be true and is simply a reflection of how we have programmed ourselves in the past.

ARE ANY OF THESE QUESTIONS FAMILIAR?

- Why am I always screwing up?
- How come I'm not good enough?
- How could I be so stupid?
- Why didn't I say something smart at the meeting?
- When will I finally learn?

The brain searches your history and comes up with pat answers such as: "I have always been a slow learner," or "I am not as smart as others," or "I am always making stupid mistakes," or "I'll never get ahead." These programmed responses make you hang your head and lose confidence. It's time to take control of the programming of negative self-talk. Let your brain search its files for a more positive, constructive, and useful answer. The questions and actions below can help you in this process.

QUESTIONS AND ACTION APPLICATIONS

- Be more aware of the questions you ask yourself. Write them down and collect them over a week.
- Ask your questions out loud. Listen, and then evaluate what you are really asking your brain to search for.
- Are your questions positive or negative?
- What kind of answers are you getting?
- Evaluate the biases in your questions. Are you leading the witness? Are you setting yourself up for failure? Would a judge allow your questions?
- Are you using over-generalized words such as "always" and "never"?
- Using the following five questions will consistently lead to better answers. Think of a situation for reflection. Now use the questions to generate positive confidence-building answers:

▲ What can I learn here?

▲ How can I be more on my side?

▲ What do I feel good about here?

▲ How do I best deal with this situation?

▲ How do I bring all my resources to this issue?

3. BUSTING PERFECTION: CREATING REALISTIC EXPECTATIONS

Success-driven people always set goals for themselves, but often these goals set them up for failure or frustration. Why? Because the goals are unrealistic to start with and constitute a pattern that is a setup for failure. This can lead to Being on Your Case and becoming dissatisfied with performance.

There are three key reasons for this pattern:

• These expectations are made automatically without the benefit of critical thinking.

• Once made, the expectations are no longer examined for their accuracy or realism.

• These unrealistic expectations are adhered to as the Golden Rule and clung to tenaciously.

Striving for perfection, a characteristic which once served as a standard for effort, quality, satisfaction, and acknowledgment, now operates as a carrier of the "more, better, faster" self-evaluation cycle. If left unexamined, perfection changes from a motivating driver to a relentless torturer.

THE PERFECTION LOOP

The Perfection Loop illustrates this now-familiar debilitating self-evaluation cycle (see Figure 3.1). How much does it reflect your behavior or the behavior of those around you?

FIGURE 3.1   SIX STAGES OF THE PERFECTION LOOP

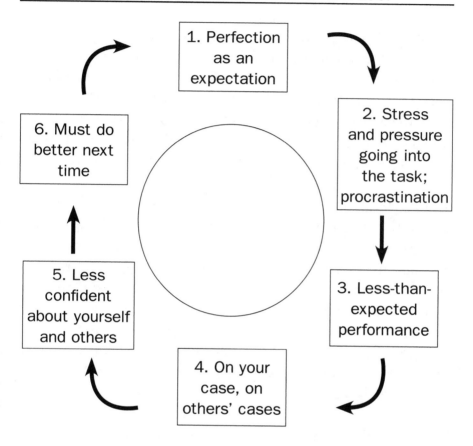

This pattern occurs unconsciously, repeatedly, and quickly. Before you know it, you are in it. The goal of identifying this loop is to:

- Become aware of the unproductive pattern
- Understand the steps that cause it and how they influence behavior and performance
- Know what to change to get different results

Perfection as an Expectation

The goals you set are very lofty and made without the benefit of critical thinking or truly examining their feasibility. "Perfection" rationalizes that you need to stretch and push yourself, so you set goals that are extreme, unrealistic, unattainable, and without the slightest margin of error. A thorough assessment of what it takes to reach them is not made, and you are doomed to complete the loop. Most of the time the effort, resources, and training you need to accomplish the goals are not taken into consideration.

In *Pure Genius*, Dan Sullivan talks about the differences between ideals and goals and how we often evaluate ourselves against the ideal and always fall short. He uses the example of the horizon, which, even though we can see it, doesn't really exist. If we chase the horizon, it keeps moving back and we never reach it. Sullivan recommends that we ask ourselves where we have come from and assess our progress in achieving our goal. This evaluation will leave us feeling better about our progress. If perfectionism is not curtailed, it will thrust you into the endless Perfection Loop, which is like being thrown into rapids where the force of the water controls where we go.

Stress and Pressure Going into the Task; Procrastination

Extreme expectations influence your state of achieving this goal. Pressure, anxiety, and stress accompany the preparation for the task and can have an impact on the focus and creativity needed to move toward the unattainable goal. On an unconscious level, you know that the task is overwhelming and that you have set yourself up for failure. This only adds to your anxiety. One typical response is procrastination disguised as giving yourself time to get ready. It's going to take all your effort so "planning" is actually worrying, "preparing" is actually avoiding, and "resting" is actually putting off. All of this leads to more procrastination. This stage of the loop compounds your performance even more.

Procrastination's Seduction

SEDUCTION	RESULT
"I better really plan."	Unproductive worry
"I have to carefully prepare."	Avoiding doing anything
"I better rest to ready myself."	Putting off effort
"If I had only had a little more time, I would . . . "	More worry, less effort

Less-Than-Expected Performance

The task is completed, and of course it is not at the level you expected. You could have done more, done a better job, started it sooner, and finished it faster. Repetitive "more, better, faster, more, better, faster" is a sign of a faulty evaluation system.

On Your Case, on Others' Cases

Your self-talk has pulled the whipping stick out. It is easy and habitual, and many leaders don't realize that their internal talk turns into the same conversation, but it can show up out loud when you communicate with your direct reports.

- "Why didn't I get this done sooner?" becomes "Why didn't you get it done sooner?"
- "How could I be so stupid?" becomes "What were you thinking?"
- "I am not cutting it and should have done a lot better" becomes "You are not cutting it or meeting my expectations."

Inside your own mind you are usually unaware of how harsh this kind of negative self-talk sounds. When you speak that way to others, your harshness can be very demotivating and detrimental. These automatic responses become who you are to the people you lead and have unintended negative consequences and repercussions.

Less Confident About Yourself and Others

There is less self-trust and trust in others as the loop continues and the estimation of success is less likely. Confidence is reduced.

Must Do Better Next Time

As a solution for stress and frustration, a leader makes the decision that, next time, "I'll try harder, start sooner, and do better." Now there is another setup put into place for the next task, which will unfortunately generate the same unrealistic expectations . . . and the loop goes on.

HOW TO COUNTER THE PERFECTION LOOP

To counter the debilitating effects of the Perfection Loop, you have to develop new behaviors early in the first or second steps— before the momentum sucks you in. Small changes at the beginning and throughout will help you break this pattern. To begin, think of a current expectation and answer the following:

- How realistic and attainable are your expectations?
- Do you thoroughly assess your expectations and plan for what it will take to get the task done?
- Rate yourself on a 1-10 scale with 10 representing your most realistic expectation. What is your rating?
- To what degree does perfection run your life or have control over you? Rate yourself from 1-100%.
- What is the first step you need to gain some control?
- Look at the Procrastination's Seduction chart (page 127). Which rationale do you use the most?
- What would be the best counter to the statement, "No, I need to develop a realistic plan and get something started now"?

- Is your evaluation system faulty?
- How is it faulty? (e.g., too rigid, uncompromising, etc.)
- What percentage of the time are you on your case after a performance?
- Refer back to some of the strategies from "Being on Your Case vs. Being on Your Side" on pages 117-122 to redirect your evaluations and self-talk.
- Once you have turned your evaluation into a learning experience, what is your plan for not getting into the Perfection Loop next time?
- How can you get others to support you?
- Who can give you feedback when they see you stuck in the loop?
- How will you know that you are listening?

4. SUCCESS RULES: WHO IS RUNNING YOU?

In this strategy, the objective is to become aware of your rules for being successful. All of us have them, but often they were made a long time ago and are outdated, too rigid, or over-generalized. It is like we have a nine-year-old inside of us who dictates what we should do and how. That is the age when we were becoming more on our own and trying to manage ourselves to get the best results. We made guidelines for ourselves such as:

- "Stay out of trouble."
- "Be polite to others."
- "Don't say anything stupid."
- "Don't make others upset."
- "Don't ever be satisfied."
- "Confidence is bragging."

When you were nine, these guidelines for good performance were probably very effective. Because you were successful, you kept using them. The problem occurs when:

- These guidelines become rules.
- Rules become calcified and are too rigid.
- Rules translate to everything, and you didn't realize how you abstracted them to cover all situations.
- You fail to update these rules to integrate your new learning and resources.

It's like you have an old version of software, let's say AOL 2.0, and are very happy knowing how everything works. It was once the best program available. Now with AOL 10.0 or higher, your email possibilities are far greater. The new version offers more services and is faster and simpler to use. You may hold on to outdated rules or programs without even realizing they are outdated. These unexamined rules leave you feeling unsatisfied and often like a failure. This little nine-year-old sits behind the steering wheel of your life, barely able to see the road, clipping parked cars along the way. How can you change and upgrade?

QUESTIONS AND ACTION APPLICATIONS

Write down the rules you live by as answers to the following: "What must happen for me to really feel successful?"

Feel free to write as many rules as come to mind.

Here are some sample answers to get you started: "To really feel successful . . . "

- "I have to be the president of whatever I do."
- "I have to be the smartest in the room."
- "I must earn . . . "
- "I have to have answers when people ask."
- "I must have the best house, car, etc."

- "I have to control everyone and everything around me."
- "I must feel happy every minute."

Next to each rule you list, write #1, #2, or #3 if true for that particular rule. It's fine to have up to three numbers per rule.

#1 = It is outdated

#2 = It is too rigid

#3 = It is over-generalized

Now, answer these questions:

- How many of your success rules are outdated? Too rigid? Over-generalized?
- What is the price for holding on to these rules?
- What is the first step to take in rewriting some of your success rules?
- If you were to refresh this particular rule, how could you make it more helpful and constructive?
- What will be the benefit for you in rewriting your rules?
- How will you know when rewriting these success rules actually makes a tangible difference?

5. SUCCESS LOG

Another strategy to enhance confidence is to write a log of past successes, broken into a chronology by age bracket. We all have had many successes in our life, which are easy to forget or minimize. These successes can leave footprints for future successes. And, you can build your confidence by simply reviewing the list.

QUESTIONS AND ACTION APPLICATIONS

Think of successes, activities, or events when you were proud of what you accomplished. These are the building blocks for confidence.

Age in Years

0-5

6-10 - sp.bee - piano

11-15 -

16-20 church and captain, 1ST job, marriage.

21-25 Kids

26-30 nursing degree

31-40 manager

41-50 BSW MSW job promotion.

51-60 new job -

61+

Go through your life from the time you were a young child and write down key successes for each age bracket. For example, you had a best friend in kindergarten, you had a lead role in a play in school, you won a Little League baseball game with your pitching, you received an award for a story you wrote in school, you were selected to give an orientation speech to incoming students, you were the editor of your high school yearbook, you were a cheerleader, you had good grades and won an award in college, you were selected team leader in your first job, you presented at a conference, you got an advanced degree, you started your own company, you wrote a book, and so on.

Now analyze your successes by answering these questions: persistent

- What efforts did you make to achieve this success? positive
- What was your preparation? research   outloud
- What obstacles did you have to overcome? support
- How did you feel about yourself afterward? successful
- What did people say about your achievement?
- How do you minimize your successes? - I don't
- What patterns or themes emerge from reviewing these successes?
- What key best practices or guidelines emerge for use in future endeavors?

6. CURRENT SUCCESS LOG

As an outgrowth of creating your Success Log, keep a current log of daily or weekly successes and achievements.

After a few months, analyze these successes by answering the same set of questions:

- What efforts did you make to achieve this success?
- What was your preparation?
- What obstacles did you have to overcome?
- How did you feel about yourself afterward?
- What did people say about your achievement?
- How do you minimize your successes?
- What patterns or themes emerge from reviewing these successes?
- What key best practices or guidelines emerge for use in future endeavors?

These successes can also help you define your strengths. What are you truly gifted at? Think about your successes against the following criteria of a strength defined by Marcus Buckingham:

1. Before the event there is a positive anticipation.
2. During the event there is a release of energy and joy and you are in "flow," a performance "sweet spot."
3. After the event there is a positive afterglow and appreciation.

QUESTION AND ACTION APPLICATION

- Which of your successes would you say meet this criteria as a strength?

7. THE FIVE PIVOTAL PEOPLE IN YOUR LIFE

A useful tool in building confidence is based on the notion of Phillip McGraw, also known as Dr. Phil, that each of us has five pivotal people in our lives who represent positive forces—people from our history who shaped our sense of self-worth and confidence.

QUESTIONS AND ACTION APPLICATIONS

Who were these five key people in your life? Write them down and then respond to the following for each key person:

- What capabilities did this person see in you?
- What did he or she say or do to motivate you?
- How did you feel in this person's presence?
- What are the main insights you received from this person?
- What have you internalized from this person?
- What have you rejected or minimized from this person?
- If this person was here today, what would he or she tell you?
- How are you sharing this learning with others today?

8. VISUALIZATION

The power of visualization has been well-documented in sports and theater performance. To improve your confidence, a regular visualization of mastering your most challenging situations will be helpful. You imagine yourself in the situation, performing exactly the way you want to perform. This kind of pre-practice informs your nervous system and helps create neural pathways to make the performance more natural.

QUESTIONS AND ACTION APPLICATIONS

- Find a quiet time to preview your day and the challenges you will encounter.
- Take five minutes to quiet yourself, take some deep breaths, and focus on the outcome you want.

- See it happening just the way you would want it to happen.
- Picture what others are saying to you, how you are feeling, and how it feels to be successful in the endeavor.

9. DECISIVENESS

In 1983, Quaker Oats bought the slumping sports drink Gatorade. CEO William Smithburg paid $220 million for Gatorade and turned it into a $3 billion business. When he came to his board to purchase Snapple in 1994, it seemed like a no-brainer. The acquisition, though, proved to be one of the most unsuccessful in American history. It cost Smithburg his job, and Quaker unloaded Snapple for $300 million in 1997 after having paid $1.8 billion for it.[8]

How could the Gatorade purchase be so successful and the Snapple deal be such a failure? The answer is: it is easy and natural to rely on old data to give us insight about a current decision. It is in our human nature to rely on historical precedent. We have a selective memory and recall what is recent or most traumatic and neglect subtle details or results.

KEY STEPS FOR DECISION-MAKING

Strong leaders do not act as the group's brain, but rather as consensus builders. When team leaders express their opinions too early in a decision-making discussion, the group generates fewer ideas and often makes poorer decisions. But when the leaders hold back and act mainly as facilitators of the group's process, without imposing their views until the end of the discussion, the outcome is a better decision.[9]

Lee Iacocca, who rebuilt Chrysler into a world-class auto company, states, "If I had to sum up in one word the qualities that make a good manager, I'd say that it all comes down to decisiveness . . . In the end you have to bring all your information together, set up a timetable, and act."

In making decisions it is crucial to:

- Cross-examine every precedent
- Clarify assumptions
- Have others challenge your thinking
- Not rely only on precedent
- Develop a disciplined process [10]

QUESTIONS AND ACTION APPLICATIONS

- What is your decision-making process?
- What kind of information, how much time, and what conditions do you need to make your best decisions?
- When you made your best decisions in the past, how did you do it?
- When you made your worst decisions, how did you do it?
- What patterns do you see?
- Do you tend to distort or over-generalize any specific type of information?
- How often do people consciously challenge your decisions?
- What could you do to make sure you get enough input? Do you play devil's advocate?
- On a scale of 1-10, how effective are you at using reflective time to mull over your major decisions?

10. THIN-SLICING

Malcolm Gladwell wrote *Blink: The Power of Thinking Without Thinking*, which immediately became a *New York Times* bestseller. The book gives fascinating examples and stories about how people make snap judgments in their decision-making, often without knowing why. He calls this "thin-slicing." Thin-slicing is "the ability of our unconscious to find patterns in situations and behavior based on narrow slices of experience."

Thin-slicing, snap judgments, and intuition all describe this phenomenon that happens unconsciously, behind the "closed door."

Researchers from Harvard suggest that people can intuitively sense, in the first 30 seconds of an encounter, basic impressions they have about a person. People watching 30-second snippets of teachers giving a lecture can assess each teacher's proficiency with approximately 80% accuracy as well.[11]

"In a study of three thousand executives, with regard to decision-making, those at the top in various fields were most adept at utilizing intuition in reaching their decisions."[12]

This nonlinear type of knowing is a good complement to the tried-and-true systematic thinking prevalent in traditional problem-solving.

QUESTIONS AND ACTION APPLICATIONS

- Do you know when you are having a gut reaction?
- How good are you at identifying your gut reactions, on a scale of 1-10, 10 being the highest?
- How good are you at honoring your gut reactions, on a scale of 1-10?
- What helps you get in touch with and listen to your gut?
- How often do you communicate these gut reactions to others?
- What do you need to do to utilize your intuition more?

STAR PERFORMER ACTION PLAN

The Star Performer Action Plan helps you integrate some of the learning from this chapter's Star Secrets and *Coach's Corner* into your overall development plan.

Read through Fisker's Star Profile and the list of other strategies that you noted to develop your confidence. Answer the following to help you make your plan.

Micro-initiatives can make a macro impact.

Which competencies or practices are you already doing that you want to continue?

1. _____ using my gut _____
2. _____ — not busting in precedence _____
3. _____

What are some new practices you want to incorporate?

1. _____ review strengths of Direct reports _____
2. _____
3. _____

What resources do you need to make this happen?

1. _____
2. _____
3. _____

Who can support you and hold you accountable?

1. _____
2. _____
3. _____

How might you sabotage your efforts and best intentions?

1. _____
2. _____
3. _____

What will be your first steps in this plan?

1. _____

2. _____

3. _____

Share this plan with your support people. Good luck!

Remember, spend a good month working with your new behaviors and actions. Don't try too much and end up getting stuck in the Perfection Loop. When you are ready, pick another competency chapter to explore, practice, and integrate.

CHAPTER FOUR

TEAMWORK AND COLLABORATION
TOOLS AND STRATEGIES

It is easy getting the players; getting them to play together is the hard part.
—Casey Stengel, Yankee Baseball Manager

This section provides tools and strategies to help you become a Star Performer in the area of Teamwork and Collaboration. It begins with a profile of Paulette Jones, Director of Technical and Strategic Business Development of NMB Technologies Corporation. Jones is a Star Performer who shares *10 Secrets & Current Practices* that help her shine as a successful team leader and player. The profile is followed by the *Coach's Corner,* which presents a series of 23 strategies and activities you can implement with your team right away to increase Star Performance in teamwork and collaboration. These include: 7 tools to improve your meetings, 2 Experiential Teambuilding Exercises, 2 Team Activities. To augment the process, take the Teamwork Ingredients Survey, which monitors positive changes.

WHAT IS THE TEAMWORK AND COLLABORATION COMPETENCY?

Teamwork and Collaboration are competencies that contribute to building an atmosphere of friendly and cooperative relationships within a team. Members are drawn into active, committed, and enthusiastic participation and exhibit respect and helpfulness. There is a team identity and an *esprit de corps*, which members work hard at developing and protecting.

141

EMOTIONAL INTELLIGENCE RESEARCH EXAMPLES

As noted in Chapter 1, for many years Robert Kelley of Carnegie-Mellon University has been asking people in various companies the following: "What percent of the knowledge for doing your job is stored in your own mind?" In *How to Be a Star at Work*, Kelley stated that the typical answer was 75%. By 1997, the percentage had slid to about 55%, and in one company it dropped as low as 10%. It is obvious that the group mind knows more than the individual mind and that teamwork or collaboration brings about better decisions than working alone.

Cambridge University Business School explored this topic further. They set up an experiment with 120 simulated management teams who were asked to make important decisions for a mock business. Some teams consisted exclusively of high-IQ members. Surprisingly, these high-IQ teams performed worse than other "less brilliant" teams. Why? The members of the high-IQ teams spent too much time debating issues and trying to outshine each other. They failed to attend to the necessary practical parts of the job, such as communicating information and coordinating a game plan.

In another study, the Center of Creative Leadership evaluated top American and European executives whose careers had derailed. It revealed that the main reasons for executive failure were the inabilities to build and lead a team. Lastly, in a study of 60 work teams operating in a large American financial services company, the behaviors that mattered most for team effectiveness came down to how members interacted and connected. Clearly, the demand for team skills will only grow in the years to come, as more and more work is done at a distance and in cross-functional project teams that form and dissolve depending on the task.

Hillary Elfenbein found that teams with greater average EI have higher team functioning than groups with lower EI. She found the ability to understand one another's emotional expressions explained 40% of the variance in team performance.[1]

Are You a Star Performer in teamwork and collaboration or just average? Do you regularly and consistently (80% of the time) encourage and draw others into an active commitment for the collective effort?

STAR PROFILE: PAULETTE JONES, DIRECTOR OF TECHNICAL AND STRATEGIC BUSINESS DEVELOPMENT, NMB TECHNOLOGIES CORPORATION

Paulette Jones from 1998 to 2002 has held a variety of leadership positions, from Director of Marketing and Sales of Keyboards in North America to General Manager of Keyboards. When I interviewed her in 2001, she was responsible for the management of an 18-person computer keyboard team, a 30-member engineering group, and a 6-person audio team. Jones's direct activities included product and program management, customer service, quality assurance, and factory coordination. She had full profit-and-loss responsibility for the company's keyboard business in the United States. Jones and her teams were successful in growing the Keyboard business by 300% from 1998 to 2004 and increasing the Audio sales by 566% during the same time period. Jones earned a B.S. in Computer Sciences, and she holds an MBA from Pepperdine University. She is a member of Mensa, is listed in International Who's Who of Business professionals, and held a Top Secret security clearance with the U.S. Navy.

Paulette Jones has one of the best initial greetings I have ever experienced and makes you feel appreciated and welcome. She has a quick sense of humor, can be self-deprecating, and makes everyone on her team feel special.

JONES WAS ASKED

- How did she learn this Teamwork competency?
- What does she do to be such an effective leader?
- What are her daily practices?
- What are the pitfalls she needs to be aware of?

EARLY LEARNING EXPERIENCES

"It seems that all of my life I have expressed [the Teamwork] competencies. I was president of my class in high school, and these leadership qualities have always seemed to be natural for me.

"Demonstrating these competencies has never been a conscious effort on my part. I can't ever remember a time in my life when I did not use them. Perhaps my perspective comes from the fact that I was one of six children growing up. (I was the fifth born out of the six children.) My father died when I was three years old and my mother raised all six of us by herself. We had to work together as a unit, and lack of teamwork was just not an option. We all learned that our strength and security lay in our numbers. It was 'us' trying to survive and we had to stick together to do it. That was my mom's message."

10 SECRETS & CURRENT PRACTICES OF
PAULETTE JONES—STAR PERFORMER

Below are strategies that Jones and other managers at NMB use to be Stars. Read through the strategies and pick one or two to try out.

1. START THE DAY WITH "AN ATTITUDE OF GRATITUDE"

"As I drive to work each day, I mentally walk through a list of things that I am grateful for (e.g., my family, health, and job). I also specifically think of individuals on the team who I am particularly grateful for. By the time I have gone through this exercise, I am ready to start the day feeling uplifted."

2. FOCUSED GREETING OF PEOPLE

"I believe it is important to greet people in such a manner as to indicate that you are glad to see them and that you view this individual as an important person. A strong handshake, direct eye contact, and a display of genuine interest in the person conveys the message that 'I am truly glad to see you.' I never actually thought about this 'skill' until it was brought to my attention. This has never been a conscious choice on my part."

3. COMMUNICATION

"It is absolutely essential to present the team with accurate and up-to-date information regarding our financial performance, achievement of stated goals, etc. We have placed a bulletin board in a central location that contains easy-to-read graphs and charts. These graphs and charts document our revenue, expenses, profitability, and inventory value compared to our budgets and goals. All members of the team have been trained in how to read and interpret these graphs and all team members share a common vision. Everyone knows how we are performing to goals at any time. In addition to these tools for tracking our performance, the bulletin board also includes easy-to-read charts that indicate the status of our sales efforts to introduce new technologies to our major customers."

4. RED FLAG MEETINGS

"Daily red flag meetings are held in the team area and are attended by all team members. These meetings are 'stand-up' meetings that usually last anywhere from 5 to 15 minutes. The purpose of these meetings is to raise red flags and to quickly identify resources to address the issues raised. These meetings are the *lifeblood* of communicating with the team members and are an essential tool for quickly sharing critical information."

5. REVENUE GAP MEETINGS

"These meetings are held immediately after the red flag meetings and are also 'stand-up' meetings that last no longer than 5 or 10 minutes. Their purpose is to identify the current revenue for each customer, the individual customer forecast for that month, and any specific actions needed to close the 'gap.' These meetings are critical for ensuring that revenue opportunities are not lost due to oversight or administrative errors."

6. BAT TEAMS (BUSINESS ACQUISITION TEAMS)

"BAT teams consist of four or five members each and are drawn from the keyboard team at large. Each team is assigned a major strategic account target. The objective of the team is to document specific information about their account. The team studies the account and identifies the decision-makers and their individual contributions to the purchasing decision, the competitors and per-centage of the business they each hold, the important purchasing criteria, the customer product road map, a strategic statement that will guide our dealings with the customer, and specific milestones that are needed to achieve our objective.

"In addition to delivering a valuable account profile and specific actions, the benefits of forming the BAT teams are apparent to those who participate. Participation in these BAT teams by members who do not normally engage in sales-related activities offers an opportunity to become involved in processes that many people in customer service, program management, and factory coordination would otherwise never be involved in. It gives the team members a sense of ownership and a valuable learning experience."

7. TEAM MEETINGS

"Held twice per month, attendance by all team members at these meetings is mandatory. They provide an opportunity to share information that is not normally shared during the daily red flag meetings. These learning experiences for the team, such as practicing Covey's *The 7 Habits of Highly Effective People* over a three-month period, are valuable ways people learn and bond together. Whenever a team member demonstrates one or more of the habits, the team recognizes them during our daily red flag meetings. The team meetings are also used to provide detailed product and financial information and provide opportunities to bring up other important issues during the 'round robin' portion."

8. CONTINUAL PROCESS REVIEW

"All processes (MRP, sales forecast, etc.) are subject to constant review and refinement and all departmental processes are well-documented and available to anyone who cares to view them. When problems are identified, a team consisting of stakeholders within that process is formed, the process is reviewed, and modifications are made by the people who will be working with that process."

9. VALUING STAFF

"I believe in the value of each individual on the team. Whenever I return from a business trip, I make it a point to go around to each and every person on the team and check in with him or her. It only takes a few minutes, but people sense that I do care about them and it sends a message that they are valued."

10. HUMOR

"I am amazed at how well the prudent application of humor can relieve tensions and bring the group closer together. We use humor constantly to build a sense of camaraderie. It's a great stress-reliever."

PITFALLS: WHAT JONES NEEDS TO BE AWARE OF

"I am aware that I may have an emotional response to a business situation. Due to real or imagined slights, my feelings may get hurt and my ego may become bruised. When this happens, I may have a tendency to want to impose my position on the business unit. I really don't like myself when I do that and I feel that it compromises my ability to be an effective leader."

ACTIONS: REVIEW JONES'S CURRENT PRACTICES

Looking at Jones's current practices, what practices can you incorporate to become a Star Performer in Teamwork and Collaboration?

Which ones do you want to add to your Star Performer Action Plan?

1. _____

2. _____

3. _____

THE COACH'S CORNER: 23 STRATEGIES FOR TEAMWORK AND COLLABORATION

Most organizations talk a lot about teamwork, but their approach is often simplistic and superficial. A group of workers is dropped together, told "You are now a team," and expected to act like one. This so-called team is marched onto the performance field of business without the skill sets to collaborate successfully. Becoming a functional and effective team that works and communicates well together is no slam dunk! It takes a great deal of discipline, planning, and practice and certainly isn't easy.

Although they desperately want it, it is uncommon in today's organizational environment for leaders to prioritize teamwork and collaboration. Take a quick look at the focus of a professional sports team or dance troupe compared to a typical organization. In the corporate world, only about 5% of an individual's time is devoted to off-line learning. Compare that to the athletes' or dancers' commitment: 95% of their time is spent practicing, standardizing routines and movements, identifying roles and responsibilities, improving communication effectiveness, and practicing coordination, alignment, and teamwork. To thrive, it is paramount that leaders devote the same kind of time and intention to teambuilding that athletes or performers do. Leaders need to help their employees practice their skills, enhance their strengths, and improve their weaknesses.

Unfortunately, the crisis of the day tends to take precedence over dedicating this quality time.

The first 10 of the following 23 strategies are key ingredients organizations must incorporate to master the competency of Collaboration and Teamwork. Each needs to become a discipline that is practiced, reinforced, and refined. Only then does Star Performance become a habit and a solid foundation for superior teamwork. The following combine to help you develop high-performance teams.

Average performers do what is easy and NATURAL. By that I mean they do what is obvious, effortless, and painless. Star Performers do what is UNNATURAL and difficult on a regular basis to develop their teams. By that I mean that, despite the pain, they do what is necessary in an organized, ritualized, and disciplined manner.

> Star Performers do what is UNNATURAL and difficult on a regular basis to develop their teams.

Notice how each of the 10 ingredients illustrates an "Average" as well as a "Star" approach, and gives specific actions designed to help you make your team succeed.

1. SHARED VISION

AVERAGE: Holds a blurry vision of where the organization is going and does not share this vision often enough throughout all of the departments.

STAR: Creates a clear and inspiring vision for the future that is communicated regularly, understood by all members, and reinforced in numerous ways.

ACTIONS to do the unnatural and be more effective: Leaders maintain a clear picture of their vision with a deliberate plan to communicate it to the team. Following are some suggestions.

- Communicate your vision at least four times a day.[2]
- Communicate what needs to be done to implement the vision and explain how the vision supports the team.
- Use the word *because* to help explain the connection between the vision and the individual team members.
- Include others, from all levels of the organization, and invite them to offer comments and clarifications. It is important to get everyone's "fingerprints" on the projects at hand. Remember, involvement equals commitment.

2. TRUST AMONG MEMBERS

AVERAGE: Relies only on him- or herself or on his or her particular department and does not expect much from others.

STAR: Develops an interdependency with others characterized by high trust and risk-taking.

ACTIONS to do the unnatural and be more effective: Leaders develop trust by trusting their people. Below are some suggestions.

- Develop trust by being vulnerable and admitting your mistakes.
- Make and keep small promises.
- Set high expectations for your team and encourage risk-taking and direct feedback.

3. EXPECTATIONS AND GUIDELINES

AVERAGE: Assumes that co-workers are on the same page and that they can read minds and so understand the desired results.

STAR: Is deliberate in clarifying reciprocal expectations and establishes guidelines for working together effectively.

ACTIONS to do the unnatural and be more effective: Leaders encourage members to co-create their expectations for themselves and communicate that they value the input. Below are some suggestions.

- Leaders and the team decide how they are going to make decisions (i.e., by majority, minority or content expert, unanimous, or consensus).

- Expectations are clarified from the leader to the team, from the team to the leader, and within the team. (See team Expectations exercise on page 180 for how to do it.)

- Meetings and team guidelines are established that flow out of agreed-upon expectations, such as "One conversation at a time," "Stay focused," and "Defer judgment." (See more about meetings beginning on page 155.)

4. COMMUNICATION SKILLS AND CONFLICT RESOLUTION

AVERAGE: Avoids conflict, jumps to conclusions, and may fail to effectively communicate his or her thoughts. Communicates the same way to everyone.

STAR: Makes thinking known and heard, identifies assumptions, acknowledges and resolves conflicts. A Star treats each person as a "chess player" with unique talents and varies his or her communication to fit the person.

ACTIONS to do the unnatural and be more effective: Leaders give the team specific tools for communication and working through conflict; otherwise, the strongest, loudest, and most senior voice tends to prevail. Below are some suggestions.

- Teach communication skills such as how to listen better, inquiry versus advocacy, and summarizing what is said.

- Appreciate differences and then communicate uniquely to each person to fit that person's style.

- Assign a devil's advocate to enliven conversations and protect against "group think."

5. SYSTEMS THINKING[3]

AVERAGE: Focuses on his or her own department to the exclusion of thinking large, across departmental boundaries. Believes his or her team's action has limited impact on others across the organization.

STAR: Looks at the big picture and recognizes how his or her department's actions affect others. Knows that customers, co-workers, vendors, and family are also intertwined as stakeholders and can have unintended impact and consequences.

ACTIONS to do the unnatural and be more effective: A leader helps the team see the big picture. Below are some suggestions.

- Make sure all sides of a situation are examined by assigning advocate roles in the conversation to customers, employees, managers, and vendors. Team members take on the roles and concerns of each of the above stakeholders.

- Encourage the team to elaborate on all possible consequences before rushing to make decisions.

- Counteract limited thinking and organizational learning disabilities such as "I am my position" and "The enemy is out there."

6. PERSONAL LEADERSHIP

AVERAGE: Stays in his or her comfort zone and only takes "safe bet" risks.

STAR: Takes risks that are consistent with values. In order to become a change leader, stretches and encourages others in spite of doubts and fears.

ACTIONS to do the unnatural and be more effective: Leaders know that the team is the playing field to try out their Emotional Intelligence skills and also the place to receive feedback on their performance. Following are some suggestions.

- Cultivate a developed point of view of your leadership style and know where you are going.
- Be aware of the different styles and preferences of your team and vary your style to meet and challenge each individual.
- Be a role model for development by sharing your current areas of focus. Ask for support and feedback from the team.
- Wear all of the hats on the team and know which hat to wear when. Key roles are initiator, coach, model, facilitator, and negotiator.
- Read the team's emotional state and create balance through attention, humor, and empathy.

7. APPRECIATION OF DIFFERENCES

AVERAGE: Values team members with similar backgrounds and opinions.

STAR: Embraces differences and creative tensions to generate better solutions and raise the "Team IQ."

Treats team members as chess players, not checkers. Matches each person's unique talents to his or her best-fit position.

The team IQ is a great indicator for the group to evaluate themselves. The IQ should be higher than the IQ of any one individual. IQ is 100 points, plus or minus 15 points. Above 115 is high average, 85-115 is average, and below 85 is low average.

ACTIONS to do the unnatural and be more effective: The leader is a powerful role model for dealing with differences. Below are some suggestions.

- Spend time thinking about and conversing with each individual, establishing his or her unique talents and deciding how that talent can best be used for the team.
- Hold a conversation with your team about their team IQ. Rate it, talk about it, and take actions to raise it.

- Encourage the team to stay with ambiguity, creative tension, and dialogue as long as possible. (See Dialogue vs. Discussion in Chapter 6.)
- Do not rush into a decision.
- Embrace differences and recognize that holding opposite and contrary ideas long enough can lead to breakthrough ideas.
- Integrate differences and transform them into innovations.

8. ACCOUNTABILITY AND CONSEQUENCES

AVERAGE: Feels disappointed with the efforts of team members, but fails to hold anyone accountable.

STAR: Discusses accountabilities and consequences up front, before a project gets underway, and reviews them throughout the project.

ACTIONS to do the unnatural and be more effective: Leaders provide the road map for dealing with obstacles before they arise. Below are some suggestions.

- Help individuals define their roles and responsibilities and make sure everyone is clear about them.
- Define and clarify what success looks like.
- To eliminate problems later, converse about accountabilities and consequences as part of the team's formation.

9. ONGOING LEARNING AND RECOGNITION

AVERAGE: Completes a task, possibly congratulates the team, and moves on to the next item on the "to do list."

STAR: Takes time to reflect to discover if what worked can be used again. Learns what not to do next time, decides who needs to know this information, disseminates it, and designs formal and informal celebrations for the win.

ACTIONS to do the unnatural and be more effective: Leaders look for every opportunity to learn and improve. Below are some suggestions.

- Hold sessions to crystallize learning and "spread the news" to the right people.

- Recognize individuals' efforts and contributions, which increases discretionary effort and raises morale.

- To keep performance focused, give timely and specific feedback.

10. MENTOR OTHERS

AVERAGE: Gets caught up with the urgent crises of the day and does little mentoring or training of key employees or colleagues.

STAR: Takes time to train and mentor others to be better performers. Keeps motivation high with career development, learning, and succession planning.

ACTIONS to do the unnatural and be more effective: Leaders enhance strengths and develop plans to improve the weaknesses of their team members. Below are some suggestions.

- Hold one-on-one meetings with your direct reports to coach and mentor. (See Chapter 5 about Developing Others for more tools on how to do this.)

- Encourage team to share core competencies by cross training.

- Spread your knowledge and develop your successors.

11. MEETING MASTERY AND MEETING MENACE

In reading Paulette Jones's Star Profile you probably noticed how many of her actions revolve around the types of meetings she holds. Meetings are the primary tools of a leader. They are the executive playing field where leadership is most on display. In many organizations, over 50% of an executive's time is spent in meetings. When used well, meetings can increase the performance of your team and build your credibility as the leader. When used poorly, in an undisciplined way, meetings can waste the organization's time and money and derail leadership.

THE MEETING MENACE: FRANK'S STORY

I have attended many corporate meetings, either facilitating or observing, and I would say that most could run better and that the members could participate more effectively. This story features "Frank," a composite of many leaders I have worked with or witnessed. I call his kind of leadership "Menacing."

Frank is a senior member in his organization and has been there for almost 10 years. He is known to have a temper that occasionally flares up. In one meeting, he was so upset about the direction his boss was taking on a particular project that he angrily tossed a wad of paper across the room, swore loudly, and shouted, "This makes absolutely no sense!" His boss happened to be at the meeting and an awkward, uncomfortable silence prevailed. No one seemed to know how to deal with him or the situation.

Meetings are the primary tools of a leader.

Frank has a history of being short and gruff. In the past, others had talked to him about his inability to be a team player, but his style continued to be confrontational. At meetings he would ask piercing questions and put others on the defensive. He would then calmly make his counterpoint, and people would feel embarrassed and humiliated. Because he is so critical and often volatile, Frank is negatively affecting the project deliverables and undermining any teamwork.

In a meeting with a cross-functional action team, Frank got overly excited and put another member of the team on the spot by asking endless questions about an interpretation of what a customer really wanted. Frank proceeded to engage others by asking them to comment on what they remembered happening in past meetings. Members stammered through their responses, and most felt and behaved anxious or uncomfortable.

Frank's boss talked to him numerous times about his temper and how it affected others, but Frank refused to apologize. Things would usually settle down, until the next blowup a few months later. Frank didn't realize how devastating these blowups were to his credibility and trustworthiness as a leader. He was unpredictable. Everyone wondered if he or she would be next to feel his wrath.

How would you deal with Frank if you were his boss? If you are Frank, it is important to realize the fear you are instilling in others and the harm you are doing to yourself. Take time to reflect and then apply some of the practical tools in the section.

QUESTIONS AND ACTION APPLICATIONS

- Did you see yourself portrayed on any level in Frank's story?
- How aware are you of your impact on others in meetings, 1-10, where 10 is totally aware?
- How would you rate your impact on others in meetings, 1-10, where 10 is very valuable and effective in meetings?
- Would you be willing to ask others about your impact?
- Did you see someone else you work with reflected in Frank's story? If so, would it be beneficial to talk to him or her about it? How might you approach this person (e.g., take the person aside and tell him or her about the impact of his or her behavior and give suggestions for alternatives)?
- Read the following Snapshots, which you may be creating, and the actions you can take.
- Take the Meeting Menace Checklist on pages 160-161 and establish actions to work on.

ꞈHOT MANAGEMENT: "THE ONE-HAND RULE"

.ɹost of the time that members of your organization spend with you is at meetings. It is here that your image as a leader gets crystallized. It exemplifies what I call "Snapshot Management." Members quickly make positive or negative fixed impressions of you as a leader. If your behavior, posture, and style are similar in three to four meeting snapshots, you can count it on "One Hand." Then you get "thin-sliced" as "that is you." People don't take time to understand your intentions or rationale. They want to know quickly if they can trust you or not. If you are unpredictable, you are untrustworthy in their eyes. Certainty, even if wrong, is more comfortable than ambivalence. These snapshots may not be accurate portraits of who you are as a leader, but unfortunately they stick in people's minds and become "reality."

> If your behavior, posture, and style are similar in three to four meeting snapshots, you can count it on "One Hand." Then you get "thin-sliced" as "that is you."

If your snapshot image is positive, your colleagues and boss will give you the benefit of the doubt if you miss a deadline or make a mistake. The problem occurs when these snapshots are negative, because once the impression is made it is almost impossible to change. If this impression was created because you have been unpredictable or impulsive in your behavior, your direct reports, peers, and boss are constantly poised for that same behavior. They can't trust that you can control yourself. Even if you make considerable changes over 6-12 months, if the same impulsive behavior happens again, in most people's minds you haven't changed at all. They think, "There goes Frank again."

I have been in meetings with executives talking about the performance of an individual victimized by Snapshot Management. The question discussed was, "If this person actually made positive changes, would the executives see and recognize him?" Original snapshots are so powerful that they can blind people to the multifaceted sides of a person. All of the person's wins, strengths, and capabilities in different settings with different people can blur the original fixed snapshot, but it is a very slow process and doesn't always stick. It is crucial to become acutely aware of how you present yourself in meetings and important to learn how to manage the snapshots you give people.

> Original snapshots are so powerful that they can blind people to the multifaceted sides of a person.

The goal is to counter the one hand of snapshots with a "collage" of all your successes and efforts. That may mean communicating more than you feel is necessary about what you have accomplished. Many executives say, "I don't want to toot my own horn" or "They will see my results." In taking the initiative to communicate in an informative and respectful way what you have been doing, you can ensure that your co-workers and boss "see" more of you than just a few snapshots. Otherwise, you are leaving your image management more in the hands and minds of others. Being more visible has been a strategy for many executives I have worked with, especially if they have negative snapshots ingrained in the minds of their supervisors or co-workers.

For example, here are some micro-initiatives you can say without boasting:

"I feel very comfortable with our progress thus far in . . . "

"The team is really performing well with . . . "

"I am very proud about . . . "

"I am excited with our direction with . . . "

QUESTIONS AND ACTION APPLICATIONS

- Do you have snapshots of people that are limiting how you see them?
- Can you inquire about other successes they have had and multiply or expand your snapshots of them?
- What are the snapshots of you? Are they more positive or negative?
- Are you taking the opportunities to present the "collage" of your successes and efforts?

Next, take the Meeting Menace Checklist to raise your awareness of the behaviors that can handicap your pursuit of being a Star Performer.

13. MEETING MENACE CHECKLIST

Check the box if you notice the behavior in yourself, a direct report, or a peer at least one time in a two-month period.

- [ ] 1. Gets irritated, upset, or angry in a meeting.
- [ ] 2. Interrupts people frequently during a meeting.
- [x] 3. Uses questions like weapons. They are not really questions, but disguised statements.
- [ ] 4. Over-talks issues advocating only one's own ideas.
- [ ] 5. Prevents people from managing or interacting with him or her. Says, "I just have one more thing to say," and then continues to talk on.
- [ ] 6. Makes disagreements a grand performance.
- [ ] 7. Fails to build on others' ideas.
- [ ] 8. Refuses to acknowledge others.
- [ ] 9. Puts others on the spot and urges them to express an opinion about a conflict.

☑ 10. Indulges in debating but doesn't realize others are uncomfortable and might see it as conflict or confrontation.

☐ 11. Is unprepared. Asks questions that have already been covered.

☐ 12. Interrogates others about their points of view in a condescending manner.

SCORE: If you made three or more checks, you are (or your direct report or peer is) a Meeting Menace.

QUESTIONS AND ACTION APPLICATIONS

What are one or two things you can do that would help you break out of being a Meeting Menace? For example:

- Take time to prepare for the meeting.
- Decide what outcomes you are looking for with each statement you make.
- Ask clarifying questions before advocating your point.
- Get a coach to help you deal with what might be blind spots and to learn new strategies.
- Work with a colleague to give you feedback if he or she notices any of the "menacing behaviors."
- Work with your supervisor on these development issues and have him or her give you feedback if he or she notices any of the behaviors.

Stars have a disciplined system for using meetings and maximizing their use. They are prepared for each meeting and appreciate the visibility that a meeting casts. Employing some of the following actions will bring about the degree of difference (D.O.D.) that moves your performance from good to great!

BECOME A MEETING MASTER

Employing the following collection of meeting tools, tips, and insights will make you a Meeting Master. This chapter focuses on

Team Meetings and shorter Stand-Up Meetings. You will discover information about how to orchestrate other kinds of meetings in the Developing Others and Communication and Empathy chapters.

14. TEAM MEETINGS

Team meetings are usually held weekly or bi-weekly. They are more frequent when you are involved in a big project. After 9/11, Rudy Giuliani held a daily morning meeting with the top 20 department heads. It was his key management tool to make sure he and everyone else knew what was happening and how they needed to respond after the tragedy.

HOW TO SET UP AND RUN AN EFFECTIVE TEAM MEETING

Here are the *key tasks* that should occur before, during, and after a team meeting:

Before

The leader or meeting owner should:

- Define the purpose and objective of the meeting.
- Select participants.
- Secure the room and equipment.
- Prepare the agenda and send it out ahead of time. Ask if there are items people want on the agenda and include them.
- Make a final check on the meeting room.

During

The leader or meeting owner should:

- Start promptly.
- Select a scribe to take minutes.
- At the start of the meeting, prioritize the agenda with time frames and then manage the time.
- Follow specific team guidelines you have created. (See page 164.)

- Hear from everyone.
- Limit or encourage discussion.
- Clarify actions to be taken.
- Summarize results.

MEETING PROCESS CHECKS

Here are various ways to make sure your meetings are effective. It is good to vary the way you perform the process check.

- On a 1-10 scale, how effective or satisfied are you with today's meeting? (Use the lowest scores to state what the team thinks needs to be improved.)
- What was good, what was bad, and what needs to be improved regarding this meeting?
- On a 1-10 scale, rate how on track the meeting was. What needs to be improved? (Use this at the halfway point of the meeting, asking each person to answer.)

After
The leader or meeting owner should:
- Restore the room.
- Make sure the scribe sends out minutes.
- Evaluate meeting and meeting feedback.
- Take agreed-upon action.
- Prepare next steps.
- Evaluate the effectiveness of the meeting. Focus on content and process. Most meetings are only content-focused, and yet what goes wrong in meetings usually has to do with "process"—the "how" versus the "what" of the meeting. By not focusing some time on the process of the meeting, you miss the critical variables to improve the meeting. (See the Meeting Checklist on pages 166-167).

15. GUIDELINES FOR RUNNING A GREAT MEETING

Following are guidelines for making meetings more effective. Have your team look at the list and add any other specific points that would be helpful. So that everyone is on the same page, hold a short meeting to discuss these guidelines.

Consider:

- Which guidelines will be hardest to comply with?
- How can you hold the accountability if someone isn't following the guidelines?
- What is the most effective way to administer these guidelines? Consider having a facilitator who rotates from meeting to meeting, or come up with other suggestions. Here are some sample guidelines.

▲ Arrive on time.

▲ Be well-prepared.

▲ Be concise. Stick to the point.

▲ Make "I" statements.

▲ Don't hold sidebar conversations.

▲ Participate in a constructive manner.

▲ Seek first to understand before seeking to be understood.

▲ Make your thinking visible.

▲ Don't interrupt.

▲ Other guidelines specific to your situation.

16. HOW TO ESTABLISH ROLES WITHIN A TEAM MEETING

To make a meeting run effectively, it is valuable to assign key roles within the meeting. Before the meeting, identify who will do what. Decide if a facilitator or another person will be the timekeeper. Also establish if people need more training in their roles before proceeding.

FACILITATOR

Your role is to keep the meeting going and to follow the agenda. State the purpose and end result of the meeting. Go through the agenda. Enforce the guidelines. Consider using a "latecomer's jar" to fine someone if he or she is late. Stop people if they go off on tangents. Honor the time limits or appoint a timekeeper to do so. Ask how much time people need on new topics. Use a "parking lot" for items that are not part of the agenda but need to be discussed at another time.

SCRIBE

Your role is to take notes (minutes) of the meeting so the facilitator can focus on the content and process. Document key issues and decisions made, with actions highlighting responsible parties. Make sure the minutes are distributed to all the participants within a 48-hour time frame.

PARTICIPANTS

All participants are expected to add value to the meeting and follow the guidelines. If you can't make it to a meeting, it is your responsibility to notify others.

17. "STAND-UPS"—SHORT TEAM MEETINGS

Short 10- to 15-minute meetings are a powerful means to promote teamwork and communication. Paulette Jones referred to them as "red flag meetings" in her Star Profile. Other people call them "huddles." The stand-ups are done standing up, thus the name. This is not time to get comfortable. Instead, your team stands in a circle, and each person has an opportunity to say something or pass. This is not a problem-solving meeting. (Use your team meeting for that.) Make sure that tangents are curtailed and topics between only two people are taken off-line.

Acceptable topics are:

- Information that will be helpful for everyone to know (e.g., a customer is coming today; he or she will be at an all-day meeting tomorrow).
- "Red flag issues" (e.g., someone needs everyone's help to get a rush product order out the door).
- What he or she is working on, or information or knowledge that is new to others.

As a leader, you can use these meetings to:

- Clarify the vision or deliverables.
- Acknowledge others.
- Celebrate small wins.

18. THE MEETING CHECKLIST

Use this checklist on a regular basis to make sure each meeting improves upon the last.

Team _____

Meeting owner _____

Date of meeting _____

Rank each item from 1 to 10 points, with 10 being the best or most productive meeting you have participated in.

1. Leadership of the meeting

☐ The agenda was clear and explained up front.

☐ The meeting owner stated the overall purpose.

☐ Time frames were honored.

☐ Overall

2. Accountability

☐ Individual team members were prepared for the meeting.

☐ Actions had a clear assignment, owner, and time deadline.

☐ Resources for the assignment or task were clarified.

☐ Other stakeholders' involvement and impact were considered.

☐ Overall

3. Communication

☐ Assumptions and interpretations were made explicit.

☐ People asked good questions and listened well.

☐ Risk-taking and challenging the process occurred.

☐ Tension and disagreements were aired, reduced, and resolved.

☐ Overall

4. Summary

☐ A summary of the decisions made was communicated.

☐ Actions and the people responsible for them were summarized.

☐ Next steps or considerations for the next meeting were stated.

☐ People evaluated the meeting and talked about improvements.

☐ Overall

5. What one thing do you want to change or improve for the next meeting?

_____

_____

_____

EXPERIENTIAL TEAMBUILDING EXERCISES

This section focuses on two experiential teambuilding exercises that you can do with your team. They are designed to give you all the information you need to set up, conduct, and process the activities successfully.

What follows is a brief rationale for experiential training. When you enter into an organization, you may be asked to explain why you believe experiential exercises have value and impact.

Whether you are a manager, coach, or trainer talking to an HR Director or giving your boss an overview of some of the exercises you will do with the team, your ability to understand and explain the power and value of these exercises will help to get buy-in.

WHY EXPERIENTIAL TRAINING?

"The premise is simple: that we have all been brainwashed by the cultural myth that learning occurs 'in our heads,' not in all of us, and that, until we challenge that belief, our capacities for any sort of deep learning are severely limited . . . Our learning is 'in our heads' but we don't seem to get it out, and apply it."[4]

Experiential training is quite different from traditional training. It involves whole-body learning and engages the physical, mental, behavioral, and even spiritual dimensions of a person, rather than focusing solely on the person's mind. Because the activities are generally unknown and unfamiliar, they can lead to unexpected outcomes and surprises, creating situations of crisis and chaos. In this way, experiential activities are a metaphor for work itself, mirroring the ups, downs, and unexpected twists and turns that take place on a daily basis.

Experiential training is a "practice field" that allows learning to happen in a setting where cause and effect are closely linked in time, and knowledge is generated to improve teamwork, communication, and collaborative problem-solving. Experiential training helps a team project their decision-making process and group intelligence onto the experience to be successful. The team has to organize itself to deal with time constraints, ambiguity of the directions, changing resources, leadership, follow-through, and vision, again mirroring a variety of work projects.

WHY EXPERIENTIAL LEARNING WORKS: 12 UNIQUE CHARACTERISTICS

1. Equality: It provides a common yet novel experience, where all participants are equal in their knowledge about the tasks or projects. One year or 20 years with the organization doesn't help an individual solve these problems.

2. Relationships Build Quickly: This is accomplished by the communication, collaboration, cooperation, and physical effort needed to solve these exercises. Participants are in close proximity all day and interacting in new ways. The end result is that they have to rely and depend on each other in clear and significant ways, which builds trust in an accelerated manner. People get to know each other more in a day than they have over the last one to two years.

3. Disequilibrium: Because of the unknown and unfamiliar quality of the challenges, participants are put into a state of disequilibrium or disorder. They are stripped of their normal status, roles, and defenses. Prior experience isn't relevant here. This creates a pure learning environment as the group has to self-organize around the challenge.

4. Projective Technique: In organizing instability or disequilibrium, the group projects their problem-solving, project management, and leadership style onto the experience. The experience provides a "gotcha" where participants are "caught" in doing what they typically do, in spite of knowing better. The learning is profound, revealing, and presented in a more meaningful and relevant way than would come from an organizational assessment. This window into their process provides unlimited information to shape team learning. This is one of the prime reasons experiential learning is an excellent "laboratory." Other methodologies don't provide such a rich projective technique.

5. Decreased Cycle Time: The space between project initiation and outcomes is compressed, so consequences of organizational decisions can be examined and improved. Typically, there is more of a time lag and more variables must be considered, so learning by doing is diluted and delayed.

6. Meta Learning: In this "learning laboratory," as the projections shed light on the managerial process, the group is asked to step back and evaluate itself. The learning is about themselves, their leadership, problem-solving skills, teamwork, communication, and ability to manage change. This time to reflect and develop lessons learned after studying themselves and their processes is usually not done with the same intensity within the organization.

7. Chaos Management (in a Safe Environment): Teams are able to experience chaos, disorder, and changing requirements for success in a safe environment where the consequences for failure are limited. The groups develop strategies or best practices to manage the change back at the work site.

8. Kinesthetic Imprint: Experiential learning anchors cognitive material. Participants have a kinesthetic imprint or whole-body learning of cognitive principles, because the learning is graphic as it involves physical, mental, behavioral, and even spiritual dimensions.

9. Common Language/Story-Making: The experience provides common language, story, and imagery that can be transferred to the workplace. This language becomes a shortcut in communicating a shared vision or "learning disability." The intense experience is storied in such a way that the participants see themselves and others in a new light. This story then becomes the catalyst for continuing the same theme, but taking it into the organization.

10. Encourages Risk-Taking: The experience allows participants to take risks, try on new roles, and make mistakes with few costs to the organization. Risks are perceived versus actual. Each person taking a risk vicariously pushes others to try something outside of their circle of comfort. In this environment, there are always individuals who shine and whose leadership hasn't been noticed at work.

11. Diversity of Strengths: The activities include physical and mental challenges requiring the resources of the whole team. Differences become necessary strengths for solving challenges. Just like on the job, one person alone could not complete most of the challenges, so the interdependencies of the team are emphasized.

12. Fun: Experiential learning provides a fun way of learning how to become a high-performance team. Fun also helps participants learn more, because they are more open to the experience and are typically more creative.

WHY TRAINING FAILS

In today's world, learning is the critical advantage that separates an organization from its competition. One reason learning needs to be improved is found in the systems perspective. Often, the learning or training is not embraced or reinforced back in the real world. Many times, the training is a solution to an undefined or complex problem. It may be a Band-Aid doomed to fall off and reopen the existing wound. Here are eight of the main barriers to the transference of learning. They are presented in rank order, with the first being the biggest impediment:

1. Lack of reinforcement at the work site

2. Interference from others (e.g., customers, co-workers, supervisors)

3. Non-supportive organizational climate

4. Training seen as impractical and irrelevant

5. Participants uncomfortable with the amount of change needed to implement the learning

6. Leaders or trainers not present as support mechanisms

7. Training perceived as poorly designed and delivered

8. Pressure from support group to resist making significant changes

CORPORATE TRAINING PRINCIPLES

Experience-based training and development as a field is continually growing and incorporating new skills and activities. As we innovate the way in which Corporate America and the international marketplace are learning and growing, we must keep in mind the basic premises of working with adults. These five principles are adapted from the *Creative Training Techniques Handbook* by Bob Pike:

1. Adults are like kids in big bodies. Like kids, adults learn the best through hands-on experiences.

2. The more you get others involved, using their own projections as the learning material, the more it stays real and relevant.

3. The more fun your participants have, the more they will learn.

4. No learning takes place until behavior changes. Everyone must learn to "walk the talk."

5. Learning has ultimately taken place only if participants can teach each other what you have taught them.

Using these experiential methodologies along with traditional training will make the entire process more lively, engaging, and fun. In the future, managers and trainers share the same bag of tricks to help develop strong and high-performance teams.

PROVEN EXPERIENTIAL EXERCISES

The following two activities are presented with instructions, materials needed, and process questions. They are designed for a team leader, outside consultant, or trainer to use for team development.

- Nails
- Performance and Accountability

These exercises can be used:

- To help "break the ice" for the team.
- To focus the team on the problem at hand, rather than doing it by yourself.
- As metaphors for how the team is working together. Leadership, teamwork, and communication prowess will be immediately evident.
- To assess strengths and weaknesses of the team and develop action plans for improvement.

19. "NAILS" TEAMBUILDING ACTIVITY

RESOURCES

- 11 3-inch 10-D nails with a head
- A small piece of wood with one nail in the center (See Figure 4.1 for the answer.)

TEAM SIZE: small groups of 2-3 people

FIGURE 4.1   SOLUTION TO THE NAILS TEAMBUILDING ACTIVITY

INSTRUCTIONS

Read these instructions aloud or print them out and hand them to the team:

- You have in front of you a bag with 10 nails and a piece of wood with one nail.
- Take the nails out of the bag.
- Your objective as a team is to get all the nails to rest self-contained on the top of the nail in the piece of wood.
- There is a configuration or pattern to make this possible.
- All you can use are the nails and your ingenuity.

GUIDELINES

- The piece of wood must remain flat and can't be turned on its side.
- No nails can touch the wood.
- No nails can touch the neck of the nail in the wood.
- Do not use extraneous tools to hold the nails together (e.g., hands, string, paper, cup, etc.). Use only your ingenuity!

TIME FRAME: 12 minutes

PROCESSING THE ACTIVITY

GOALS

- To help your team master teamwork and collaboration
- To make your team more cohesive and high-performing
- To reach consensus on the key ingredients of a Star team
- To assess your team on these key ingredients
- To affirm your team strengths
- To pick a few key areas to focus on for team improvement

TIME FRAME: 2 hours

MATERIALS NEEDED

White board or flip chart and pens

PROCEDURE

Focus: After 12 minutes ask the small group how they felt doing the exercise, especially if they were not successful.

- What did the curve of their energy and focus look like?
- Was it:
  - ▲ Constantly going up?
  - ▲ Did it plateau?
  - ▲ Did it dip and go down?
- Would they want their team or staff to respond in this way to a hard project?

Metaphor: Have each small group recreate the design or pattern in front of them, even if they didn't get the answer initially. (Usually you will have to create it and have them copy it.) Ask: "What do you notice about this pattern?"

Sample responses:

- It is a picture of interdependence.
- One definition of a team is a group of people who "hang together well," just like you see with this design.
- Each nail can represent your team members or your departments and how they fit or "hang together," relying on one another.

Consensus Exercise: If the nail in the wood represented the key foundation or ingredient that holds the whole team together, what does that nail represent?

- Have each person individually write his or her "top three ingredients for a high-performance team" on a piece of paper.
- Then ask each small group to get a consensus and come up with their "top three ingredients for a high-performance team."
- Have one person report for each group. He or she writes the answers on a flip chart.
- Go around to each group and hear one ingredient from each team until you have all the key ingredients.
- Look at your list and consolidate any of the ingredients, where possible. The ideal number should be around seven. If you have many more, it will be cumbersome for the next steps.

Team Assessment: Have each group write all the key ingredients you have on the flip chart onto their paper.

- Now have each group assess your whole team on these items. "Where is the team today, on a scale of 1-10, where 10 is high?"
- Give the small group 10 minutes to discuss it and come up with a score on each ingredient you have on the flip chart. The whole team will have to reach a consensus on each one.
- Pick one ingredient and get each group's score for it.
- Then ask for more details about why the group selected that number from both the highest score and lowest score.
- Continue this process for each item. Then get an average of the small groups' scores for each key ingredient.

Team Actions:

- As a whole team, look over your list and find where you are highest and lowest.
- Pick the two highest scores and ask two small groups to each take one strength and come up with actions to enhance

it. (You may have more than one group work on an area if they have a lot of members.)

- Pick the two lowest scores and ask two groups to each take one ingredient and come up with actions to improve their weaknesses.

- Each group reports their actions to the whole team.

- Collect all the actions on the flip chart.

- Decide which actions would get you the biggest results. Remember the 80/20 rule: 20% of your efforts yield 80% of your results. You can vote if you have too many; ideally you should have two enhancers and two development areas to begin with.

- Each action team should have an owner, a key deliverable, a small team, and a time frame. Plan to report on progress in a few weeks.

- Schedule the follow-ups so you continually support the efforts.

Follow-Ups:

- Have each action team report their progress.

- Ask how you can support each team's effort.

- Plan small win celebrations and spread the news.

20. "PERFORMANCE AND ACCOUNTABILITY" TEAMBUILDING ACTIVITY

RESOURCES

20-30 soft kush balls or any kind of small, soft ball

TEAM SIZE: Ideal size is 8-12

GOAL

To forecast how many balls you will catch and assess how successful you were.

GUIDELINES

- Catch as many balls as you can.
- The balls must be thrown up in the air at the same time.
- Say, "Ready on the outside?" "Ready on the inside?"

TIME FRAME

Go until you finish. Depending on the size of your group, it will take 10-15 minutes.

PROCEDURE AND INSTRUCTIONS

- Distribute the balls in such a way that everyone has at least two balls.
- Everyone gets into a circle.

Round One

- ▲ Ask for two volunteers from your group to come into the middle of the circle.
- ▲ Have them give their balls to others.
- ▲ Ask them to decide how many balls between them they will catch. They will announce their forecast.
- ▲ Have the rest of the group throw the balls all at once and count how many were caught.
- ▲ Let the group self-organize. Only reiterate the guidelines; they must decide how to proceed.

Round Two

- ▲ Same as above with two different volunteers.

Round Three and On

- ▲ Continue as above with as many rounds as you need until you have only two people left.

Last Round

- ▲ Now say that you received a message from the corporate office: "You now must catch all the balls. The balls represent your customers, and you can't afford to let even one fall through the cracks."

▲ If successful, the two people in the middle will receive a bonus of 25% of their salary.

▲ If balls are dropped, both people in the middle will be fired (again, let them self-organize, and reiterate only the guidelines).

PROCESSING THE ACTIVITY

TIME FRAME: 20 minutes

QUESTIONS

- What did you notice?
- What roles did you see?
- What assumptions were there?
- How did things change when you had stiffer consequences?
- Did you use any of the innovations from other groups?
- How creative were you in using your resources?
- What did you notice about your role?
- How assertive were the individuals who offered ideas?
- Were there any ideas that were not heard? Why not?
- What would the team need to do better to make sure all inputs are heard?
- How does this experience relate to what happens at work?
- What are some of your insights and applications back at work?

KEY POINTS IF NOT BROUGHT UP BY THE GROUP

- Unclarified assumptions in your team can be a poison and can curtail your ability to innovate.
- All ideas have to be heard for a maximum of creativity.

- It is easier to go along with others and be unsuccessful than it is to be a change leader and challenge the process.
- Leadership is not about having all the answers, but rather utilizing all the resources effectively.
- "Thinking outside the box" requires that people challenge the process, take initiative, and get buy-in from others.

Following are three activities you can do with your team to foster teamwork and collaboration. Each one is laid out to assist you in leading the 1.5- to 2-hour session. The topics will help you clarify expectations, assess your team on specific Star ingredients that the team created, and establish what stage of group development your team is in. Specific actions help keep the momentum to develop a Star team.

At the end of the chapter, there is a Teamwork Ingredients Survey, followed by a Star Performer Action Planning sheet.

21. "EXPECTATIONS" ACTIVITY

"Sixty percent of business problems come with unclear expectations."—Stephen Covey

GOALS

- To help your team become more cohesive and high-performing
- To make your expectations as the leader visible and clear to others
- To hear from your team what they expect of you as their leader
- For your team to clarify expectations of each other

TIME FRAME: 2 hours

MATERIALS NEEDED

White board or flip chart and pens

PROCEDURE

- Ask the leader to prepare ahead of time a list of what he or she expects from the team (e.g., open and honest communication, they come to you with recommendations versus problems, they give above and beyond the call of duty).

- Have your team prepare their expectations of you and each other. Send out an email or tell them about this exercise a week before the meeting.

- Read your list slowly to the team. Let them ask questions and try to engage them in a dialogue about your expectations.

- Now, have each person state one expectation of you and write it down on the flip chart. Stop when more clarification is needed and get examples, where possible. Go around the room until you have heard from everyone.

- Look at the list and give your comments. Is there anything on the list that you can't do for some reason? Tell the team you'll work on meeting their expectations.

- Then have the team share their expectations of each other (e.g., get back in touch with each other within 24 hours for emails, support each other in meetings). Things that get repeated often can be guidelines for your team.

- Again, hear from one person and go around the group as many times as needed to finish hearing all the expectations from everyone. Encourage discussion and clarification. If things were communicated negatively, have them give an example and ask what they would rather see.

- Send out the notes so everyone has a copy of the expectations.

- Within two months check back on how you and the group are living up to meeting the expectations.
- Go through each item and ask, "How are we doing on this one?" Use a scale from 1-10 to get a measurement. If someone gives it a 5, ask what it would need to get it a 6. Look for small wins.

22. TEAM ASSESSMENT

GOALS

- To help your team become more cohesive and high-performing
- To reach consensus on the key ingredients of a Star team
- To assess your team on these key ingredients
- To affirm your team strengths
- To pick a few key areas to focus on for team improvement

TIME FRAME: 2 hours

MATERIALS NEEDED

White board or flip chart and pens

PROCEDURE

- Have each person write his or her "top three ingredients for a high-performing team."
- Break up the team into groups of three and ask each group to "Come up with your top three ingredients for a high-performance team." Have one person report for each team.
- Go around to each group and hear one ingredient from each team until you have all the key ingredients. Write the ingredients on a flip chart.

- Look at your list and consolidate ingredients where possible. The ideal number should be around seven. If you have many more it will be cumbersome to get to the next steps.
- Now, have each group assess your team on these items. "Where are we today on a 1-10 scale, where 10 is high?" Give the group 10 minutes or so to discuss it and come up with a score on each ingredient you have on the flip chart. The team will have to reach a consensus on each one.
- Pick one ingredient and get each team's score for it.
- Then, from both the highest score and lowest score, ask for more details about why the group selected that number.
- Continue this process for each item. Then get an average for each key ingredient.
- As a whole team, look over your list at where you are highest and lowest.
- Pick the two highest scores and ask two groups to take one strength each and come up with actions to enhance your strengths. (You may have more than one group work on an area if your team has many members.)
- Pick the two lowest scores and ask two groups to take one ingredient each and come up with actions to improve your weaknesses.
- Each group reports their actions to the whole team. Collect all the actions on the flip chart.
- Decide which actions would get you the biggest results. Remember the 80/20 rule: 20% of your efforts yield 80% of your results. You can vote if you have too many; ideally you should have two enhancers and two development areas to begin with.
- Each action should have an owner, a key deliverable, a small team, and a time frame. Plan to report on progress in a few weeks.

- Schedule the follow-ups so you continually support the efforts. Ask, "What can you as their leader do to support each team's effort?"
- Plan small win celebrations and spread the news.

23. TEAMWORK INGREDIENTS SURVEY

For each of these questions, please rank on a 1-5 scale as follows.

1 = *it never happens*

2 = *it happens infrequently*

3 = *it happens occasionally*

4 = *it happens frequently*

5 = *it always happens*

Never	Infrequently	Occasionally	Frequently	Always
1	**2**	**3**	**4**	**5**

1. Our team has a shared vision that we understand and accept.

2. There is high trust among team members.

3. Communication is open, thinking is made visible, people listen well, and differing ideas are encouraged and accepted.

4. Conflict is dealt with openly and resolved.

5. Our team is able to establish, prioritize, and work on what is most important.

6. Risk-taking and being proactive are encouraged and supported among team members.

7. Collaboration is high and team members seek win-win solutions.

8. Our team maintains a "one-team" perspective (i.e., all individuals and departments are one big team).

9. Our team is constantly learning and trying to improve.

10. Leadership is participative, shared by all, and no one person dominates.

11. Our team has established values and guidelines for how we operate.

12. We are able to hold each other accountable for the performances.

13. I receive recognition or praise for good work within every seven days.

14. My opinion counts at work.

15. I am clear about what is expected of me at work.

NARRATIVE QUESTIONS

16. Which items from the 15 above work well on your team?

17. Which items from the 15 above do not work on your team?

18. On a 1-10 scale where 10 is the highest, how would you rank your teamwork?

19. From 1-10, how would you rank the leadership on your team?

20. What could your leaders do to improve your teamwork?

21. What are a few things you would like to see changed that would significantly improve the way your team performs?

22. Other comments?

STAR PERFORMER ACTION PLAN

Read through the Star Profile and *Coach's Corner* to develop your teamwork and collaboration skills. Now, answer the following questions to help you make your plan. Remember, micro-initiatives can make a macro impact.

Which competencies or practices do you already do that you want to continue?

1. _____
2. _____
3. _____

Which new practices do you want to incorporate?

1. _____
2. _____
3. _____

What resources do you need to make this happen?

1. _____
2. _____
3. _____

Who can support you and hold you accountable?

1. _____
2. _____
3. _____

What will be your first steps in this plan?

1. _____
2. _____
3. _____

How might you sabotage your efforts and best intentions?

1. _____

2. _____

3. _____

Share this plan with your support people. Good luck!

CHAPTER FIVE

DEVELOPING OTHERS
TOOLS AND STRATEGIES

Keep away from people who try to belittle your ambitions.
Small people always do that, but the really great make you
feel that you too can become great.

—Mark Twain

Thisis section provides the tools and strategies to help you become a Star Performer in the area of Developing Others. It begins with a profile of Mark French, retired Women's Basketball Head Coach for University of California at Santa Barbara. French shares *13 Secrets & Current Practices* that help him shine as a Star Performer. The profile is followed by the *Coach's Corner,* which presents a series of 11 strategies and activities you can implement with your team right away to increase developing others in your organization.

WHAT IS THE DEVELOPING OTHERS COMPETENCY?

Developing Others is a key component in leading others to become Star Performers. It is the process of identifying the strengths and potential of others and then designing and implementing a plan to help them succeed. It provides support, timely feedback, and mentoring to bolster their career development.

EMOTIONAL INTELLIGENCE RESEARCH EXAMPLES

Strong coaching and mentoring, two methods of developing others, help the individual and the organization in many ways, including better employee performance, higher levels of loyalty

189

and job satisfaction, more opportunities for promotion and pay increases, and lower rates of turnover.[1]

Developing Others is a vital skill for all levels within your organization, but a study of supervisors, managers, and executives in 12 large companies reveals that the greatest impact is with supervisors and also affects both sales people and line staff.[2] Research shows that as managers and executives move up in their careers, they spend a greater amount of time away from the line (and their specific job skills) and their leadership skills become more essential.

In superior managers, excellence in Developing Others is second next to team leadership.[3] Star Performers understand the value of this competence. The relationship with one's boss is one of the best predictors for how long a person stays at a job, and an essential part of that relationship is the sense that your boss sees your potential and wants you to succeed. Spherion and Lou Harris Associates found that only 11% of the employees who rated their bosses as "excellent" said they were likely to look for a different job in the next year. However, 40% of those who rated their bosses as "poor" said they were likely to leave. So, people with good bosses are four times less likely to leave than are those with poor bosses.[4]

One of the questions I ask in many of my leadership trainings is about a person's best boss. What did he or she do and say? How did he or she influence you? It is always enlightening to hear the specific practices, some micro and some macro, that have had a powerful impact on these individuals. After asking these questions of hundreds of leaders, a pattern has emerged. The individuals adopt the practices of their "best boss." Their thinking is, "It worked well for me and should work well for others I supervise." Typically these are essential practices like the ones we are discussing here. The fact that people remember and repeat these practices illuminates the power and influence every leader has on his or her people. If you start doing a few micro-initiatives right now, not only are you having an immediate impact on your people but you are also influencing the next generation of leaders who will pass your practices on to their followers.

In *The One Thing You Need to Know*, Marcus Buckingham states that great managers make a point of discovering the uniqueness in each of their workers and then capitalize their findings. He identified the three things that great managers need to know about their people:

- What are their strengths?
- What are their motivators or triggers?
- What is their particular style of learning?

As noted, the average manager views his or her employees like generic checkers on a black-and-red board—all basically the same and able to move only one space at a time in only one direction. Stars see their employees as "chess players," each with unique skills and talent who can move in different ways and cover more territory than one space at a time. The challenge is to discover your "chess-playing" employees' uniqueness and then learn how to implement their strengths for the sake of the organization as well as the development of the individual.

Are You a Star Performer in developing others or just average? Do you regularly and consistently (at least 80% of the time) give timely and constructive feedback and mentor others?

STAR PROFILE: MARK FRENCH, UNIVERSITY OF CALIFORNIA AT SANTA BARBARA (UCSB) RETIRED HEAD COACH, WOMEN'S BASKETBALL TEAM

Why a basketball coach as the Star Profile? Most leaders have a difficult time focusing on developing others. They are juggling their own meetings, deliverables, as well as administrative and operational tasks. Depending on their role, they may spend as little as 25% of their time on development, some possibly a tad more. A college coach's success is totally dependent on his team's performance. It makes sense that a smart coach would devote a great deal of time to developing others. Approximately 75-80% of French's workload is built around nurturing the talents of each person, in practice or conversation, focusing on performance issues, stretching each team member to his or her physical and mental limit, and orchestrating his or her unique abilities to create one high-performance, winning team. Mark French's 25 years of experience and secrets are a goldmine of information and inspiration for leaders to study and practice.

French retired in 2008 after 28 years as a Division I Head Basketball Coach. He has more than 500 career wins and 438 wins in 21 years at UCSB. French had taken UCSB to 12 NCAA appearances and 12 straight Big West titles.

In the 2003-2004 season, they made it into the Sweet 16 in the NCAA finals, losing to the eventual winner, University of Connecticut. Coach French has been the Big West Coach of the Year seven times and in 2002-2003 was the WBCA District Coach of the Year and the Naismith National Coach of the Year finalist.

French is very proud that UCSB players have a 98% graduation rate and that 63% of the players go on to graduate school. There are even five graduates who play or played in the Women's National Basketball Association. More than 20 of French's players were recognized as Big West scholar athletes, tops in the conference. He states, "I'm more of an educator than a coach," and he is more concerned that his players "have world-class people skills and be good people than just excel on the basketball court."

As an athlete, French was a two-sport letter winner at University of California at Santa Barbara. He was an all-league pitcher for the baseball team and played two seasons on the basketball team. French earned a B.A. in Political Science from UCSB and received a master's degree from the University of the Pacific in Physical Education.

In looking over the 20 Emotional Intelligence competencies, Coach French added, "Most of our star players have a lot of these."

COACH FRENCH WAS ASKED

- How did he learn the Developing Others competency?
- What does he do to be such an effective leader?

- What are his daily practices?
- What are the pitfalls he needs to be aware of?

EARLY LEARNING EXPERIENCES

"Both of my parents were teachers. My mother taught English and my father was a baseball coach. My mother helped me understand the value of language and how to talk about my feelings. She constantly told me it was OK to share how I felt and convinced me I'd be more successful and satisfied if I were really in touch with other people. I think that's why I'm particularly successful coaching women. My father was an old school coach for 41 years and was highly organized and competitive. I spent a lot of time watching and learning from him. I believe I had the best of both influences."

Coach French had great role models for many of the EI competencies. His father demonstrated conscientiousness, initiative, leadership, and achievement orientation, while his mother taught empathy, communication, accurate self-assessment, and emotional self-awareness. This blend of utilizing and integrating both logical and emotional aspects of the brain continued in his formative training.

As a graduate student at the University of the Pacific, French became the pitching coach for the baseball team. The head coach, Tom Stubbs, a lot like French's father, was very efficient and organized. He knew all the relevant statistics of the players and the game and was quite structured. In his graduate classes, Coach French was learning about coaching theory, sports psychology, and the body-mind connection.

Fortunately, Coach Stubbs was a strong believer in developing others, and he let Coach French teach and practice visualization, meditation, and progressive relaxation with the pitchers in particular. The team won games and, as French remembers, "The players felt like I really cared." His experimenting and risk-taking were paying off.

Coach French was building a philosophy and practice for educating the whole person—physical, mental, and emotional—and he received immediate positive feedback on his techniques. The success of the team's performance, the intimate relationships he was developing with the players, and the constant commitment to development truly put Coach French on the road to becoming a Star.

In 1978, French was asked to be the head coach of the women's basketball team at University of the Pacific. He took the job and found, "I really liked working with the women, and it fit me better. Women value other things than just being the star. They are there to be a part of a team." In his first season the team won 16 games and lost 11. The second season they were 20 and 7, and Coach French proclaimed, "I can do this."

Another key influence for Coach French was Stephen Covey's *The 7 Habits of Highly Effective People*. It helped him in his personal life, and he was able to integrate the practical habits into his coaching philosophy as well. To be an effective coach or player he learned, "You have to win the inner battle and work interiorly first to become trustworthy and confident." This is in line with focusing on the personal competencies of Self-Awareness and Self-Management before addressing the social competencies of Social Awareness and Relationship Management.

13 SECRETS & CURRENT PRACTICES OF MARK FRENCH—STAR PERFORMER

Coach French took his early learning experiences and created a successful coaching philosophy and strategy, not just for basketball players but also for being Star Performers in all aspects of life. You are probably not developing Star basketball players in your role, but season after season Coach French has honed the development process, and you can borrow some of his strategies.

Think about these practices and how to apply them to your own business or setting to help develop and guide your Stars. Read through the strategies and pick one or two to try out. (Note that each secret is followed by a set of business applications you can use for your organization.)

1. LEADER'S POINT OF VIEW (POV): BASKETBALL AS A METAPHOR FOR LIFE

Coach French says, "Basketball helps my players learn about themselves." A recent NCAA study states that the average woman athlete spends 3,000 hours with her sport, but only 4% of her time dedicated to playing the game itself. The other 96% revolves around "What we are really about," as Coach French says. "That's communicating, bouncing back from adversity, and dealing with stress."

When asked, "Is this journey better if you are the Star or the 14th player," French smiles. "Our program is for both." French focuses on this philosophy every day, to help his players develop "habits of excellence." (A Covey term.) "We are what we repeatedly do." This organizing principle helps Coach French keep perspective and inspires how he communicates his program to new prospects and the community. A Leadership Point of View is incredibly important because it is the cornerstone of how you perceive and practice developing others.

BUSINESS APPLICATION

- As a leader, what is your POV regarding work and fellowship?
- What is your leadership POV in developing your people?
- Do they know your POV?
- How often do you talk and act on your POV?

2. PRACTICE

Practice is a critical piece in the development of people and teams. This is the one big difference between sports and the business world. In sports, people spend 95% or more of their time practicing and only 5% of the time performing. In the business world it is the exact opposite, where 95% if not more is spent performing and very little time practicing. As mentioned in Chapter 4, we can learn and adopt a great deal of useful techniques from sports and the performing arts regarding practice.

During the season, Coach French's teams practice two to three hours a day, and he assigns a specific focus for each session. During practice, French studies the development of each player and also builds individualized training programs to improve each player's game. (For example, some may need to work on their defense, others on rebounding and boxing out.) He feels his players shine at game time because they focus on staying with what they do best rather than letting the opponent dictate what they do.

BUSINESS APPLICATION

- How prepared are your people for their meetings and presentations?

- Do you regularly have "dry runs" or practice sessions for important presentations or meetings? (Most organizations do not.)

- Are your people clear where they are in their learning curve and when they must perform?

- How are your people encouraged to try new risks and practice something that will pay off for them and the organization in the future?

3. BONDING AND TEAM MEETINGS

At the start of every season the team has a bonding weekend. To help the players get to know one another, they participate in a variety of teambuilding and community events. Coach French has each of them talk about themselves, their past, family, and current aspirations. He encourages starting the season with meaningful activities. Many have done rope courses, spent time at community soup kitchens, and then spent the night together sleeping on the basketball court. These rituals are created to help individuals get to know each other as people as well as basketball players. One of the most positive results is a heartfelt commitment each player feels toward one another and to the team as a whole.

BUSINESS APPLICATION

- What rituals do you have to bring your team together?
- How do you encourage your team to get to know each other?
- Do you have a team formation process to start a new project or orient new players to each other? (See Chapter 4, *Coach's Corner* for some ideas of things to do with your team.)
- What is your process for orienting new employees? Are they able to quickly feel connected to people and your company's culture?

4. RECRUITING STARS

In the business world, hiring the wrong person can cost a company three times his or her annual salary. For UCSB's Women's Basketball team, the wrong player can affect the team chemistry and the success of the season. The coaching staff has an elaborate process for selecting and recruiting their future Stars. They have to be able to have "successors" for all the positions, and naturally they go after their recruits in a focused manner. The pinnacle of the recruiting effort is the home visit. According to NCAA rules, a prospective player can only have five home visits from universities or colleges. UCSB is competing with Stanford, Virginia, Georgia Tech, and other top-tier basketball schools for these players. The visit is limited to two and a half hours and is highly orchestrated.

In order to structure their visit, the coaching staff spends a great deal of time researching the specific recruit to understand what is important to the recruit and his or her family. The research results in a three-page outline for each visit, followed by role-playing the visit while videotaping it. To cap things off, they review their efforts. A win for Coach French results in the family having had a positive experience and saying, "This was a nice visit and a great conversation."

Some families wonder if their child can keep up with the academics at UCSB. Coach French and his top assistants will talk about "special admits," support available, and the overall grade point averages. Understanding Coach French's philosophy or point of view (POV) is important. Many times he is the differentiator who influences the recruit to select UCSB.

The home visit is the playoff game for using Emotional Intelligence. Reading their audience, coming prepared, using empathy, asking questions, having a good give-and-take, inspiring the family, building bonds, and developing a trusting relationship are paramount in this game. Getting their recruits to enroll at UCSB is the ultimate win.

BUSINESS APPLICATION

- What kind of Stars do you need in your organization?
- Is your interviewing and hiring method as clear and practiced as Coach French's?
- What do you need to do to enhance your process of hiring Stars?
- How capable are you at understanding the needs of new employees and providing challenging positions to meet their needs?
- Are you able to paint the picture of what your culture is like and what is expected of them as employees? (Strategies for hiring are found in the *Coach's Corner* on page 207.)

5. BUILDING EFFECTIVE RELATIONSHIPS

Coach French understands that to develop his players he needs to build a relationship with them. One solid way to do so is to act as a mentor, one of the Star competencies. French states that women often define having a good relationship with him as "Knowing he is someone I can talk to." This description is far different from what male basketball players find important, such as top-notch facilities, details about the schedule, and being informed about the amount of playing time they will have.

One key in building a real relationship is to support the women as they deal with their "inner battles," an issue that affects their performance and life in general. Some of these battles include lack of confidence, parental pressure, or the boyfriend back home. French works with the women to solve these conflicts so that they feel cared for and can then focus more intently on their performance on the court.

BUSINESS APPLICATION

- How are your relationships with your co-workers?
- Do you know your direct reports very well?
- Do you have an open and honest relationship with each one?
- Do you know what is causing your direct reports' performance to be less than desirable?
- Do your direct reports trust you to share their real concerns?
- Do your direct reports feel you care about them and that their opinion counts?

6. SELF-ASSESSMENTS AND GOAL SETTING

Coach French uses the Myers-Briggs Type Indicator and Strong Campbell Interest Test with all the players. They share their results to determine what they need to work on as individuals and also as a team. Each player is encouraged to acknowledge that she needs help in specific areas. "Athletes don't learn this naturally," French states. Some of the goals may be developing "trustworthiness, selflessness, patience, tolerance, or leadership." The players are then encouraged to reach out to each other to provide support in these key areas.

BUSINESS APPLICATION

- Do your team members know the strengths and weaknesses of each individual person?
- Have you encouraged them to help each other?

- Do you know your direct reports' strengths?
- Do you know what each of your people's career aspirations are?
- As a leader, do you know what motivates your reports to their peak performance?
- Do you know each of your people's specific learning style?
- What style assessments do you use to help determine your people's uniqueness?

7. ONE-ON-ONES

Each week in season and out, Coach French meets with his players individually. These one-on-one conversations provide the place for French to act as mentor to help his players deal with their "inner battles." He uses a Socratic approach where he asks questions and lets the player explore her own answers. He also takes opportunities to give feedback on each player's progress. This is an anchor to his program and contributes greatly to truly knowing and developing each player year after year.

BUSINESS APPLICATION

- Do you come to one-on-ones with your leader prepared and able to bring up pertinent issues to your development?
- Do you have one-on-ones with your people?
- Are there specific goals your reports are working on for their development along with the tasks for their position?
- Are the one-on-ones valuable for you and your reports?

(Read more about one-on-ones in the *Coach's Corner* on pages 222-226.)

8. SUPPORTIVE LEARNING

Ongoing learning is important to Coach French because it supports his philosophy and program. He expects his players to read and report on books such as Stephen Covey's *The 7 Habits of Highly Effective People*. He also has his players attend diversity training so that they can appreciate the differences in their teammates as well as in other people who will show up in the rest of their lives. A highlight of the year was the afternoon spent with the late, legendary Coach John Wooden of UCLA. Coach Wooden and the players exchanged questions and he read poetry to them. Wooden discussed his Pyramid of Success, which has 15 building blocks, many identical to the EI competencies, such as confidence, team spirit, self-control, initiative, industriousness, conscientiousness, cooperation, and loyalty.

Wooden's principles are evident in all of his actions. During one of the meetings, he received two phone calls. One was from Roone Arledge, the creator of ABC Monday Night Sports as well as the ABC news division. Coach Wooden let the call go directly into voicemail because he didn't want to interrupt his visit with the players. The second call was from his granddaughter. He jumped up to answer that one!

BUSINESS APPLICATION

- As an employee, do you have specific ideas on what training and education you want?
- As a leader, what learning do you provide for your employees?
- How are you checking in with your employees to reinforce and hold them accountable? (As their leader, your support for their training is the key to their retention and application of the training.)
- Do you pass along articles or books you think would be helpful to your employees?

9. TIMELY FEEDBACK

According to the EI competency model, Stars give timely feedback and act as mentors. Coach French quotes a study that charts the type of feedback Coach Wooden gave in his winning history. Wooden's feedback to his players was 80% positive; while the average coach's feedback is 80% negative and only 20% positive.

Coach French thought he and his staff were pretty positive, but then he checked videotapes of the practices and scored it for positive and negative feedback. He was surprised to find out that 60% was negative! French immediately made changes and the next season he got it up to 50% positive, with the goal for the next year being to increase it to 60%.

In the business world, it is very rare for teams to examine their performance to decide what works and what they can do differently, let alone watch themselves on videotape.

BUSINESS APPLICATION

- How often are you giving positive feedback to co-workers and direct reports?
- Is the feedback immediate and helpful?
- Is your feedback successfully received?
- How often does your team as a whole evaluate your performance?

(Chapter 4 gives specific tools for your team to assess its effectiveness.)

10. FOCUS ON STRENGTHS

Coach French makes sure that he shows film clips of the team doing their offense and defense correctly. He knows that, from a motivational standpoint, he will get more effort from them if they focus on what they are doing right.

An athlete's confidence is critical to his or her performance, and focusing on strengths while balancing negative feedback ensures a confident performer. In the business world, your performer's confidence level is also critical, although many managers don't take this into consideration when interacting with employees. It can hardly be said enough: Your *relationship* with your subordinates is the critical factor that contributes to their feeling valued and wanting to stay at the organization.

BUSINESS APPLICATION

- Where is most of your focus with your people—on their strengths or development areas?
- Do you spend time talking about their strengths and ways to use them more?
- Are your decisions about tasks for your people dictated by what they do best and thinking about them as chess players? If not, how can you make more time to do so?

11. TAKE PERSONAL RESPONSIBILITY

Coach French said, "I would never yell at my team about something we haven't made a big deal about in practice. We never do anything in games that we haven't done in practice." If there is a mistake or letdown, Coach French looks at where he might have let the team down. French is willing to take responsibility for it.

Dean Smith, the famous University of North Carolina (UNC) basketball coach with 879 victories, more than any other coach in college basketball history, has a similar philosophy. Scott Williams, a UNC graduate who went on to win three NBA championships with the Chicago Bulls, said about Smith, " . . . he never took credit for our wins but went out of his way to take the blame for all our losses, claiming he hadn't prepared us properly." [5]

How often have you heard of leaders or employees taking responsibility for a mistake by admitting they had not prepared enough? Just because nobody takes responsibility for the mistake does not mean the mistake did not happen. In many organizations, the exact opposite occurs—people spend time and energy blaming someone else for the problem.

BUSINESS APPLICATION

It is crucial to ask yourself if the following statements are heard enough in your organization.

I need help.

I don't know.

I made a mistake.

If you don't hear these often enough, you do not have the optimum climate for positive and responsible learning. Ask yourself:

- How often are these statements made in my organization?
- What would help to make them safer to say in my organization?
- How can I take more responsibility for the preparation and performance of my employees?

12. PERFORMANCE REVIEW

All of French's team games are videotaped, and then the teamwork and individual player performances are studied and discussed. Usually, the highlights are accompanied with music and humorous commentary. Typically, the team strengths are emphasized. This is immediate feedback for the team. When mistakes are shown, they are framed in a context of learning with the idea of improvement in mind, so that they will not be repeated. In addition, the coaches are always taking the players aside during practice, to talk about their performance and what they need to work on. Each coach tailors his feedback to the individual player, in terms of her unique requirements for help with motivation, confidence, or specific play instruction.

BUSINESS APPLICATION

Athletic teams require continual reviews for daily improvement. In many business organizations, there is only one yearly review. Others expect the leader to talk to their employees every month about their performance. Because leaders are too busy responding to "the crisis of the day," this often does not happen regularly or in depth. Leaders often make uninformed assumptions that everybody is doing just fine. Here are some of the basic review practices used successfully in the world of sports that leaders can apply to their businesses:

1. Communicate and give feedback daily.

2. Tailor communication to the individual.

3. Balance strengths with development.

4. Offer experiential teaching. Make sure "correct" actions are repeated along with support and guidance.

5. Give feedback immediately after the next performance in the developed area.

Which practices can you use to improve your performance reviews?

- Are there ways you can shadow or witness a direct report's performance?

- How can you incorporate feedback from others, such as peers?

13. BRIEFINGS BEFORE AND AFTER THE GAME

BEFORE THE GAME

Coach French always focuses on what his team does well and how they can continue to execute what they already know. He doesn't focus or worry as much on what their opponent does. Coach Smith at the University of North Carolina had a similar philosophy. Before games he would repeat the phrases: "play hard," "play together," and "play smart."[6]

AFTER THE GAME

Coach French and the team talk about what they did well and what led to their successes. This discussion reinforces the practices and disciplines the team has employed. It is important for French to hear from his players about their perception of the game. This helps him gauge their confidence level and motivation and often begets new insights and practices. The successes are written down so they can be referred to at a later date.

BUSINESS APPLICATION

- Do you consciously prepare your team for a new endeavor?
- Do you clarify your expectations with them and hear from your people what they think they need to succeed?
- Do you practice for this new endeavor?
- What kind of feedback do you give and get after a performance? It may be a meeting with a new client, a presentation in front of your executive team, or solving a conflict with co-workers. In many companies, this is called an "after-action review" or a "postmortem."
- Would this be helpful in your organization?
- What do you need to do to start this process for your team or organization?

PITFALLS: WHAT FRENCH NEEDS TO BE AWARE OF

Coach French identified a few of the pitfalls that can get in the way of developing his players:

- He can become too sensitive about being liked by his team, the administration, and the fans and fail to stick with his gut feelings about what the right thing to do is.
- At the risk of not being liked as much, he might not challenge the players as much as he could.
- He can be too helpful in solving players' problems instead of letting them struggle to find their own answers.

ACTIONS: REVIEW FRENCH'S CURRENT PRACTICES

Looking at Coach French's current practices, what practices can you incorporate to become a Star Performer in Developing Others?

Which ones do you want to add to your Star Performer Action Plan?

1. _____

2. _____

3. _____

THE COACH'S CORNER: 11 STRATEGIES
FOR DEVELOPING OTHERS

The Center for Creative Leadership has trained and written a great deal about the development process for executives and managers. They state: "Managers are critical to the development process. They have a number of roles that they must endorse, understand, and have the skills to carry out. These include: making development real, providing development experiences, providing support and feedback, and accessing organizational resources." [7]

Here are 11 strategies I use in executive coaching when focusing on developing others. Read through each of the tools, pick one or two to try out, and then incorporate them into your plan.

1. HIRING STARS: EMOTIONALLY INTELLIGENT LEADERS ARE MORE LIKELY TO BE HIRED AND BECOME STARS

Increase your success rate by hiring executives with strong EI competencies. They are far more likely to perform in the top third based on salary bonuses for performance of the divisions they lead (87% are in the top third). In addition, division leaders with these competencies outperform their targets by 15-20%. Those who lacked these strengths under-performed by almost 20%. [8]

One of the most important activities in hiring is being clear about what the position requires. Every position is unique—some require high interaction and collaboration; others require much individual planning and effort.

Behavioral Questions for EI Competencies: Behavioral interviewing techniques are a way to relate a candidate's answers to past experiences and to develop indicators for how this candidate may respond and perform in the future.[9] Remember, the best predictor for future behavior is past behavior. Some of the benefits of behavioral questioning are:

- Spontaneity, as the candidate cannot give you a "canned, prepared" response.
- The ability to watch the candidate's thought process as he or she selects an experience to speak about.
- The opportunity to see the candidate think and communicate on his or her feet.
- Less exaggeration, as the response is tied to past concrete experiences.
- Ease in establishing his or her lack of experience in an area.

2. BEHAVIORAL QUESTION LIST

Select two or three questions from the competencies below that you feel are most important. After each set of questions is a list of assessments to help you delve deeper. When you finish each interview, rate the candidate using the Interview Rating Scale.

INITIATIVE

- Give me an example of extra efforts you have taken to get a sale. What did you do or say?
- What is the biggest initiative you have taken and championed at work?
- How did it work out? On a scale of 1-10, where 10 is the highest, how would you rate the result? What would you have done differently?

Assessment

- Did he/she appear to take risks and initiate actions on his/her own?

- Does this seem to be a habit for him/her; does he/she regularly and consistently act this way?

- How would you rate the candidate for Initiative—Star or average?

SELF-CONTROL

- Give me an example of a time when you were very frustrated with a customer or co-worker. What did you do or say?

- What methods do you use to control yourself or keep yourself in check? How effective are you at managing your emotions, on a 1-10 scale?

- What triggers you or pushes your buttons the most with customers?

Assessment

- Did the candidate give responses that indicate he/she responds calmly and calms others as a regular habit?

- How would you rate the interviewee for Self-Control—Star or average?

EMPATHY

- How do you read others' non-verbals?

- Give me an example of how you demonstrate that you are open to new ways of looking at things.

- Tell me of a time when a customer, co-worker, or employee was very upset with you. What did you do or say?

Assessment

- Did the respondent give indications of understanding where the customer was coming from or why he/she was feeling that way?

- Did he/she report any empathic responses, such as "You must have felt . . . " or "That sounds very challenging, rewarding, exciting . . . "
- How would you rate this candidate for Empathy—Star or average?

BUILDING BONDS

- Give me some examples of what you do or say to build strong relationships with customers and co-workers.
- Tell me an example of an opportunity you received from networking.
- Who is the best person you know at building and cultivating relationships? What does he/she do or say?

Assessment

- Did it appear as a habit or an irregularity that the interviewee used strong mutual relationships as a tool in influencing or selling?
- Did it seem he/she understood the importance of networking for success?
- How would you rate this candidate for Building Bonds—Star or average?

SELF-CONFIDENCE

- Give me an example of a time that you had to be very decisive. What did you do or say?
- What do you do to ready yourself for a big project, meeting, or presentation?
- What do you do to maintain your confidence?

Assessment

- Did the candidate appear to speak and behave in an unhesitating manner?

- How confident did this person seem to you?
- How would you rate him/her for Self-Confidence—Star or average?

ADAPTABILITY

- Give me an example of a time you had to totally change or adopt a new strategy in working with someone. What did you do or say?
- What do you find to be the hardest part in dealing with change?
- Give me an example of a time you changed your strategy or ideas based on what someone else told you.
- On a 1-10 scale, how adaptable are you? What else could you do to improve?

Assessment

- Did this candidate seem to have a tolerance for ambiguity and the ability to change as a strong habit?
- How would you rate him/her for Adaptability—Star or average?

ACHIEVEMENT ORIENTATION

- What has been the most challenging goal that you set for yourself and achieved?
- What has been your most challenging goal that you set for yourself and didn't achieve?
- What is an example of a calculated risk you have taken recently?
- Explain how you decide if you will take a calculated risk.
- In this position, what obstacles do you anticipate you will have to deal with?
- How long do you think it will take before you make a significant contribution to the team and company?

Assessment

- Does it seem as though these behaviors are a habit for this candidate?
- How would you rate him/her for Achievement Orientation— Star or average?

SERVICE ORIENTATION

- How do you know that your customers are satisfied with the service you are providing?
- Give me an example of satisfying a customer need that was beyond his or her expectation.
- How do you find out what the customer really needs? Is there an example of providing for a need that the customer didn't initially think of?
- How well do your customers trust you, 1-10? What makes you say that?

Assessment

- Does the interviewee seem very customer-focused?
- Do you think customers will relate well to him/her?
- How would you rate this person for Service Orientation— Star or average?

INFLUENCE SKILLS

- Give me an example of your best and worst persuasion experiences.
- What do you find is the best way to persuade someone?
- How do you deal with objections to what you are trying to sell?
- Give me an example of your strategy for selling a new idea to a client or your team.

Assessment

- Are there indications that this person anticipates the impact of his/her words and actions?
- Are there indications of using indirect influences (e.g., others internal and external, research information, articles, and stories)?
- Are there any examples of using complex influence strategies to meet his/her goals?
- How would you rate this candidate for Influence Skills—Star or average?

TEAMWORK

- Give an example of how you dealt with someone who strongly opposed some ideas you had.
- What would be your initial strategies to build relationships?
- What kind of questions would you like to ask people?
- What is the main thing you want to convey about yourself to people on your team or to a new customer?

Assessment

- Does it seem that this person values teamwork for getting things done or is he/she more of an individual performer?
- From your interview, will he/she solicit input from others?
- How encouraging does he/she seem of others?
- Will this person be able to build a strong team?
- How would you rate him/her for Teamwork—Star or average?

TRUSTWORTHINESS

- Tell me about a time that was challenging for you to follow your own values, when there was pressure to do otherwise.
- Tell me a time you made a mistake and how you deal with situations when you don't know or need advice.

- How would you develop your credibility in this organization?
- In many organizations, it is difficult to ask for help. How do you deal with that?

Assessment

- Does this person seem open to admitting his/her mistakes and asking for help?
- Does it seem like this candidate would stick to his/her values or bend them under pressure from others?
- What is your gut reaction about this person?
- How would you rate him/her for Trustworthiness—Star or average?

COMMUNICATION

- Tell me about a time when you were a new leader. What things did you communicate to your team, the customer, or the organization?
- How would you describe your communication style?
- What do you find is the best way to engage your audience?
- What has been the hardest thing for you to communicate as a professional? How well do you do it? What would you do differently?
- How would you communicate differently between an internal and external customer?

Assessment

- In your interview, was there an effective give-and-take?
- Did the candidate ask you good questions?
- Did he/she appear to have the skill to communicate in different ways for different people?
- How would you rate this person for Communication—Star or average?

ORGANIZATIONAL AWARENESS

- Give me an example of how you might use the politics of the organization to help get something done.
- What would you do to find out about how this company really works?
- How long do you think it would take you to understand the underlying structures of this organization?

Assessment

- Does it feel as though this person is sophisticated in understanding the underlying issues of the organization?
- Did he/she demonstrate organizational savvy in getting things done?
- How would you rate this candidate for Organizational Awareness—Star or average?

DEVELOPING OTHERS

- Give me an example of how you go about developing your people.
- What is the best example of your successfully mentoring someone?
- Give me an example of the most challenging person you were developing.
- What was the most challenging part for you?
- When do you find is the best time to give someone feedback?

Assessment

- Does it seem like the candidate is good at giving people feedback?
- Do you think he/she could be an effective mentor?
- How would you feel being mentored by him/her?
- Would people be able to relate to this person as their leader?

EMOTIONAL SELF-AWARENESS

- Give me an example of a time you had mixed feelings about something and how you sorted through it.
- Give me an example of a time your feelings had an impact on your experience or others' experience.
- Is there a specific emotional signal you have that helps identify what you are feeling?
- What are the top three feelings you most frequently have?
- Tell me about a time you had a negative feeling at work. Why did you have it and what did you do about it?

Assessment

- How was this person's emotional vocabulary—fair, good, or excellent?
- Did it seem that he/she knew why his/her feelings occurred?
- Did this candidate demonstrate understanding of the implication of his/her feelings?
- How would you rate this person on Emotional Self-Awareness—Star or average?

ACCURATE SELF-ASSESSMENT

- Give me an example of feedback you received at a past job and how you used that feedback.
- What goals for improvement have you made the most progress in? Least progress?
- What was the hardest feedback you ever heard from a co-worker or boss? What did you do about it?

Assessment

- Did you feel that the interviewee is open to feedback?
- How well does this person appear to leverage feedback and awareness?

- Does he/she seem to regularly make long-term self-development plans?
- How would you rate this candidate on Accurate Self-Assessment—Star or average?

CHANGE CATALYST

- Tell me a time that you personally led a change effort. How did it go?
- What strategies did you use to get people on board?
- How did you execute the change effort?
- What was the most successful change initiative you have been involved in and what made it so successful?
- How would you rate yourself as a change agent, on a 1-10 scale, where 10 is the highest? Why?

Assessment

- Did you feel that the candidate took full responsibility for promoting and championing this change?
- Did it seem like he/she had effective strategies for getting people involved in the change initiative?
- How effective were this person's communication strategies?
- How would you rate him/her on being a Change Catalyst—Star or average?

INSPIRATIONAL LEADERSHIP

- Describe a situation where you were the leader of an initiative.
- What strategies did you use to position yourself as the leader?
- What methods did you use to communicate your vision?
- How did you stimulate enthusiasm and make the vision compelling?
- Describe a situation where your leadership was lacking. What would you do differently?

Assessment

- Did you feel this person took a confident and powerful role in the situation described?
- Would you feel inspired and enthusiastic, listening to him/her?
- As a follower, would you follow his/her lead into new territory?
- How would you rate this candidate on being an Inspirational Leader—Star or average?

CONFLICT MANAGEMENT

- Describe a situation at work that was conflictual for you. What did you do to de-escalate the conflict?
- Give me an example of a solution you created that was a win-win for the people involved?
- Tell me what steps you take to resolve conflicts.

Assessment

- Does it feel to you that this person is comfortable with conflict?
- Does he/she seem to have a plan on how to deal with conflict?
- Is it a habit for him/her to de-escalate conflict and orchestrate win-wins?
- How would you rate this person on Conflict Management—Star or average?

CONSCIENTIOUSNESS

- Give me an example of a project where follow-through was very important. What systems did you employ to carry it out?
- Tell me a time that you had to personally take responsibility for getting something major done. What did you do? How did it turn out?

- Tell me a time when something dropped through the cracks in a project. How did you correct it? What would you have done differently?

- What is your method for time management? What is the most challenging thing for you with time management?

Assessment

- Did it seem to you that this person manages follow-through?

- How easy was it for him/her to acknowledge a mistake in the third bullet?

- Does this candidate seem to you to have a strong habit in taking responsibility for tasks?

- How would you rate this person in Conscientiousness—Star or average?

HOW TO USE THE INTERVIEW RATING SCALE

Following is a rating scale to help you determine which competencies are needed for each position. Rate the competencies first for importance and then rate the interviewee using a score. This is helpful because when you are talking with other interviewers you can be more specific about what you are looking for and what each interviewer's opinion is about a certain competency. The result is a focused and poignant conversation about competencies, rather than the general, "So what do you think?"

INTERVIEW RATING SCALE

Use the Interview Rating Scale for each of your employees and each of your positions.

First, RANK each of these characteristics for its IMPORTANCE to the particular position.

3 = Must have   2 = Like to have   1 = Not necessary

Next, SCORE the individual on each characteristic.

4 = Excellent   3 = Good   2 = Fair   1 = Poor

Now, MULTIPY the two numbers (IMPORTANCE times SCORE) for the TOTAL

Name: _____

Characteristic	Importance	Score	Total
Organizational Awareness			
Proactive Initiative			
Energy Level			
Self-Control			
Acceptance of Others/Empathy			
Trustworthiness/Integrity			
Communication: Internal			
Communication: External to Clients			
Intelligence			
Conflict Resolution			
Self-Awareness			
Building Bonds/Rapport			
Self-Confidence			
Accept Things as a Challenge/Adaptability			
Motivation/Achievement Orientation			
Service Orientation			
Voice of Reason in Chaos			

Leadership			
Teamwork and Team Player			
Software Tools: Microsoft Excel, Microsoft Project, Quickbooks			
Fit for Our Culture			
Influence Skills			
Technical Skills			
Developing Others			
Conscientiousness/Work Ethic			
Financial Knowledge & Experience			
Creativity			
Other Characteristics: _____			
TOTAL SCORE			

Assessment:

- What I like best about the candidate is . . .
- I think he/she can help us in the following areas . . .
- Concerns I have about the candidate are . . .
- Overall rating:

Don't hire!   Good.   Adds value.   We must have!   (Circle One)

Gregg Butterfield, an executive project manager in Dealership Facilities Services working for General Motors, has been extremely innovative in the project development process. He uses this form and these types of behavioral questions to evaluate and select architects, engineers, and contractors for dealership development projects. He says, "I ask the questions that people are not prepared to answer in the normal interview process for this type of work. What this yields is an indication of how this person may function with other members of the team." This information about their Emotional Intelligence, paired with their experience and their bids, has allowed him to select the best teams. He has saved General Motors hundreds of thousands of dollars and untold hours of conflicts and headaches. Butterfield says, "Every project that goes wrong is usually driven by mismatched expectations. That's why this selection process is so important."

3. ONE-ON-ONE MEETINGS

This is the heart and soul of development. If you don't have one-on-ones with your people, you are missing the primary tool for moving your people from good to great.

Jim Snell is the president and COO of Shield Healthcare, Inc., a national distributor of medical products. He has one-on-ones every Tuesday with all of his direct reports. When asked about the value and content of these meetings, he replies:

"The one-on-ones are a good opportunity for me to stay current with what the department is working on and allow me to offer suggestive input on the direction of significant initiatives. Often the initiatives cross functional boundaries, and if I perceive inconsistencies between departments I can suggest the managers get together and do a reality check between them.

"We establish due dates, timelines, and significant events to determine 'go' and 'no go' decisions. These conversations go a long way in helping us learn about each other. They are essential to team-building and creating meaningful long-term business relationships."

Paul Collins is the Director of Client Services at Shield Healthcare, Inc., and has reported to Jim Snell for almost nine years. In that time he missed only a handful of Tuesday morning meetings because of vacation, sickness, or out-of-town trips. "Jim is the one who is so diligent about keeping these meetings," Paul states. "He lets you know this is our time and he is brutal at holding it."

Paul described the impact of the meeting. "It puts the onus on me to give him information I think he wants, and it gives me a valuable opportunity to see where I am." Paul also has one-on-ones with his people. He confesses, "I found out how hard it is to commit to these weekly meetings. There is always a good reason to reschedule, but I don't." It takes time, commitment, and discipline to keep meetings with your direct reports, but Jim Snell and Paul Collins see these as a mainstay to successfully developing their people and company.

Myron Jones, the president of NMB Technologies Corporation, a computer peripheral company, also uses one-on-ones as his key management and development tool. He truly believes in the value of the one-on-one.

"I know the lack of these meetings can cause misalignment in the company. In the one-on-one—I call it a Performance Review—we talk about four elements:

1. Major Job Responsibilities

Talking about the Major Job Responsibilities helps us grade the performance at that point in the fiscal year.

2. Our Win-Win Agreement under the Covey guidelines

The Win-Win is a complementary tool to Job Responsibilities and allows me to focus on the cultural and behavioral actions of the employee.

3. Bonus Plan Progress: Performance Metrics and Management by Objectives (MBOs)

The Bonus Plan review is cool because it is a document employees typically ignore until the last month of the year. A well-written MBO should potentially have an impact on short- and long-term company performance. Reviewing them quarterly allows more top-of-mind thinking.

4. Course Corrections

Course corrections make sure there are no surprises at annual review time. It ensures that the employee and I are aligned on what is most important to the company.

These quarterly meetings can have a powerful impact because my staff members can be aligned, and then you can go into the Business Units and replicate the process."

SOME BENEFITS FROM HOLDING REGULAR ONE-ON-ONES WITH YOUR DIRECT REPORTS

- You demonstrate you care about their development by dedicating time, your most valuable commodity.
- You truly understand what they are doing as well as what their key challenges are.
- You value them by observing and highlighting their strengths.
- You recognize their accomplishments and validate their efforts.
- You can give and clarify information about where you and the organization want to go.
- You can coach them about specific "inner battles" or "other battles" they are having.
- You can teach them about the company and its culture.
- You can have more influence and make more of a contribution with the organization by helping them be better workers, managers, and leaders.
- You can prevent crises by helping them think and plan ahead.
- You can teach about your POV and give specific data about products, customers, bosses, etc.

THE AGENDA AND TIME FRAME: You and your direct reports should both create the agenda for your one-on-ones to help meet your needs. To stay abreast of their direct reports, many successful executives have their one-on-ones once a week. Some hold them every other week or once a month. You have to decide what will work best for you. You may start off with more frequent meetings and then spread them out. To make it is easy to stay focused, take notes and keep a file on each person.

KEY AGENDA ITEMS SHOULD INCLUDE

- Progress on deliverables or tasks. Helps to get a "% completed" number.
- Challenges or obstacles they have; anything they want to add to the agenda.
- How can you help as their leader (e.g., resources, talking to department heads, training, etc.)?
- Critical information you want to make sure they get.
- Recognition and acknowledgment you can give for what they are doing.
- Identify and stretch their strengths. (See pages 226-227.)
- Feedback and coaching on issues.
- Clarity of vision and answering any questions they have.
- Stretch goals, projects, and positions for your direct reports to keep them growing.
- Next steps and actions.

The Center for Creative Leadership (CCL) has identified five broad categories of experiences that lead to growth and personal development. Here are additional topics to talk about in your one-on-ones to solidify the learning.

- Being given a challenging job was rated as the number one source of development by managers at CCL. Challenging jobs force rapid growth and development for your direct reports.[10]
- Experiences off the job such as community service, serving on boards, or leading church and youth projects can be valuable lessons in leadership.

- Learning from bosses, both "best bosses" and Dementors, can help in identifying the characteristics to emulate or avoid.

- Hardships can teach about limits, mistakes, resilience, and courage. Integrating these learning experiences can let your direct reports see themselves in a new light. Also, it can cast a new perspective on life matters.

- Traditional training classes are a means to self-development. They can give participants tips, strategies, shortcuts, and a comparison of how they stack up against others in the class.[11]

QUESTIONS AND ACTION APPLICATIONS

- Decide how often you want to have one-on-ones with your direct reports.

- Prepare the first meeting agenda from the previous list.

- See what agenda items your direct reports want and ask how you can best use the time.

- Use the time to truly explore thinking and learning on many of the topics above.

- Discuss and evaluate the meeting together. How was this meeting, what worked well, and what could be better?

- Re-establish the frequency required for the meetings to remain beneficial.

4. SOARING WITH STRENGTHS

When working with your direct reports, scan for their strengths, help them stretch them, and teach them to apply them to other areas as well. In their book *Soar with Your Strengths*, Clifton and Nelson identified five characteristics of strengths:

LISTEN FOR YEARNINGS: This is a pull or an attaction toward something. It may come from watching someone else and saying,

"I'd like to do that." Leaders use yearnings as a clue for strengths. Talking about their dreams, aspirations, or future goals will help to identify these aspirations.

WATCH FOR SATISFACTIONS: "Satisfactions are experiences where the emotional and psychic rewards are great; typically they are the activities we 'get a kick out of doing.'" [12]

WATCH FOR RAPID LEARNING: When someone catches on quickly to something, this is an indication of a strength or talent. It comes easy to the person and it feels like he or she has always known how to do it.

Slow learning, where a person just doesn't get the hang of something, is also very significant. It is an indication of a nonstrength.

GLIMPSES OF EXCELLENCE: Within each task there are a series of moments or subtasks where someone can demonstrate excellence. This can be a glimpse of a strength. My son and I were taking guitar lessons, and our teacher demonstrated what she wanted us to do. As I was trying to memorize the sequence, my son just listened and was able to repeat it perfectly. As I toiled away, he got it effortlessly—a glimpse of excellence.

These glimpses can be nurtured to develop the talent. Examples include an ability to know just the right time to ask for the sale, or an ability to make people feel very comfortable, or thinking on one's feet in a presentation, responding to hard questions, or an ability to simplify complex tasks.

TOTAL PERFORMANCE OF EXCELLENCE: This isn't a glimpse of excellence, but rather when the whole task is done with excellence. In sports, for example, the person may be experiencing "flow," where the performance is effortless.

Notice that the aforementioned five characteristics for strengths involve your watching and listening. You will need to listen with one ear for strengths and one for development opportunities.

5. INPUT + 1

This strategy has to do with learning theory. Do you know how each person learns? Do you know when and why people get into overwhelm? It is important for you to help stretch your direct reports by giving them new information, and thus the moniker "Input + 1." Dr. John Luckner, a professor of Deaf Education at University of Northern Colorado, stresses the importance of teaching to the specific level and style of the learner. If matched well, the student will learn more and develop better self-esteem. Keeping the new material at Input + 1 is critical for this to happen.

If your direct reports are at Input + 3, they are on overwhelm and can't integrate all the information or learn well. Their eyes are glazed over, and they may be just nodding their head. They may be asking vague questions, or their results may be far from what you expected. The average performer may think it is his or her direct report's fault for not understanding. The Star Performer will take responsibility, like Coach French and Coach Smith, for not meeting the direct report's needs. The Star will figure out where the employee comfort zone lies and how to push just the right amount so that he or she can be successful. What may be Input + 3 for one person can be Input + 1 for someone else.

QUESTIONS AND ACTION APPLICATIONS

- In your one-on-ones, assess or ask about their learning styles.
- Get feedback on how much you are stretching them. Find out if it is working.
- Use the Myers-Briggs Type Indicator (MBTI), the Kolbe, or the DISC to delineate learning styles.
- Hold conversations with your team about learning styles, preferences, and how they best take in and assimilate information.

6. CIRCLE OF INFLUENCE

This term was first used in Stephen Covey's *The 7 Habits of Highly Effective People*. It is useful in establishing responsibility and in deciding when to refocus your energy on more fruitful endeavors. (See Figure 5.1.)

CIRCLE OF CONCERN: These are concerns that are important to you but that you don't have any control over. They begin to be a distractive noise that takes the place of truly focusing on what you can actually do.

CIRCLE OF INFLUENCE (OR POWER): These are things you do have control over and where you feel empowered. Put your energy and effort here.

CIRCLE OF FOCUS: These are the key areas where you need to focus. It is important to clarify a plan and the first steps.

FIGURE 5.1 CIRCLE OF INFLUENCE

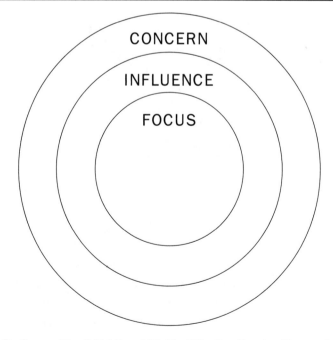

Stephen R. Covey. The 7 Habits of Highly Effective People. *Simon & Schuster, copyright 1989. Used by permission.*

USING THE CIRCLE OF INFLUENCE

When working with your direct reports, show the Circle of Influence and ask questions about their concerns. The goal is to move them from the Circle of Concern (see Figure 5.2) into the Circle of Influence. If people stay in the Circle of Concern for a long time, they become victims who feel helpless, powerless, anxious, and insecure. They have many concerns that can and do affect them, but they feel there isn't anything they can do about the situation. Their Circle of Influence is very miniscule, and everything is impinging on them. Their Circle of Influence can feel like the diagram that follows:

FIGURE 5.2   CIRCLE OF CONCERN

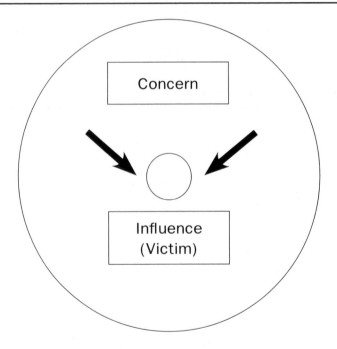

As a leader, you need to listen to your direct reports about their concerns. You need to really hear them, show empathy, and evaluate the situation. Once they feel heard, you want to shift them from areas of concern to areas of influence and power. These questions can help:

- Is there anything you can do about this situation that will help?

- Is there anything anyone else can do that would help you?

- Is there any part of this situation where you have some influence?

- Is there anything you can do right *now* about this?

If the answer to all four questions is no, you want to help them let go of the concern and focus on something else, something that is under their influence. Some of these questions may help:

- What will it take for you to let go of this concern?

- What are you getting out of putting your energy into something you can't change or influence?

- Is it your choice to put your energy on something that won't or can't change?

- Where else could you be putting your energy and focus if you weren't so absorbed in this situation, which you can't change or alter?

- What are you missing out on by staying in the Circle of Concern?

Now take your direct reports into answering some focusing questions:

- What do you have influence over that you can do now?

- What is the first step?

- What is the rest of your plan?

- What support or resources do you need to get this done?

- How can anyone support you?

- What would prevent you from taking action?

TEAM APPLICATION: Hold a meeting with your team and go over the key concerns they face. First, have each person evaluate whether each item is a concern or something he or she has influence over.

Hold a discussion to talk about differences of opinion. Second, talk about what actions you can take for the areas under your influence.

QUESTIONS AND ACTION APPLICATIONS

- How can you implement the Circle of Influence tool with your team or team members?
- Think of examples from your experience that will illuminate the Circle of Influence.
- Practice explaining the Circle of Influence to another person first before working with your whole team.

7. PERFORMANCE = POTENTIAL – INTERFERENCES, OR P = P – I

In *The Inner Game of Work,* Tim Gallwey introduces a simple and effective technique he uses with professional athletes. It begins by focusing and expanding on one's strengths. Once you have your strengths identified and stretched, you can then look at the main interferences that seem to create limitations. The goal is to have performance equal potential. Examples of interferences that may limit one's performance are:

- Lack of closure
- Time management
- Not including others in decisions
- Avoidance of conflict
- Being overly on your case
- Lack of focus
- Poor listening
- Low self-control
- Not open to new ideas
- Talking down to people

QUESTIONS AND ACTION APPLICATIONS

- In your one-on-ones, ask your direct reports to list their interferences.
- How aware are they of their interferences?
- Are there one or two things they can do differently that would have a big impact?

8. DELEGATION

Delegation is a key skill that Star Performers excel at and practice daily. The following model adopted from Covey's Win-Win Agreements has five steps that can help ensure that your delegations are clear, empowering, and effective if performed sequentially and in depth.

The "Recommend, and Then Act" and "Act and Advise," following, can be used as a separate *check-in strategy*. Have both you and your direct reports fill out what they need to come to you with first for recommendation before acting on. With these, you have to give them the green light *(Recommend, and Then Act)*. Then, fill in what they are empowered to do and just inform you on *(Act and Advise)*. The resulting conversation can be very clarifying and can ensure that your direct reports are empowered and checking in with you appropriately.

Often when I am talking with leaders, they complain that their direct reports are not taking enough initiative. Or, on the other side, their direct reports have made decisions the leader wished they had known about ahead of time. I ask, "Have you told them what they can and can't do (as explained above)?" Usually this conversation hasn't happened. This is another example of a micro-initiative that can make you a Star and separate you from the average performers.

Usually impacts don't get talked about. This gives you an opportunity to tie in the value to the greater cause of what they are doing. Employees want to know how they are contributing to the bigger picture, and the impacts of their actions give them that feedback. An example of a negative impact may be: "If you don't get this done on time, it will slow down the production line and cost the company money. Plus, you and I will be to blame and that won't work for what we are trying to accomplish. Come to me if you need more support or resources."

DESIRED RESULTS

The big picture, beginning with the end in mind.

- What are you trying to accomplish?
- What are the key goals or deliverables?
- What kind of relationship do you want with your direct reports?

GUIDELINES

More specifics, how to get it done.

- Key do's and don'ts.
- Check in with you at what points?
- Don't spend more than X amount of time or money.

LEVELS OF INITIATIVE: WHEN TO CHECK BACK RECOMMEND, AND THEN ACT

For example: Personnel issues, changes that affect the project, budget, or timeline.

ACT AND ADVISE

People are empowered to make their own decisions and keep you informed periodically or immediately.

For example: Daily routines, clarify up to what amount of money, time, and resources they can use.

RESOURCES

What people, time, money, training, software, consultants, etc., can be used to achieve the desired result?

ACCOUNTABILITIES

- What metrics do you have to measure the desired results?
- How will you know if they are being successful or not?
- When and where will they be measured?
- Others also act as accountabilities (e.g., executive feedback).

IMPACTS

What are the positive impacts on you, the team, and the individual from achieving the desired results? For example: More challenging projects, better leadership, eligible for more training, make budget, quality product, helping the team, more respect, and progress in their career goals.

NEGATIVE IMPACTS: The opposite of the positive ones given above. It's better to talk about them before negative consequences happen.

QUESTIONS AND ACTION APPLICATIONS

- Try out the delegation steps when you next delegate.
- Get feedback on how the delegation went.
- Ask if there is a way you could be clearer in the next delegation.
- Encourage your direct reports to use the delegation steps when they delegate to others.

9. COACHING FOR PERFORMANCE

This model has been used for almost 20 years as a way of developing people. When coaching, it is important that you save your advice or feedback until the end of your session. Often people are not looking for expert advice, but instead want validation or acknowledgment for what they are already doing. Many leaders miss this and go right to Step Five, advice!

When I ask leaders, "How long do you wait before answering questions from direct reports?" Often they laugh and say, "If I don't interrupt them, maybe I'll wait three to five seconds."

Then I ask, "How long do you think this person thought about his or her issues before coming to you for an answer?" They usually respond, "Anywhere from one to three days."

Often people are not looking for expert advice, but instead want validation or acknowledgment for what they are already doing.

So I say, "What are the chances, with three to five seconds of thought, that you are going to be right?" and "What is the possible impact on the employee?" Obviously the longer you understand the issue, what the direct report's take is on it, and what he or she has already tried, the more accurate you can be with your advice. When you race to advise, the impact on the direct report can be negative, from feeling insulted, devalued, or not heard.

The values of not jumping to advice, or Step Five, until the end of this process are:

- The employee feels heard and understood.
- You will have more time to truly think.
- The employee can feel acknowledged and honored for the problem-solving he or she has already completed.
- You have an opportunity to see how your direct report thinks and problem-solves.
- Your employee can demonstrate his or her strengths to you.
- If placed at the end, your answer or advice has a better chance of being helpful and accepted.

Step One: Hear the Problem or Issue Fully

- What happened?
- When did it happen?

- Why do they think it occurred?
- Reflect back the content and emotions you have heard.

Step Two: Get More Details

- Find out what they have tried.
- How long has it been going on?
- Who has been affected or impacted by the problem?
- What does anyone else think the problem is?
- Is there something that worked even part of the time?
- Reflect back the content and emotions you have heard.

Step Three: Honor Their Ideas for a Solution

- If it is their problem, what do they think should be done next?
- What is the benefit of their idea?
- How long do they think it will take?
- What major obstacles do they see with this solution?
- What other resources will they need?
- How will they know if it's working or not?
- If there is more than one solution, ask about the merit of each. If they had to rank each answer, which is the highest, and why?

Step Four: Ask If They Want Your Feedback

- If not, just confirm what they will do.
- If you feel they really need it but don't want to hear it, offer it.

Step Five: Give Your Advice or Feedback and Make a Plan

- Don't just give the answer, but also use this as a *mentoring moment*.
- Make your thinking visible to them.
- What are your considerations for this choice?
- Why did you select this?
- What did you consider but rule out, and why?

- In a similar experience you might have had, what was the impact of that decision?
- How would you have improved on it knowing what you know today?
- What things did they *not* consider with their choice— unintended consequences, impact on stakeholders, resources needed, time needed to implement it, skills needed?

PLAN

- What will be the next step?
- When should they check back with you?
- How will they know it is working?

10. SCALING QUESTIONS

These questions ask candidates to rate where they are in various situations. It is a helpful strategy to see how people rate themselves. When you are going through your goals in the review, it will also help you see if there have been gains. Scaling questions bring some metrics to the development process, even if it is a self-report.

Ask questions from your direct reports and request that they rate themselves on a scale from 1 to 10, where 10 is the highest. When you get a number, say a 6, you want to follow with the question: "What will bring it to a 7," not a 10. This will help in getting some micro-intiatives to help them move forward. Another benefit when you review their goals with them using scaling questions is that people typically don't remember what number they gave months ago. They are surprised and encouraged when their self-report has increased.

Carl was a client who worked for a design firm, and we developed the following goals for his coaching. Here, the ratings are 1-10, where 10 is the highest:

- Be an inspiring leader = 4
- Set strategic direction = 2
- Communicate frequently = 6

- Become a better listener = 6
- Time management = 3

On two separate occasions we reviewed Carl's goals and modified his actions to continue his development. At the end of the coaching, Carl's progress on the goals was as follows:

- Be an inspiring leader = 7
- Set strategic direction = 5
- Communicate frequently = 7.5
- Become a better listener = 8
- Time management = 6

Carl was satisfied with his progress, as was I. He was very clear about what he needed to do to maintain his gains and what actions to focus on to continue his improvement in the areas listed. The scaling questions helped in identifying gains, rewarding progress, and clarifying areas for continued development. They also helped by bringing some metrics and evaluation to the coaching process.

DEVELOPMENT CHART

Use this chart to organize the information about your direct reports and to clarify the best ways to lead them.

Name: _____

Strengths:

Weaknesses:

Motivations:

Learning style:

Leadership style to use:

Plan:

Resources:

Accountability metrics:

11. DEVELOPMENT FIRST

In 1995 David Peterson and Mary Dee Hicks wrote *Development F.I.R.S.T.* It gives simple yet powerful steps for implementing a development plan that will help you or your direct report make sure your big ideas have staying power so that they do not disappear like last year's well-intentioned New Year's resolution. Include these topics in your conversations with your direct reports or have them bring these answers to your one-on-ones. For your own development, write out your answers to further illuminate the process.

Each step follows the F.I.R.S.T. acronym:

1. FOCUS ON PRIORITIES: What are the most important issues or competencies to focus on in your development plan? Remember, one or two key areas are enough. It's a good idea to work with them for a month or two until you have them mastered.

- Where are you now and where do you want to go?
- What are you actually going to do differently?
- How will these things benefit you and the organization?

2. IMPLEMENT SOMETHING EVERY DAY: Peterson and Hicks suggest spending five minutes a day on development. These micro-initiatives can lead to macro impacts. They suggest finding situations that have *high stakes* and visibility, *novelty* to stretch your comfort zone, *challenges* where you have to do more than in the past, and *interaction* where you have to work through others over whom you don't have position power.

- Can you take a risk each day?
- What is one small step toward your goal?
- How can you employ your strengths?
- What resources or training will help you take these steps?
- What do you need to face?

3. REFLECT ON YOUR EXPERIENCE: This involves spending time really thinking about what has and hasn't worked in the past.

- What have you learned from your successes and mistakes?
- Write down what has been the highlight of each day.
- Write down what you feel most proud of each day.
- What patterns do you see with this daily reflection?
- What have you learned from your hardships?

4. SEEK FEEDBACK AND SUPPORT: The more people you involve in your development plan, the more able you will be to hit your targets. Can you get feedback to make sure you are on the right track? They can provide: 1) feedback, 2) direction, 3) new strategies, 4) support, 5) motivation, and 6) accountability.

- Who are the best people to get feedback from?
- Who are the best people to get support from? (They may be different.)
- Can you tell them exactly what you need and how they can support you?
- What kind of feedback will not be useful to you? Let them know that also.
- How can you support and foster mentoring relationships with them?

5. TRANSFER LEARNING INTO NEXT STEPS: When you have successes, how do you best codify them so you can see the patterns, efforts, and support that allowed you to move forward? Often in seminars or training I will ask participants how they had a success, and their first answer is: "I don't know, I just did it." I want their second, third, and fourth answers to what steps, training, and support made this possible, so they can replicate it.

- Write down your success steps.
- Ask others to list what they saw you do that was helpful.
- To highlight the "how," teach someone else what you did.
- Teach your learning to your team so they can benefit from it.
- Ask others to help hold you accountable for your new behaviors by giving you feedback when you fall back into old habits.

- What are some ways to celebrate your successes?
- What are your next goals to which you can generalize this learning?

STAR PERFORMER ACTION PLAN

Review the Star Profile and *Coach's Corner* strategies to assist you in developing others. Now answer the following questions to help you make your Star Performer Action Plan. Remember, micro-initiatives create macro impacts.

Which competencies or practices are you already doing that you want to continue?

1. _____
2. _____
3. _____

What new practices do you want to incorporate?

1. _____
2. _____
3. _____

What resources do you need to make this happen?

1. _____
2. _____
3. _____

Who can support you and hold you accountable?

1. _____
2. _____
3. _____

How might you sabotage your efforts and best intentions?

   1. _____

   2. _____

   3. _____

What will be your first steps in this plan?

   1. _____

   2. _____

   3. _____

Share this plan with your support people. Good luck!

CHAPTER SIX

COMMUNICATION AND EMPATHY
TOOLS AND STRATEGIES

*The single biggest problem in communication is the illusion
that it has taken place.*

—George Bernard Shaw (Nobel Prize–winning playwright)

This section provides the tools and strategies to help you
become a Star Performer in the areas of Communication and
Empathy. Communication and Empathy are the foundation
of all social or relationship skills. A definition of Communication is illustrated with a research example followed by a Star Profile of
John Davies, founder of Davies Public Relations, a top communication
and public relations firm. Davies shares *11 Secrets & Current Practices* that help him shine as a Star Performer in Communication. He
also describes some of the pitfalls he encounters in his business.

The *Coach's Corner* presents a definition of Empathy, the research
that supports how important it is for peak performance, and 12 proven
strategies used by executives and leaders for the development of these
skills. It also includes a Star Performer Action Plan, which will help
you transform general ideas and concepts into tangible applications for
guaranteed performance as a Star Performer.

WHAT IS THE COMMUNICATION COMPETENCY?

The Communication competency includes listening with an open
mind, sending convincing and clear messages, and cultivating an empa-

thetic give-and-take. A speaker reads the emotional cues expressed by the listener and meets the listener by fine-tuning his message. For communication to be effective, the message has to be received with the intent intact, just as the sender had planned. Difficult situations and delivering bad news are not easy communications, but a Star Performer knows how to express information diplomatically and directly by creating a free flow and exchange that goes back and forth, until there is mutual understanding of each person's perspective.[1]

EMOTIONAL INTELLIGENCE RESEARCH EXAMPLES

The biggest single complaint of Americans in the job force is poor communication with their managers. Two-thirds of those interviewed believe this problem actually prevents them from doing their best work. Another study of 130 executives and managers shows that people prefer working with and relating to others who know how to successfully handle and communicate their emotions and requests.[2]

What makes a good communicator? There are five basic skills that determine whether a co-worker is an effective communicator: listening skills, such as asking good questions; being open-minded; understanding the other; not interrupting; and asking for suggestions.[3]

Are You a Star Performer in communication or just average? Do you regularly and consistently (at least 80% of the time) have an effective give-and-take with others, continually fine-tuning your delivery?

STAR PROFILE: JOHN DAVIES, CEO AND FOUNDER, DAVIES PUBLIC RELATIONS

In 1985 John Davies founded Davies Public Relations, one of the most successful strategic communications firms in the country. The company has won over 250 awards for excellence in advertising, design, and communications and is the third-largest public relations firm in the state and the top 20 in the nation.

For 20 years, Davies ran numerous political campaigns and had an 85% win ratio. His focus has always been on studying human behavior and effective communications strategies to influence decision-making processes, no matter the venue. Whether it is helping a politician refine his or her remarks and presentation or designing a public relations campaign over heated political and environmental issues, John Davies is one of the best. His seminars and coaching have consistently received the highest ratings from audiences all over the country.

DAVIES WAS ASKED

- How did he learn these communication competencies?
- What does he do to be such an effective communicator?
- What are his daily practices?
- What are the pitfalls he needs to be aware of?

EARLY LEARNING EXPERIENCES

John wasn't always a Star in Communication. As a matter of fact, he was unable to speak intelligibly until the age of 10 or 11 due to a speech impediment now called verbal apraxia, a condition that kept him from feeling how his tongue moved around in his mouth. Davies simply couldn't be understood, so he developed an avoidant pattern, specifically to make sure he didn't have to speak in public. "People treated me as stupid, and then I seemed to believe maybe I was stupid," he told me. "I couldn't spell or read well and was in a special remedial reading class." Young Davies decided he wanted to learn how to speak like others, but after hundreds of hours studying people's communication skills he came to realize that most people were actually poor communicators! This insight informed his future decisions about the importance of clear expression.

Davies said that after two years of speech therapy he "got his voice" and claims he hasn't stopped talking since! "Once I got my voice I experimented, and at one point became the class clown. But I flunked eighth grade and had to stay back a year. I felt like a loser again, but staying back turned out to be a gift. Since I was older than everyone else, I naturally had more physical and emotional maturity. And so, I decided I had to get my act together and stop being a loser."

Sports helped build his confidence. He played football, ran track and cross-country, and wrestled. During sixth grade his gym teacher, Don Edick, had kind words for him just as he was beginning to feel his oats. He shared with Davies that he was a late bloomer and would be good in sports someday because he was fast. "You are just like my son; you are smart but no one has figured it out including you, and you are a really fast runner!" Edick's comments were a moment that Davies remembered as he faced Round Two of his communication challenges.

Another defining moment for Davies was being part of the wrestling team, with a coach who happened to teach the advanced English courses and recruited his students for the team. So Davies ended up on a team that featured an unusually high percentage of the smartest kids in the school. He realized he could actually keep up with them and began to embrace more of his own strengths. At the age of 17 or so, he became involved in the student government and ran for president. Naturally, he had to make a speech. He pulled it off but lost by one vote. Why? He admitted he didn't vote for himself! But Davies became the vice president and this turned out to be a critical learning period as he immersed himself in the political arena.

Davies was one of the student officers who dealt with state issues through the Principals' Association. He realized then that the school principals were hesitant to take a stand on important issues because of political ramifications. This was frustrating for Davies because he wanted to get things done. Important ideas that foretold his future began to crystallize in his mind as he came to understand that, in order to succeed, a person needed to learn how to craft a message and deliver powerful communications.

11 SECRETS & CURRENT PRACTICES OF
JOHN DAVIES—STAR PERFORMER

In interviewing Davies, *11 Secrets & Current Practices* emerged that help make him a Star. Think about these practices and how to apply them to your own business or setting. Pick one or two to try out.

1. TOUCH THE HEART

Davies agrees that engaging the audience, clarifying or emphasizing a message, effective give-and-take, and fine-tuning your delivery are crucial elements in successful communication. He also strongly believes that Stars "touch people's hearts" with their words. Effective communication is really more emotional than logical. Davies is always searching for the passage into the heart. Many of the strategies below synergize to arouse other people's emotions.

2. UNDERSTAND WHAT PEOPLE WANT

Davies is deeply concerned about what his clients want.

In an initial meeting, instead of talking about his capabilities and interests as many firms do, he focuses on asking pertinent questions of his client, to better understand their needs, goals, and vision of success. Davies wants to assess whether or not there is a good fit, to make sure he can add real value. He calls himself in this role "The Server of the Question."

3. FIND YOUR PASSION

Davies defines passion as "Being your best without any compromise or change." He firmly believes, "The anatomy of powerful communication is about passion. Passion needs to ooze out of every pore of your body." Davies knows that when a person is passionate, his message is convincing, persuasive, and genuine. In his speech training for politicians, Davies teaches candidates to get in touch with their passion on a physical level. Once they know what it feels like in their body, they can access and retrieve it more easily. They also work to discover what they are most passionate about, beyond speaking points, and delve into other juicy areas of their lives such as their personal relationships, a sport they love, places they've traveled to, and art. To further spark their passion he asks, "When are you most happy?" Getting in touch with the answer to this question provides a wellspring of core energy, which the candidate can develop and use as fuel to feed the feeling tone behind his or her speeches.

Davies also asks more pertinent questions such as:

- Why should I vote for you?
- How is my life going to be better because of you?

If a candidate cannot find his passion, Davies often suggests he not run. Period.

Davies thought John Kerry was neither passionate nor believable in the 2004 campaign. Kerry appeared to be in conflict during his speeches, and Davies believes he looked like he wasn't 100% behind what he said.

It is no surprise that people wondered, "Will he protect us?" In fact, Davies has video clips of Kerry speaking, nodding yes and then saying NO. Other tapes show Kerry often changing his blink rate—getting more rapid with issues that he did not believe—leaving the audience with a bad impression.

Bush, on the other hand, who is not as polished nor as good a speaker as Kerry, appeared confident and passionate and therefore believable.

Davies shares his perceptions of these two candidates, knowing that a person's perception is his or her reality. He coined the term *perceptioneering*, which he uses as his tag line, to describe one of the things his company does.

4. FIND YOUR UNIQUENESS

Davies is always interested in accessing people's strengths and unique abilities. His goal is to use those capabilities in the most effective manner. When Davies is working with clients, he pays close attention to the skills and capabilities that set them apart from others. His focus is to discover their unique talent and skill set, and then he and his team craft these findings into the most effective and compelling message and marketing campaign.

In his own company Davies uses people's unique abilities to synergize talents. He believes that each person contributes in his or her own way to the success of a project, and he looks for a multitalented combination rather than insisting that everyone be the same.

Davies has a demanding and rigorous hiring process that includes using the Kolbe Assessment (to look at preferred instincts in action), other assessments, and multiple interviews. He is always looking for a full complement of abilities across his company. The new hires see from the interview process that Davies Public Relations is unique in its approach, values, and climate. They report that the "challenge and the people" are the key reasons to join the team.

5. READ PEOPLE

In a recent training of community leaders, Davies discussed how touching or scratching one's nose while speaking is an indication of lying (think Pinocchio). He illustrated his point by showing a video of George Bush Sr. telling his audience, "We are winning the war against drugs," while unconsciously rubbing his nose close to 10 times, almost on cue! Davies is aware of how people reveal themselves in countless non-verbal ways when we closely tune in to their message.

In his own company, Davies is able to read which employees need "touches" or personal contact from him or Brandon Edwards, a principal in the firm and the COO. Edwards states, "I don't pick up these cues, but John sees them or senses them, and we are able to connect with people in a 'just in time' process that lets them see we know them and value them."

When Davies is unable to read his audience or their reaction, he conducts a focus group or gives a survey. He knows it is crucial to establish what the audience is feeling and thinking. Davies emphasizes that to be a strategic communicator you must be clear about the target you are trying to hit.

COACHING EXAMPLE

As an Executive Coach, I worked with an executive who had great difficulty reading his audience's reactions to his talks. He was unable to tell if people were receptive, bored, or irritated. On some unconscious level he was able to read that something was going on, but unable to discern what it was or what to do differently. Instead of finding out, he would just talk more and more. The audience felt talked at versus engaged. Because of his inability to read his audience and change his strategy, his efforts to communicate were backfiring on him.

This executive's career began to derail, as he was simply trying too hard. All he had to do was stop, ask some questions, and find out what they needed. The cues were there, but a micro-initiative in a different direction would have a major impact on his effectiveness and his career.

6. ACKNOWLEDGE/DO NOT OFFEND

Davies believes it is important to acknowledge what other people say. Acknowledging also lets the listener know that he or she is being heard and that his or her ideas count. Davies is generous in giving clients credit for coming up with ideas and strategies, rather than having to toot his own horn. He also refuses to threaten or offend people at a meeting and is extremely concerned that everyone feels safe when with him. He makes a point, though, of switching what he is saying or how he is saying it if he is working with a "Contrarian."

This is a person who will disagree and take the opposite opinion just for the sake of discussion.

7. SUMMARIZE AND INTEGRATE

Davies wants his clients to feel that he totally understands their concerns and where they want to go. He does this by summarizing what he hears them say and feeding it back to them. This is an effective way to establish successful give-and-take in a conversation. He will then integrate new information and strategies to help move them forward. Stephen Covey's Fifth Habit says it all: "Seek first to understand, before you are understood."

8. BE PREPARED

Davies believes preparation is the key to being a Star Communicator. That means:

- Review the client goals.
- Research all the relevant issues.
- Know all sides of the story.
- Prepare for rebuttals to client and community responses.
- Review presentations.
- Prep staff for what they need to do to support you and the client.
- Make sure all the details are covered before a client meeting or presentation.

Davies has trained his staff to be well-prepared and proactive. He also expects them to provide all the back research and support he needs before working with clients.

9. TRAINING AND PERSONAL GROWTH

Davies is dedicated to taking time out every year to have several offsite retreats with his staff. These sessions help align the company in the "Davies Way" and give everyone a chance to master the urgency, complexity, and change that takes place at work. He also realizes that his team needs "practice time" away from the demands of their clients to provide the service and quality that bears his name. Although some of these retreats cost up to $20,000 in lost billing, Davies is confident that the investment in his people and the Davies brand results in the excellence and integrity he requires.

One recent training was designed to practice teamwork and give new leaders time to interact with their team by doing business simulations in a non-client setting. Davies, Edwards, and the facilitators gave the team feedback on their results. On one activity, the teams assembled a series of nuts and bolts from memory after brief exposure to a model. They then compared their product to the model for errors. Each team did it numerous times and decreased their time and errors to near perfection. The teams were competitive, enthusiastic, and committed. The conversation after the exercise was about what the teams learned about their leadership, teamwork, project management, communication, and how to improve these in work projects.

Davies is also personally committed to learning and has been a part of the "Strategic Coach" for over 10 years. This organization holds quarterly meetings that focus on business and personal innovation and success. As part of the process, Davies feels that writing down his personal and business goals every year and reviewing them four times a year is very beneficial. He reports, "When I review them I discover that most are already accomplished and some I believe get done simply by writing them down."

10. QUALITY IN ALL

Davies takes a great deal of time mentoring his staff on the "Davies Way" to guarantee that all of the products they create reflect the highest quality. There are hundreds of details to be attended to that require meticulous care, such as writing a quality cover letter for a campaign; working with graphic artists and printers; stuffing envelopes; putting on labels; meeting deadlines; communicating clearly and timely with clients; and dealing effectively with vendors, mishaps, and changes.

Davies wants his staff to be proactive, accountable, and responsible for serving the clients in a superb manner. Not only is Davies's name on everything that leaves the office, but so is his touch.

11. FINDING THE "NEEDLE IN THE HAYSTACK"

Davies believes it is crucial to: "Find a way for us and our clients to be successful by uncovering and creating a perception and a message that work. We then uncover the best and most visible means to deliver those so-called needles to our clients."

The needles are the output, gems, and strategies that accumulate from doing all of the strategies, 1-10 on the previous pages. The campaigns are built around these elements. They include:

- The question that has not been asked
- The hidden reason for or against a cause
- Identifying the main leverage point(s) to influence people
- The unique abilities of the client
- The passion that needs stoking and stroking

Davies's team comes up with numerous approaches for a client and then refines them over and over again. Aside from John Davies, his staff is made up of experts in communication, public relations, media, political campaigns, and crisis communication. In crafting the message, the team looks for stories, metaphors, graphics, and images that make a passionate appeal, one that touches people's hearts and will leave a lasting impression.

Davies's toolbox contains all of the most compelling practices including influence and persuasion theories, change strategies, psychology, sociology, media, leadership, non-verbal communication, crisis communication, and relationship building.

This section is about communication, but you can see that Davies is also a Star in many of the other EI competencies, such as Accurate Self-Assessment, Confidence, Trustworthiness, Achievement Orientation, Initiative, Conscientiousness, Adaptability, Service Orientation, Empathy, Conflict Management, Teamwork and Collaboration, and Influence.

WHAT PITFALLS DOES DAVIES NEED TO BE AWARE OF IN COMMUNICATION?

Davies knows that communication is a highly interpretative process. In his business, people are very emotional and highly committed to the projects at hand. When asked about his potential pitfalls or blind spots, he mentioned the following four, which are applicable to all of us.

- "Being blinded by your passion and losing your discriminatory process." Passion can be overused, and it is possible to be seen as a bully instead of exuberant.

- "Timing of when to speak." It is sometimes tricky to know when to speak and when not to speak. People want to be heard, and managing your need to be heard with that of the client's need is critical.

- "Being condescending or threatening. Managing your emotions is critical, and it is important to be aware of any subtle tones or irritation in your voice, because it can affect or even subvert the entire message being communicated."

- "Trying to get credit for things and not giving appropriate credit." In the "idea world" it is crucial to acknowledge the source of good ideas and to only take credit for something if it is true. If you are in doubt about how the idea was actually created, it is best to give others credit.

ACTIONS: REVIEW DAVIES'S CURRENT PRACTICES

Looking at Davies's current practices, what practices can you incorporate to become a Star Performer in Communication?

Which ones do you want to add to your Star Performer Action Plan?

1. _____

2. _____

3. _____

THE COACH'S CORNER: 12 STRATEGIES FOR ENHANCING COMMUNICATION AND EMPATHY

Below are 12 proven strategies that you can use to improve your communication and empathy. Every leader has to communicate to get his or her points across. Stars have a set of tools that they use judiciously to be effective. Below are key strategies I teach to executives to incorporate into their daily routines. As you read through the list, be aware of what you are already doing and what actions or micro-initiatives you could do more of.

Communication is important to all of us, but leaders especially need to be understood and to have empathy for others. Here are eight of the basic premises that make this such a challenging endeavor:

1. You are always communicating, even if you are not saying anything.

2. Everything you say counts. There are no second attempts, editing, or deleting of what you say.

3. When your words leave your mouth, you have no control over how they are going to be interpreted.

Everything you say counts. There are no second attempts, editing, or deleting of what you say.

4. Listeners are constantly constructing or "storymaking." That means they are always interpreting what you say.

5. Your words are transformed or reorganized to fit into the listener's personal story or preconceived idea of you and/or similar situations.

6. There will be more than one story. Each listener will create his or her own.

7. The story that is created from your communication determines the meaning, not what you actually say.

8. It is the story, not what you say, that will be remembered, passed on, and communicated to others.[4]

> . . . the likely outcome of your communication is that you will be misunderstood, and therefore you need to be very clear, deliberate, and focused in your communication.

Given these premises, the likely outcome of your communication is that you will be *misunderstood*, and therefore you need to be very clear, deliberate, and focused in your communication. Following are strategies and tools to help you win the empathy and communication battle to reach your targets. These strategies deal with listening, empathy, delivery, and other skills to use with your team or groups.

Read through the following strategies and think about how these behaviors will help you or your direct reports become Star Performers. Pick one or two to try out.

1. EMPATHY SKILLS

Empathy is one of the 20 EI competencies. It is presented here as part of Communication because the skills to enhance empathy are many of the same ones for improving communication. Empathy is one of the building blocks for many of the other competencies including Communication, Trustworthiness, Self-Awareness, Building Bonds, Conflict Resolution, Service Orientation, Leadership, Change Catalyst, and Influence.

WHAT IS THE EMPATHY COMPETENCY?

Empathy is the ability to 1) understand other people, and 2) accurately hear the unspoken or partly expressed thoughts, feelings, and concerns of others. It implies taking an active interest in other people's concerns. For people to believe you *see* their perspective, you have to *say* their perspective.

EMOTIONAL INTELLIGENCE RESEARCH EXAMPLES

Empathy requires self-awareness, as our sensitivity to others' feelings derives from our ability to be aware and sensitive to our own feelings.

Physicians who are better at recognizing emotions of patients are more successful at treating them than their less sensitive counterparts.[5] Spencer and Spencer found the ability to read others' needs appears to come naturally to the most successful managers of product teams. Empathy was found to be effective for sales in small and large retailers.[6] Empathy was also found to reduce stereotyping that can cause anxiety and poorer performance by the stereotyped individual.[7]

Are You a Star Performer in empathy or just average? Do you regularly and consistently (at least 80% of the time) understand others' perspectives and say their perspective first, and are you open to diversity?

HOW TO LISTEN

EXPRESSED AND UNEXPRESSED FEELINGS

The Star "sees others' perspectives and understands them." This includes the content of what they are saying and the feelings they are having. The content of what someone is saying is the easier of the two. For someone to really feel heard, knowing how he or she feels allows a deeper sense of being understood. This is challenging

FIGURE 6.1 FLUSHING OUT FEELINGS

EXPRESSED	UNEXPRESSED
1 Known to self and expressed	2 Known to self, and known to others
	3 Not known to self, but known to others
	4 Not known to self and not known to others

because often people don't know how they feel, so besides being invisible to you their feelings are also unknown to them.

What can help with this process is a modification of what is called the Johari Window, first conceived in 1955 by Joseph Luft and Harry Ingram. It is a visualization (see Figure 6.1) that helps to give voice to people's feelings, including those that are known and expressed as well as those that are unknown and unexpressed. What to do depends on the expression of feelings and whether or not they are known.

QUADRANT 1: FEELINGS ARE KNOWN TO SELF AND EXPRESSED

- **Listen for the "blinking words":** The blinking words are the feelings; they have the emotional content. You want your ear to be sensitized to them as though they are flashing brightly. Consider: "I am so *frustrated* with the project, I don't know what to do next." "Frustrated" is the blinking word. You can hear how it stands out in the sentence. Here are two possible responses:

▲ "What are you thinking about doing next?"

▲ Or, "Tell me what is making you so frustrated."
This one is much better.

QUADRANT 2: FEELINGS ARE KNOWN TO SELF AND OTHERS BUT ARE UNEXPRESSED

- **Observe body language:** Do you pick up any gestures or poses that may illuminate what is going on for this person? Slumped body, low voice, flat affect, irritated when talking?

- **Ask questions:** Try to understand what is happening for the other person by inquiring. "You seem down today. What is going on?" "You seem tense today. Can I help you with anything?"

- **Put yourself in the other person's shoes:** If you were in the same situation, what might you be feeling? "If I were in your situation, I would be feeling overwhelmed. How is this for you?"

QUADRANT 3: FEELINGS ARE NOT KNOWN TO SELF, BUT ARE KNOWN TO OTHERS AND UNEXPRESSED

- **This is known as a "blind spot":** Ask the person if he or she wants some feedback and use the SSBIR Feedback model on pages 284-289. It is ideal if you make the issue part of his or her development plan.

- **Be sensitive. Do not pry:** Remember, you can make a mental note of what is going on for the person and bring it up at another, more appropriate time. "I noticed the other day in the meeting that you were unusually quiet. What was going on for you?"

- **Observe body language:** Do you pick up anything that may get at what is going on for this person? Slumped body, low voice, flat affect, irritated when talking?

- **Ask questions:** Try to understand what is happening for the other person by inquiring. "You seem down today. What is going on?" "You seem tense today. Can I help you with anything?"

- **Put yourself in the other person's shoes:** If you were in the same situation, what might you be feeling? "If I were in your situation, I would be feeling overwhelmed. How is this for you?"

QUADRANT 4: FEELINGS ARE NOT KNOWN BY SELF OR OTHERS

For the obvious reasons, these will not be addressed.

LISTENING AT LEVEL 3

When I was a doctoral student, I helped Dr. Byron Norton train master level students in their counseling skills using the Carkuff Model. The students would listen to a counselee and then paraphrase what they just heard, without asking questions or giving advice. This kind of listening is a lot more difficult than it sounds. The natural tendency is to want to give advice and help the person. In this context, helping is not just listening. You can really help once the person truly feels heard. In order to get an "A" in the class, students were required to make sure at least 75% of their responses were at what is called "Level 3." It takes a lot of concentration and skill, but the people talking really feel understood.

THE FOUR LEVELS OF LISTENING

Level 1: Paraphrase content

Level 2: Paraphrase feelings

Level 3: Paraphrase feelings and content

Level 4: Paraphrase feelings, content, and meaning

Leaders benefit greatly by training in Level 3 and Level 4 listening. Here is an example:

Susan is Vice President of Marketing for a California Internet health products company that just acquired a smaller company that manufactures unique items to add to her company's line. She will be picking up three new direct reports from the acquired company. In addition, Susan has a family of three kids and a husband, who also works.

Susan has been asked to assess the new company's marketing staff back at their home offices in North Carolina.

She has a brief talk with her boss, Helen.

Susan: "I am not looking forward to this trip. I am on total overwhelm and feel pulled in so many different directions between my staff, the new people, and my family. I'm sunk because I feel like I can't please all of them and I'm really upset because my son's game is Friday and I have to be on a plane that day."

Helen can come back with any of the following four levels of Listening and Response.

LEVEL 1: PARAPHRASE CONTENT

"You have a lot on your plate. Can you take another flight?"

LEVEL 2: PARAPHRASE FEELINGS

"You seem very stressed and upset."

LEVEL 3: PARAPHRASE FEELINGS AND CONTENT

"You seem very overwhelmed and stressed with trying to please your team, the new staff, plus your family. You also seem disappointed that you will miss your son's game."

LEVEL 4: PARAPHRASE FEELINGS, CONTENT, AND MEANING

"You seem very overwhelmed and stressed with trying to please your team, the new staff, plus your family. You are afraid that someone will be upset and let down. It is hard for you to not be all things to all people."

For you to be a Star Performer in Empathy, the majority of your responses should be coming from Level 3, highlighting the content and the other person's dominant feelings. Level 4 is even better because it goes deeper and incorporates patterns and themes that you know about the person.

QUESTIONS AND ACTION APPLICATIONS

- Practice Level 3 responses with your family and children.
- Then practice Level 3 responses with your team or staff.
- Teach your staff the Level 3 responses and provide a practice session.
- Use Level 3 responses with your clients or customers.
- Do you feel you are getting more adept at reading into others' unexpressed emotions?
- Evaluate your empathy skills weekly and ask a trusted colleague or direct report if he or she feels you are demonstrating a good understanding of the person.

2. LISTENING AND RAPPORT-BUILDING SKILLS

Stephen Covey says, "Most people do not listen with the intent to understand; they listen with the intent to reply."

This is one reason many people and leaders are poor listeners. Empathy is the foundation of listening, and this section presents listening strategies and tips to help you become a Star in Communication and Empathy.

THINKING INSTEAD OF LISTENING: The average person can speak at about 150 words per minute but can think a lot faster, between 450 and 600 words a minute. There is obviously plenty of room to multi-think with your mind busy chattering away while so-called listening. For example, while you are sitting at a meeting, this abundance of nonstop thinking may be going through your mind: "What am I going to have for lunch? Why is this person taking so long to get to the point? Should I buy that new car or wait till the end of the year? I wonder who is going to fill the marketing role. What can I do to get out of here earlier to make my son's game?"

See if any of the following barriers to effective listening happen for you or your team. Check the ones that you or your team exhibit and start changing them today.

SEVEN BARRIERS TO LISTENING

Put a check next to the ones you use the most.

☐ **REHEARSING A RESPONSE:** All of your thoughts are on putting together a response to the questions that might come up. Or you are practicing how you are going to say your piece.

☐ **FALSE REASSURANCES:** You nod your head or say "Yeah," while looking for that tiny opening when you can jump in and speak.

☐ **CLICHÉS:** You offer all kinds of clichés, such as "I'm with you" or "I totally understand," when you really aren't or don't.

☐ **MISDIRECTED QUESTIONS:** You ask questions that divert or interrupt the person speaking and fail to really explore what the person is saying.

☐ **NOT FOCUSING:** You pay attention to something or someone just outside of the conversation, such as the person who just walked by the window or the sounds of conversation in the next room.

☐ **DAYDREAMING:** Your mind is elsewhere—on your next vacation, your next meal, or playing tennis on the weekend.

☐ **SELECTIVE LISTENING:** You only catch a few words and pretend to listen.

LISTENING AND RAPPORT-BUILDING TIPS

PSYCHOLOGICAL BREATH OF THE RELATIONSHIP

Listening is to a relationship like breath is to the body. Without air we cannot survive. Think about a time you were holding your breath while under water. One minute can feel like an eternity. Remember how you forced yourself up to the surface and were gasping for air. If you are a leader and are not listening well to your people, they can suffocate in their feelings of insignificance. For you to establish a vital and thriving relationship, they must know you are listening to them.

INCREASE THE "EMOTIONAL BANK ACCOUNT"

This metaphor was first introduced in Stephen Covey's *The 7 Habits of Highly Effective People*. Each interaction with your people adds to the so-called mutual "emotional bank account" you have with them. By listening, acknowledging, asking for their ideas, supporting, and providing resources for them, you contribute to their account, maybe $50 at a time. You want the account to have $800-$1,000 or more and keep growing. There will be times when you want them to stay late or do something that you know they don't want to do. Because you have built this emotional bank account, you now have the funds to withdraw, say, $150 or $200 and not go bankrupt. Your people will be willing to be there for you because of the strength of your relationship or emotional bank account. (The Debilitating Boss, on the other hand, is constantly withdrawing money and has bankrupt accounts.)

PEOPLE TEND TO LIKE PEOPLE WHO ARE LIKE THEM

It is smart to have something besides work in common with each of your direct reports. For your team to feel connected with you, part of your conversations should be around what you have in common with them. For one person it may be family, for someone else it might be a favorite sports team, cars, music, or travel. Find at least one area of shared interest or passion outside of the workplace to cultivate real rapport.

ATTENDING BEHAVIOR

I worked with an executive who listened intensely but always exhibited a frown on his face. He also failed to physically acknowledge who he was talking with by nodding his head or even raising his eyebrows. When I was coaching him, I quickly noticed this intense behavior, felt uncomfortable with his response to me, and talked to him about it. It turned out that he was neither unhappy nor critical. Unfortunately, when this executive paid deep attention to another person he just frowned. He never realized that he appeared so off-putting. He was grateful for the blunt feedback and made it his primary coaching goal to become more aware of his attending behavior and change his expression when dealing with others.

For many years before the executive succeeded in changing his attending behavior, most of his direct reports had misinterpreted his expression. They dreaded having a meeting with him because, under his cold glare and frown, they thought:

- "He doesn't like me."
- "He thinks I'm an idiot and not making any sense."
- "He is mad at me for something I did."

By making one simple micro-initiative, this executive allowed his people to feel listened to and understood by him instead of judged or criticized.

TO DEMONSTRATE GOOD LISTENING, YOU NEED TO

- Not talk. (This is not so obvious for some people.)
- Nod your head occasionally.

- Softly look at the person, gazing more at the top part of his or her face. Do not stare.
- Move away from the computer screen and face whomever you are listening to.
- Open your body posture. Avoid crossed arms. Don't keep looking at your watch.

GIVE BRIEF VERBAL ACKNOWLEDGMENTS

Brief verbal acknowledgments let people know you are listening. These are not the clichés from the barriers listed on page 265. Say "ah-hah," "yeah," "mmmm," "wow," "interesting," "really," "OK," "that's nice" periodically during the conversation. This is very subtle and another example of micro-initiatives.

Pace your responses. If you keep interjecting, "That's nice . . . ," it will make whomever you are speaking to think you want him or her to stop or that you are bored.

MATCHING AND MIRRORING

You can use many kinds of assessments, from the Myers-Briggs Typing Indicator to the Kolbe, DISC, or Sensory Preference VAK style (see pages 280-281) to discover how your people operate and gather information. You can then match or mirror back their particular orientation to understanding and processing data and make a strong connection.

The effort you make to identify and use this information with your team, direct reports, managers, and peers will help propel you into the top 10% of Star Performers.

QUESTIONS AND ACTION APPLICATIONS

- Which barriers to listening do you do the most?
- Practice adding to the emotional bank account with all direct reports and key stakeholders.

- Get feedback from a trusted co-worker on the effectiveness of your attending behavior.

- Establish commonalities or interests outside of work that you can talk with your people about that can help build the relationship.

- Identify the specific language to use with each of your people that matches their way of taking in information.

3. WHITE SPACE ISSUES

"If you are not sick and tired of saying the same thing over and over again, you are not saying it enough."

The word *intelligence* comes from a Latin derivation meaning "entering through the lines." People are always using their intelligence to enter or read into the lines of what you are saying or not saying. They fill in the white spaces between your words almost automatically, because it gives them a sense of understanding, control, or security. In the caveman days, gossip served a similar function. It was information that gave tribes the sense of understanding the meaning of things. They could "connect the dots," which helped their survival.

Today, gossip or "making stories" serves a similar purpose. Whether you like it or not, people will always put a personal spin on everything you say, and they do it almost instantaneously. Are their interpretations positive, accurate, or constructive? Probably not! Following is an illustration of what usually happens when you speak and others "listen."

AN EXECUTIVE SAYS ABOUT A POSSIBLE ACQUISITION

"We are looking into all kinds of possibilities that will help us maintain our viability and profitability."

HOW PEOPLE FILL IN THE WHITE SPACE

"I didn't think we were in such trouble. This may be worse than I thought. I wonder if I should start looking elsewhere."

"If we are looking to purchase another company, that means there will be layoffs and my job could be in jeopardy."

"Oh no, with this going on in the executive office, they will never have time to focus on my project. This is going to hurt my career advancement."

If you don't fill in the white space, your people will, and you will be reacting to all the misinterpretation.

Here is how you can fill in the white space with what is positive, accurate, and constructive.

AN EXECUTIVE SAYS ABOUT A POSSIBLE ACQUISITION

"We are looking into all kinds of possibilities that will help us maintain our viability and profitability. Right now there are a few exciting opportunities. Now, because of due diligence, I can't tell you exactly what. But what I can tell you is our process. We have a small team of seasoned executives who are looking at all the facts. This will be a well-thought-out and informed decision. Our criteria in the decision are that we:

"First, don't interrupt our day-to-day business and focus.

"Second, that we keep all the talent here.

"Third, we want this to be growth for you and the company. We want you to be a part of any changes that go on.

"We plan to have a monthly lunch meeting to answer your questions and keep you informed. Contact me or my office if you have questions."

In this scenario, the leader tried to fill in the white space to the best of his or her ability, answering many of the questions people may have. If you can respond to the "unasked questions," you build credibility and security. People won't have to "create their own stories" as much.

WHITE SPACE

The following visual will help you see and remember the process. The bold line indicates what you said:

The minus or hyphen signs indicate what gets filled in quickly by others. Remember, they are entering through the lines to grasp what it seems you have said. Again, it is usually inaccurate and judgmental, and rarely gives you the benefit of the doubt.

Positive signs indicate what you say when you proactively fill in the white space with accurate and positive data, talking about opportunities.

++

++

++

White space is always going to get filled in by others. You can plan ahead and inform your people of what you know and prevent too many misunderstandings.

QUESTIONS AND ACTION APPLICATIONS

- Explain to your staff how filling in white space is natural and how you want them to become conscious of how they are doing it.

- Ask, "What are the ways you can become more aware of how you and others fill in the white space?"

- Challenge yourself and others on some of their assumptions as you and they fill in the white space.

- Constantly ask for feedback about your communications. Ask, "What did you hear?" Then re-clarify.

- Ask your team to let you know if they are not hearing enough from you and are beginning to fill in white space negatively.

- Evaluate whether their interpretations are Positive, Accurate, and Constructive. This is called a PAC interpretation. If what you read or hear is not accurate and constructive, make sure you clarify.

- Remember, white space is going to get filled in by others anyway. You can be preventative and informing by telling your people what you know.

- Use the term *white space* so it remains a viable image and concept for your team.

4. INTENTION/INTERPRETATION GAP

Everything you say has *inferred intention* and *direction* to it. Even if you didn't mean to, the receiver hears a message and intended action to your words. For example:

Mary is an executive with a high-tech company. She talks fast, is extremely busy, is always multitasking, and is driven to get results. She has a meeting with her staff to motivate them to finish a project, so they can enjoy a long weekend. She begins:

"I'm working my tail off to get this project done. I'm sure you don't want me breathing down your neck to see how well you are doing. We missed our last deadline, and I won't let this happen again. Mike here has put together a nice template for all of us to follow."

This is what her people hear

- "Does she think she is the only one here who is working hard? Doesn't she see what everyone else is doing?"

- "Yeah, breathing down my neck is just what I want from her. Oh no."

- "Does she think I blew the last deadline? I know she looked right at me when she said that."

- "Look at all the work I do, and Mike gets all the credit. She doesn't know I exist."

- "She thinks I am the weak link here and that I don't know what I'm doing. She hasn't talked to me in a month. I'm just as good as Mike."

Mary didn't put much time into thinking about what she wanted to say to the group. As a consequence, she easily gets misinterpreted by what *she didn't say* as much as by what *she did say*. Her intention to motivate the group backfired. She would have been more successful if she would have: 1) taken 3-4 minutes preparing what to say and how to say it, 2) initially asked them how they were doing with the project, and 3) delivered what she had prepared to say.

It is natural to have a gap between what your intention is as the speaker and what the interpretation of what you said

The listeners assume that you *really thought about this* and there is something *specific* you are saying.

is as the listener. Many leaders live by faulty assumptions that can cause many problems such as: "Because I said it, everyone has received it." The listeners assume that *you really thought about this* and there is something *specific* you are saying. In other words, they are inferring that you have clarity in your communication.

RECEIVER'S INFERENCES INCLUDE

- You spent time thinking about this situation.
- You know exactly what you want.
- There is a clear purpose in all of your communications.
- You know what they can do or not do to add value.
- You have all the answers.

These inferences are based on what you say, your behavior, and your non-verbals. As leaders, we know that many of these assumptions are false, but these are the expectations of your followers as they are listening to you, *at least initially*. If these expectations are not met, then the opposite of these inferences are made and then validated and revalidated.

For example:

- You don't know what you are doing.
- You don't have the answers.
- You don't think anyone has any value.
- You are not clear about where you, the team, or the organization are going.
- You are not a leader who is credible and respected.

INTENTION/INTERPRETATION GAP

Everything you say has inferred intention and direction to it, as shown in Figure 6.2.

FIGURE 6.2   INTENTION/INTERPRETATION GAP

Sender Intention	What Is Said Behaviors Non-Verbals	Receiver Interpretation

To abate this gap, it is important for both the sender and receiver to be proactive in their parts of the communication. The key questions to ask are:

- Was the communication delivered in a clear, intentional manner?

- Did the communication get received as intended?

To assist in this process, it is necessary to take specific steps. The Intention/Interpretation Quotient (iiQ) was developed as a tool to delineate the steps and evaluate the process. The goal is to use this as a measurement when directions are given by a leader to his or her team or after a problem-solving discussion. The U.S. Army has found that flawed execution comes from flawed assumptions. The iiQ helps elucidate these assumptions.

INTENTION/INTERPRETATION QUOTIENT (iiQ)

Each of the following questions is worth up to 10 points. Mark a number between 1 and 10, where 10 is highest, to show the effectiveness of a particular communication and listening session. Add up the Intention and Interpretation points to come up with an overall iiQ.

Intention: Did the speaker and speakers . . . 1-10 pts	
1. Make their intentions and expectations known?	
2. Communicate to match their listener's style?	
3. Express their assumptions?	
4. Check to see if they were understood?	
5. Have clear directions?	
Total Intention Points	
Interpretation: Did the listener and listeners . . . **1-10 pts**	
1. Hear all the communication?	
2. Ask clarifying questions?	
3. Express their assumptions?	
4. Add to and build on the conversation?	
5. Challenge in an effective manner?	
Total Interpretation Points	

Intention Quotient =

Interpretation Quotient =

Overall iiQ =

There are a number of ways to decrease the gap between intention and interpretation.

QUESTIONS AND ACTION APPLICATIONS

- Introduce the Intention/Interpretation Quotient and use it. Have one person assess your meetings, and rotate that responsibility.
- Where is the gap between intention and interpretation? Which side has the biggest score?
- What gap patterns exist in your team?
- Discuss the scores and ways to lessen the gap.

- As a leader, take time to truly prepare what and how you are going to communicate your points.
- Get feedback from your team about your effectiveness in delivering messages.

5. POWER OF LANGUAGE: METAPHORS, STORIES, AND WORDS

How a leader uses language is critical to effective communication. The choice of metaphors, stories, words, and visual pictures separates the Star communicator from the average. As Mark Twain said, "The difference between the right word and almost the right word is the difference between lightning and a lightning bug."

People remember a metaphor or story more than any other form of communication. Tune in to utilizing these two communication strategies and you will successfully hit the communication target with your direct reports.

METAPHORS

A metaphor is defined as a mental bridge that links the unknown with the known, describing one thing in terms of another.[8] When someone says, "X is like Y" a metaphor usually follows. For example:

"My boss's feedback feels **like** a two-by-four against my head."

"The culture here is **like** everyone is breathing in lattes."

"Great leaders and managers treat their direct reports **like** chess players rather than checkers."

"Star communicators fine-tune their delivery **like** an archer spending extra seconds aiming to ensure he hits the bull's-eye."

It is important to train your ears to recognize people's metaphors and then incorporate these metaphors into your responses. Using your followers' metaphors will help them know they have been heard and honored. People have a special relationship with their metaphors, just like they do with their name. We know communication can be enhanced when we use a person's name. The same is true for metaphors because they are your windows into how people perceive their world.[9]

Metaphorical communication is ambiguous and open to interpretation. Because people crave stability and want to avoid imbalance, they will listen closer, think harder, and become more experientially involved.[10]

REMEMBER

"A single word can possess multiple meanings, yet as the common saying goes, one picture can be worth a thousand words. And if one picture can be worth a thousand words, then one experience can be worth a thousand pictures, and then one metaphor can be worth a thousand experiences.

"But in the end, a metaphor only possesses value when:

- It is able to interpret the experiences . . .
- In a manner that provides the picture . . .
- That produces words . . .
- That have meaning . . .
- For that particular person."[11]

Luckner and Nadler's *Processing the Experience* presents a guide for using metaphorical language, metaphor-making questions, and metaphor themes that leaders can use to enhance their communication. The themes for creating metaphors include:

Journey theme—"Our train is just leaving the station and we are not sure what the next stop will be with this product."

Systems theme—"You won't be able to race at the same unbearable speed without taking time to change your oil or the spark plugs. What will help you recharge?"

Healing theme—"This loss of our key employee is a big wound for us. It will take time to close up and develop new skin and move forward as we have."

Cyclic and Natural Phenomena theme—"The best way for us to be prepared for this storm of new interest in our products is to be prepared. What will we need in our first-aid kits to get through this next month?"

STORIES

A story is the development and elaboration of a metaphor into more of a discourse. It is also rich with visual pictures and innuendo that asks the listener to engage by filling in the blanks with his or her imagination. The individual must search through a number of stored or imagined experiences in order to find personal meaning. The searching stimulates mental associations, which make the communication more memorable and meaningful. The creative process involved in searching through and reorganizing new experiences helps individuals become active collaborators in processing and generalizing their learning.[12]

In 1974 I was working on my Master's thesis. It involved creating a curriculum of facilitative activities to do with Outward Bound courses to enhance awareness and personal relevance that could transfer back easily to home and work environments. The curriculum involved applying Emotional Intelligence competencies to the Outward Bound experience some 16 years before the term *Emotional Intelligence* was coined.

The research design involved four experimental groups and four control groups. I was anxious and apprehensive about my ability to do the courses, implement the curriculum, and gather the research. A few days before I left for the summer project, I bumped into my faculty advisor, Dr. George Brown, the founder and program chair of the Confluent Education program. I bombarded him with my worries and fears for about 10 minutes. When I finally took a breath he said, "Let me see your hand." I stretched out my hand, and he put his fist on top and declared, "You have my seal of approval. I know you will do great and whatever you don't know you will be able to figure out." He then smiled and walked away.

I felt totally bewildered. What had just happened? Over the next day or two I realized that Dr. Brown had expressed his faith in my ability to find my own answers and implement them. This brief interaction was a significant learning for me. His faith in me translated to more faith in myself to stay with what is ambiguous and uncertain until I figure it out.

This story illustrates how the simple sharing of an experience opens up poignant questions and invites personal responses from your listeners.

- Who are the people that have faith in you?
- Who is in your corner?
- Whom do you need to express your faith in?

This story also elucidates George Brown's ability to use Emotional Intelligence—his empathy, trustworthiness, service orientation, leadership, influence, and communication—in a micro-initiative that yielded macro impacts for me.

WORDS: HOW YOU TAKE IN AND RELATE TO THE WORLD

Another excellent configuration for understanding different people's communication styles comes from Neuro-Linguistic Programming (NLP), an application used in numerous settings, including sales, education, psychotherapy, and trainings of all sorts. NLP originated when researchers studied Star communicators in the 1970s and teased out powerfully effective strategies that they were using and defined them according to their sensory preferences. People take in and digest information about their world in three ways: Visual (V), Auditory (A), and Kinesthetic (K). Look, listen, and watch your team members and learn how to discern whether they are V, A, or K. Then, to have the most impact, feed them your information tailored specifically to their preference.

THREE SENSORY PREFERENCE STYLES FOR TAKING IN AND REPRESENTING THE WORLD:

V = VISUAL STYLE: **Revolves around vision and sight**

Talks fast, uses visual phrases such as "I can *see* clearly . . . " "let me paint you the picture . . . " "see what I'm saying . . . " "in view of . . . " "it looks like . . . " and "It is still cloudy to me . . . "

A = AUDITORY STYLE: **Revolves around hearing**

Talks methodically and carefully selects words. Uses phrases such as "to tell the truth . . . " "clear as a bell," "that clicks with me," "I *hear* what you are saying," "what an earful," "it sounds good," and "loud and clear."

K = KINESTHETIC STYLE: **Revolves around tactileness and motion**

May talk slowly, sometimes painfully so. Uses phrases such as "catch my drift," "sharp as a tack," "get in touch," "come to grips," "get a handle on it," "hang in there," and "cool and calm."

QUESTIONS AND ACTION APPLICATIONS

- When preparing to talk to your team, think of stories or metaphors from your own experience that give your talk more vividness and highlight your points.

- Really listen hard to the words and metaphors of your people and mirror them back to them when communicating.

- What are your preferences for taking in information and communicating? Are you a V? An A? A K?

- Write down the ways each of your people takes in information from the VAK above. When speaking to each person, make sure you start with his or her preference before falling back to your own.

- When you speak before a group, make sure you dip into all three sensory preference styles so that you successfully reach the entire audience. See it. Hear it. Feel it.

6. CLARITY: CONNECTING THE DOTS
TO A BETTER FUTURE

"Clarity is king" should be the motto for every leader. In each of your communications, you should be connecting the dots for your team members. Given the communication challenges and the Intention/Interpretation Gap, leaders need to over-communicate and employ a variety of methods to get the job done.

**More clarity = More security = Better work =
More job satisfaction**

In *The One Thing You Need to Know,* Marcus Buckingham focuses on the key initiatives of a leader as it relates to creating a better future. He says:

"Their job is to rally people to a better future . . . They are instigators. Driven by the compulsion for a better future, their challenge is to do everything in their power to get other people to join together to make this future come true. They (need to) find a way to make many people . . . excited by and confident in this better future. If, through their words, actions, images, pictures, and scores, they can tap into those things we all share, they will succeed as leaders."

Connecting the dots is a way to keep employees informed (see Figure 6.3). People want to feel significant, get involved in something greater than themselves, and contribute as vital members of the team. If you don't connect the individual to key purposes and goals, he or she will feel disconnected and unmotivated. Make sure you ask the following questions to clarify your future:

1. Who do we serve?
   - Customers, employees, or shareholders?
   - Is there a specific type of customer you are going after?
2. What is our core strength?
   - What is our unique strength that others don't have?
   - How do you keep it in focus?

FIGURE 6.3 CONNECTING THE DOTS: WHAT TO COMMUNICATE ABOUT FREQUENTLY

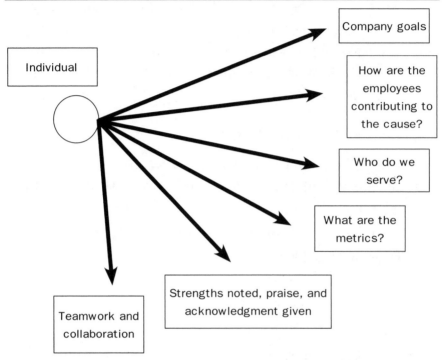

3. What is our core score?

- What metrics are useful to track and keep improving?
- How do you continually share the scores and keep everyone current? [13]

QUESTIONS AND ACTION APPLICATIONS

- Decide what methods you can utilize and how often you can connect the dots for your team and organization.
- How can you get each of your leaders and team members to pass the communications about connecting the dots into the organization?
- How do you get people who don't have clarity to speak up so they can get the answers?

- Design a "clarity meter" and ask your people on a 1-10 scale, 10 being the highest, to rate your clarity with them. Inquire what could be better, regardless of the scores they give you.
- Use a "brief back," like the army does. This is where, after you have said something, you ask your people to give you the "brief back" or to summarize back to you briefly what they heard or will do.

7. GIVING FEEDBACK: SSBIR

Like delegation and coaching, giving feedback is another skill that can greatly enhance performance when both delivered and received well.

Sometimes it is difficult to give feedback. Why? Ask yourself:

- Does the individual want to hear the feedback?
- How honest can I be?
- Will I hurt the person's feelings?
- What if he or she gets defensive?
- Will there be retribution?
- What will the person do with the feedback?
- What if he or she doesn't hear it and the same things keep happening?
- Will this hinder our relationship?
- Is this worth my risk?

THE PROCESS

The following model is adapted from the Center for Creative Leadership. This model can help in giving effective feedback. The goal of the feedback is for the person to both receive and use it. First the summary steps are listed with sentence stubs of what you say; then each step is explained in more detail.

GIVING FEEDBACK

Set the Stage: Intention/readiness to listen

- "I'd like to talk to you about something. Will this time work?"
- "My intention is to help you develop."
- "Can I give you some feedback?"

State the Situation: What happened and where?

- "In the meeting today . . . "
- "When you spoke to . . . "
- "In the report you wrote . . . "

State the Behavior: What did you see or hear, without interpretations?

- "When you came late to the meeting . . . "
- "When you said . . . "
- "Three people said . . . "
- "I saw two errors . . . "
- "When the report was late . . . "

State the Impact: On multiple stakeholders and time frames

- "The customer was disappointed . . . "
- "Others on the team were angry . . . "
- "This is a poor reflection on you, because . . . "
- "The organization wondered if . . . "
- "We lost money and time . . . "
- "I was disappointed and embarrassed . . . "
- "My boss asked me what was happening and was concerned . . . "

Resolution: How would you like to see the situation resolved?

- "What thoughts do you have on how this can be resolved?"
- "How can we prevent this from happening again?"
- "Next time I'd like to see this happen . . . "
- "Instead can you do . . . ?"

FEEDBACK TOOL EXPLANATION

STEP ONE: SET THE STAGE

This step gives listeners an opportunity to get ready to hear the feedback. Or, they may say that now is not a good time. If they are ready, they will be less reactive. This is usually just one sentence. If the timing doesn't work for them, ask them to specify when it will work.

STEP TWO: STATE THE SITUATION

The second step anchors what you are specifically talking about. It is the "what," "where," or "when."

STEP THREE: STATE THE BEHAVIOR WITHOUT INTERPRETATIONS

This third step is very challenging. It helps to write out what you will say before you give the feedback. You want to have it stated as a videotape would capture it. You do not want them to say, "No, I didn't," in response; instead, the behavior should be irrefutable.

Here are some BAD examples of how to state behavior:

- "Your attitude has gotten worse."
  They could say, "No it hasn't."
- "Your work is sloppy."
  They could say, "No it isn't."

- "I don't think you are putting your all into it."

  They could say, "Yes I am."

  Here are some good examples for stating behavior:

- "In the meeting today you raised your voice and were pointing fingers at people."

- "The customer reports that you were acting rude and were slow in responding to her."

- "You told me that you would let me know if you were going to be late with the project and you never mentioned it."

The recipients could still try to deny these, but their ground would be less stable as you are reporting facts rather than interpretations.

STEP FOUR: STATING THE IMPACT

This is the most important step. Ideally you should have 3-4 impacts. The more impacts the better. This is your leverage to demonstrate all the people or situations, time, and money that have been impacted.

- "The customer was disappointed . . . "
- "Others on the team were angry . . . "
- "This is a poor reflection on you, because . . . "
- "Waiting for you to arrive has cost us hundreds of dollars in wasted time."
- "We won't see the impact of this mistake immediately, but six months from now when we go to renew the order, the customer may not want to do business with us again."

STEP FIVE: RESOLUTION

This last step starts with a quiz.

- "What thoughts do you have on how this can be resolved?"
- "How can we prevent this from happening again?"

If they have accepted the feedback, they will be able to give you some ideas of how to prevent these behaviors in the future. If they have *NOT* accepted the feedback, you will have to be more assertive and tell them what you want to see them do instead.

If you receive feedback and do not change for the better, you will be perceived more negatively than if you had not received the feedback.

In using this model, take a few moments to write down your notes before giving feedback. This micro-initiative will increase your chances of them hearing the feedback and having them be less defensive.

If you receive feedback and do not change for the better, you will be perceived more negatively than if you had not received the feedback.

WHEN TO GIVE FEEDBACK

1. FREQUENTLY: This gives you the best chance to reinforce positive behavior and influence changes in acceptable behavior. It makes it easier to focus on a specific behavior. So that your people don't only think feedback is negative, surprise them as much as you can with positive feedback.

2. TIMELY: Speak to employees when the experience is fresh. Don't give feedback only on exceptionally positive or negative things. Remember successive approximation or to give feedback when they are approaching the goal, not only when they have reached the goal.

3. OPPORTUNITY FOR DEVELOPMENT: Make employees aware of potential opportunities and provide steps to achieve their goals.

4. TO SOLVE PERFORMANCE PROBLEMS: Regular and frequent feedback puts money in the emotional bank account between people. It also makes it easier to be direct on a performance problem. When trust and respect have been built, it is easier to make a withdrawal from the account.

SUMMARY TIPS FOR GIVING FEEDBACK

- If it is important, make an appointment to give the feedback.
- Be sensitive to the power imbalance (i.e., doing it in your office versus a neutral ground).
- Keep it simple.
- Leverage their strengths.
- Prepare the feedback to fit the learning style.
- Offer suggestions and support.
- Get their feedback about the feedback.

QUESTIONS AND ACTION APPLICATIONS

- How would you rate how well you give feedback?
- Practice the SSBIR model and ask for feedback on how well you communicated.
- Teach the feedback model to your team and practice giving feedback using real-life scenarios. Discuss which statements seemed to best hit the mark.
- Make feedback a process that you are getting feedback on and continually try to improve it.

8. ASSUMPTION LADDER: ARRIVING AND DELIVERING COMMUNICATION

Communication is the mechanism to deliver your thoughts to others. These next strategies are all about our thinking process and how to communicate our thoughts. We will start off with defining mental models—how did you *arrive* at them and how can you *deliver* them to others to be most effective.

WHAT IS A MENTAL MODEL?

Deepak Chopra stated that we have as many as 60,000 thoughts a day. Ninety-five percent of those thoughts are the same ones we had yesterday.[14] Why is that? The same thoughts keep recycling, and that is one reason we use only 5-10% of our brainpower. These same or similar thoughts form patterns or clusters of our beliefs, yet leave out a plethora of other possible views. Senge defines "mental models" as "deeply ingrained assumptions, generalizations, or even pictures or images that influence how we understand the world and how we take action."

> . . . we have as many as 60,000 thoughts a day. Ninety-five percent of those thoughts are the same ones we had yesterday.

The term *mental model* has been used by psychologists since the 1940s. Cognitive psychologists, cognitive scientists, and more recently managers use the term. In his book *The Fifth Discipline,* Senge popularized the term as one of his five disciplines. In the *Fifth Discipline Fieldbook*, "mental model" is defined as "both the semi-permanent tacit 'maps' of the world which people hold in their long-term memory, and the short-term perceptions which people build up as part of their everyday reasoning process."[15]

WHY IS UNDERSTANDING OUR MENTAL MODELS IMPORTANT?

The mental models we carry around are usually *invisible* to us and others yet are very powerful in their influence over our actions and responses to anything that occurs in our world. Often these mental models hold us prisoners to the "same old story" when openness to new learning is necessary to grow and advance in our careers. To continually learn and grow we must *think* and *act* differently, and our invisible mental models hold us back like a prisoner's ball and chain.

As a leader, it is important to make explicit your thinking. We have the tendency to take shortcuts when we think and speak. People don't have the benefit of seeing our thinking process, what we focused in on, what we discounted, or what building blocks we crafted to support our thoughts and decisions. So isn't it natural that people may have a difficult time following our ideas or suggestions? We reach a destination, but no one knows what roads we took, where we stopped along the way, or how long it took us. We leave out important parts of how we arrived at these ideas. Thus, our buy-in from others can be minimized.

> People don't have the benefit of seeing our thinking process, what we focused in on, what we discounted, or what building blocks we crafted to support our thoughts and decisions.

HOW DO WE USE THE LADDER?

The Assumption Ladder (see Figure 6.4) is a modification of Chris Argyris's Ladder of Inference, introduced in Senge's *The Fifth Discipline.* I have been using it in organizations for over 10 years with great success. When I return a year later and do follow-up assessments on the changes that took place, the Assumption Ladder is usually the tool that gets rave reviews. It has staying power because it is visual, makes sense to people, brings self-awareness to their thinking process, and helps in communicating their ideas.

The goal is to walk people up the ladder. It allows you to lay out your thinking process and mental models. You want to invite people up the ladder, as well, to see if they agree with your data, selection of data, assumptions about the data, conclusions, and then the actions you suggest. If they know how you arrived, they may be more willing to go along with you. Or they may disagree, but it is more constructive to disagree with your selection of data and your assumptions than to argue with you about your conclusions.

In summary, the ladder gives you the steps or rungs to describe how you arrived at your decision and to deliver it for maximizing buy-in.

FIGURE 6.4   ASSUMPTION LADDER

The goal is to make your thinking visible to
others as you walk up the ladder.

I take
ACTIONS
based on my
conclusions.

I draw
CONCLUSIONS.

I make
ASSUMPTIONS
based on what
I've selected.

I
SELECT
data to
observe.

AVAILABLE
DATA
and experiences
(as a video
recorder
might capture it)

The Reactive
Trap (Our
conclusions and
actions affect what
data we select
next time.)

Adapted from Luckner, J.L. and Nadler, R.S. *Processing the Experience.* Dubuque,
Iowa: Kendall/Hunt Publishing Company, 1997.

SOME POINTERS

- Once a decision or conclusion is made it becomes a force that looks for self-validation, and it is hard to entertain new data or ideas.
- The ladder slows down the thinking process, and with more people commenting on the data and their assumptions you can get more creative and sound decisions. Your team can help ensure quality decisions.
- If two people are at the top of their ladders, you get debate and disagreement. If both people are low on the ladder, you will get more of a dialogue before people are fixed to their positions and defending them.
- The Assumption Ladder Applications tool (see Figure 6.5) gives you sentence stubs to walk up and down the ladder. It is especially helpful when a direct report or client is at the top of the ladder and you want to find out how he or she arrived there. It gives you an opportunity to insert a new selection of data, which opens up thinking and other viable possibilities.
- The ladder is a universal EI tool. It helps with:

    Self-Awareness, Accurate Self-Assessment, Empathy, Service Orientation, Communication, Influence, Leadership, Conflict Management, Change Catalyst, Teamwork and Collaboration, and Developing Others.

LADDER CARRIER

It is a good idea to introduce the ladder as a tool to enhance communication and understanding of others' viewpoints. To utilize the ladder to its fullest, you, the leader, a facilitator, or another leader should bring the ladder into your conversations. This person can be the "ladder carrier" and use terms that will help the team visualize the ladder.

FIGURE 6.5 ASSUMPTION LADDER APPLICATIONS

**Examples of sentences and sentence stubs
that will help you walk up and down the ladder**

As a listener:

I hear your actions
What are they based on?
How did you arrive at these plans?

Tell me what conclusion you are drawing . . .
Could it be possible that . . .

Tell me what your assumptions are . . .
I'm curious, tell me more . . .
Is that the only way to look at it?

What piece are you looking at?
I see you're focusing on . . .
What is standing out to you from the data?

Give me all the facts . . .
What are all the findings?

As a speaker:

Therefore, this is my plan . . .
These are steps I am taking . . .

It's obvious to me . . .
Therefore, I feel . . .
As a result . . .
To summarize . .
Here we go again . . .

So, I'm assuming . . .
Here's what I attribute . . .
The next step for me is . . .

I am focusing on this piece . . .
Here's what I see happening . . .
Here's what I'm selecting . . .
This stands out to me . . .

Here are all the facts . . .
Here are all the findings . . .

ACTIONS
CONCLUSIONS
ASSUMPTIONS
SELECTED DATA
AVAILABLE DATA

Pay attention to intentions. Make your thinking visible.

Adapted from Luckner, J.L. and Nadler, R.S. *Processing the Experience*. Dubuque, Iowa: Kendall/Hunt Publishing Company, 1997.

- "You are up on the ladder on this one."
- "Can you make your thinking more visible?"
- "What are your assumptions in this decision?"

DO'S AND DON'TS WHEN USING THE LADDER

DO	DON'T
Get people to hold your ladder as you go up	Use the ladder as a weapon
Open up for multiple viewpoints	Try to knock others off their ladder
Invite others to challenge you	Get defensive
Practice walking up and down the ladder	Expect this to be easy
Listen and inquire versus just advocating	Advocate without inquiry

QUESTIONS AND ACTION APPLICATIONS

- Introduce mental models and the ladder to your team.
- Pick a facilitator to help integrate the ladder by inquiring which rung people are on and encouraging them to walk up the ladder.
- Get copies of the ladder for everyone to use and get a poster of the ladder for your conference room.
- Use the ladder if there is a disagreement and see if the data and selection of data are the same. If so, go to the varying assumptions and locate where the disagreement lies.

9. BALANCING INQUIRY AND ADVOCACY

In *The Fifth Discipline*, Senge introduces the concept of balancing inquiry and advocacy. This is where you ask more about the other person's viewpoints instead of only advocating your own. This concept is borrowed from "action science," a field of inquiry developed by Chris Argyris and Donald Schon. Their goal is to explore the reasoning and attitudes that underlie human interaction. It uncovers a person's "mental models," those tacit assumptions and stories we carry in our mind about people, places, things, and every aspect of our world. These mental models are mental maps, usually untested and unexamined.

Balancing inquiry and advocacy is another tool to help unearth and get a tangible handle on what people's mental models are. Without imposing discipline on teams engaged in a discussion, what we generally hear are the propositions, ideas, or recommendations that people are advocating. Often this stuff is expressed with a great deal of passion, and so instead of inquiring about the recommendations and specific assumptions made, there is often passionate disagreement as well, without any resolution or clarity.

What is needed is to balance the natural emotional process of advocating with the unnatural, more rational process of inquiry. It is a good idea to question people about how they arrived at their decision and then dig into their assumptions to understand more. The best way to proceed is to improve the team's inquiry process. Ask the following questions:

- Tell me, how did you make this decision or recommendation?
- What things were you considering with this idea?
- What assumptions underlie this recommendation?
- Is there a time this solution wouldn't work?
- What would you need to make this successful?
- How long do you think this process would take?
- What potential risks have you considered?

QUESTIONS AND ACTION APPLICATIONS

- In one of your meetings, introduce the concept of balancing inquiry and advocacy.
- Have people use inquiry with the existing ideas on the table before going on to the next idea.

- Work on and practice your inquiry skills.
- Evaluate the team meeting's effectiveness. (See Team Meetings in Chapter 4, page 162.)

10. THE LEFT-HAND COLUMN

This is another strategy, introduced by Senge in *The Fifth Discipline*, to illuminate our mental models. On a single piece of paper, draw one line down the middle. On the right-hand side, title the column "WHAT WAS SAID." Fill in the column with the actual dialogue of what was said in a recent conversation with a co-worker. On the top of the left-hand column, write "WHAT WAS THOUGHT, BUT NOT EXPRESSED" and fill in this column with thoughts you had that were not spoken. The reason the left-hand column is not expressed is usually because of *trust issues* or skill issues on *how to say* what is difficult to another. So this becomes the first step in identifying what is in the left-hand column. The team can brainstorm examples of how to best express the left-hand column.

LEFT-HAND COLUMN	RIGHT-HAND COLUMN
What was thought, but not expressed	What was said

QUESTIONS AND ACTION APPLICATIONS

- Work with your team and choose one conversation that may have caused some conflict. Have people write the actual right-column conversation and then the left-hand column of what was thought but not said. This can be done anonymously. Then you can exchange or read people's left-hand column. Discuss how the left-hand column can be expressed in a constructive manner. Use discretion depending on the level of conflict and how blunt people are with their left-hand column.

- If trust is the issue and you are not sure if people want to hear about your left-hand column, talk about trust in your team and ways to enhance it.

- One exercise that helps is to have people complete the following statement and share with a partner or in the group. The answer to this statement is usually in the left-hand column. "For me to trust, you should . . . "

- Fill in 5-10 responses, the later responses force you to dig deep into what you need for trust.

11. DIALOGUE VS. DISCUSSION

Dialogue is a way of thinking and reflecting together to come up with better ideas, more creativity, and innovation. It focuses on learning from one another and building shared meaning, making sure to include everyone's perspective in the mix.[16] Dialogue means the "flow of meaning" between people and "to gather together." With shared meaning come shared actions. Dialogue is about evoking insight, which is a way of reordering knowledge, usually around the taken-for-granted assumptions that people bring to the table. Better decisions and execution result when decisions start with a dialogue. Thinking together will produce better results than thinking alone will.

In most organizations, dialogues do not happen because of:

- time constraints
- hierarchies
- strong opinions and trying to be the smartest person in the room
- poor listening
- competition and defensiveness
- political agendas
- "un-discussable" topics

A discussion is a conversation that is focused on getting closure, usually with only one or a limited perspective. Discussion comes from the same word root as *concussion* or *percussion*. It evokes an image of something being beaten or shaken, and the result is something that is not whole, but rather is shattered or broken. Only pieces or fragments are left. A discussion is what generally takes place in most organizations because they are driving to find one answer, and usually driving too fast and expecting an answer too quickly. We know how to drive to one solution, but what we don't know as well is how to stay with

We know how to drive to one solution, but what we don't know as well is how to stay with the ambiguity and entertain multiple solutions to get the best answer.

the ambiguity and entertain multiple solutions to get the best answer. That's where dialogue comes in. There is a time for discussion, but not at the exclusion of dialogue (which is usually the result).

Here is a continuum that illustrates the process from debate and discussion to dialogue.[17]

DISCUSSION-DIALOGUE CONTINUUM

DEBATE AND DISCUSSION	DIALOGUE
Breaking issues into pieces and fragments	Seeing the whole among parts
Finding distinctions and exceptions	Finding connection and patterns
Taking stands and justifying	Inquiring into assumptions
Telling and selling	Learning and seeking understanding
Finding one answer	Creating shared meaning through multiple descriptions

Adapted from Ellinor and Gerard, *Dialogue: Rediscovering the Transforming Power of Conversation* (1998).

QUESTIONS AND ACTION APPLICATIONS

- Talk with your team about the differences between a dialogue and a discussion.
- Establish when you should have a dialogue versus a discussion.
- Clearly identify when you are in the dialogue process versus the discussion process.

12. DIALOGUE ROLES

In order to make quality decisions, it is useful to identify and clarify the following four dialogue roles. Ideally, each role should have a voice. This ensures that you are engaged in a lively dialogue rather than a discussion.

Dialogue roles raise the awareness of the team so that decisions are not just coming from the loudest or most confident person. In some meetings, people feel that their responsibility is only to "move" new ideas and thus fail to integrate them with other responses or determine how to implement them effectively.

THE FOUR KEY DIALOGUE ROLES ARE:

MOVER—Moves a new idea forward to the group.

OPPOSER—Opposes or disagrees with the moved idea.

SUPPORTER—Supports either the moved or opposed idea and may add onto another idea.

INTEGRATOR—Pulls together the differing ideas, looks for "both/and" solutions, summarizes and refocuses the group, and keeps the end in mind. The integrator role is the one the facilitator usually takes, but anyone on your team can take it on.

QUESTIONS AND ACTION APPLICATIONS

- Ask: Which roles are most prevalent in your team meetings? Which roles are under-utilized? Why?

- Assess what % of time people advocate their ideas versus inquiring or asking questions. Ask the group to call out their best guess. What can your team do to inquire more?

- An observer can track how many mover, opposer, supporter, and integrator statements along with questions were made during a meeting. At the end of the meeting, share what is called the "Dialogue Metric" to see if you can increase the questions and also determine which role is underrepresented.

STAR PERFORMER ACTION PLAN

Review the Star Profile and *Coach's Corner* strategies to assist you in mastering Communication and Empathy. Now answer the following questions to help you make your Star Performer Action Plan.

Which competencies or practices are you already doing that you want to continue?

1. _____
2. _____
3. _____

What new practices do you want to incorporate?

1. _____
2. _____
3. _____

What resources do you need to make this happen?

1. _____
2. _____
3. _____

Who can support you and hold you accountable?

1. _____
2. _____
3. _____

How might you sabotage your efforts and best intentions?

1. _____
2. _____
3. _____

What will be your first steps in this plan?

1. _____
2. _____
3. _____

Share this plan with your support people. Good luck!

CHAPTER SEVEN

THE GAME PLAN

G reat leadership starts with you—by choosing a few actions that you can initiate today. Keeping Score helps you pull together some of the activities and goals you've highlighted along the way and gets you on track to get them done! Like a coach, your ability to have a game plan, follow it, and stay committed will move you into the top 10%. The average performer may make a plan, but won't stay committed to it.

You have read how the Stars who were interviewed had habits or rituals of specific actions that made them Stars. Henrik Fisker's confidence included his decisiveness and capturing the moment of empowering his people. Paulette Jones's teamwork and collaboration was highlighted by her strategic use of meetings. Mark French's prowess in the development of others centered on his recruitment of Stars, using one-on-ones, and giving feedback. John Davies's communication expertise focused on finding the client's passion and unique talents and communicating in a way that touched people's hearts.

Throughout the book I have described powerful micro-initiatives, seemingly small and doable tasks that create macro impact. With the Scorecard, you will select a few of these micro-initiatives to ingrain as daily practices. Knowing your score is important reinforcement. Many leaders see these initiatives as their "second checklist" to do *after* their primary job responsibilities are over. If that remains the case, these critical actions to improve yourself and others get done haphazardly and infrequently. You will remain good, but you will not become great.

GOAL: The goal of this book is to give you and the people you lead specific skills and actions to raise your Emotional Intelligence, thus creating more Stars in your organization.

BENEFITS: Why take the time to improve your Emotional Intelligence and do a few things more frequently?

- Leaders high in Emotional Intelligence are more productive.[1]
- Great leaders also have a positive impact on profitability, turnover, employee commitment, customer satisfaction, and retention.[2]
- The more great leaders an organization develops, the more it will become an outstanding organization.[3]
- Emotions are contagious. As a top leader, you influence the whole climate of your team as much as 50-70%.[4]
- Gallup has found that if U.S. workers were 5% more engaged, it would boost national productivity by $79 billion a year.
- As a leader, you pass on your leadership legacy. As we have seen, new leaders emulate the practices of their best bosses.
- The best way to retain your good people is to have positive and productive relationships with them.
- People who are positive have been shown to live longer.[5]
- The Department of Labor has found that job satisfaction is a better predictor of longevity than smoking or exercise habits.[6]

Consequences for Not Raising Emotional Intelligence

- The reasons for losing customers and clients are 70% EQ-related.[7]
- 50% of time wasted in business is due to lack of trust.[8]

- Key executive derailers include lack of impulse control and the inability to work on teams.[9]
- The cost to replace a manager or sales position is 250% of his or her compensation package.[10]

STRATEGY: REVIEW YOUR STAR PERFORMER ACTION PLANS

Hopefully, you have already implemented a few of these activities and have seen significant and positive changes in your leadership skills as well as a new focus, dedication, and collaborative spirit on the part of your team.

Now it's time to review your Star Performer Action Plans and take your concepts about change and improvement onto the playing field. Spend some quality time studying your plans from each chapter. Then pick no more than two activities/goals that you think will benefit you the most right now. Remember the 80-20 rule: 20% of your effort can lead to 80% of your results.

As an alternative, your team can choose some of the strategies to do as a team, where everyone is working on implementing tools such as giving feedback, using the delegation tool, or implementing the leadership checklist, and teambuilding. Then as a team you can assess your result, talk about your learnings, and adjust the process.

Your focus should be on what you can realistically accomplish over the next month. Use SMART goals, which stands for Specific, Measurable, Actionable, Realistic, and Time dependent. When you have mastered these goals, take on new activities, tools, or goals from another chapter until those are mastered. Mastering a skill or tool here means that you are doing it 80% of the time; it is a habit for you. So your scores on the Scorecard should be consistently 8-10.

THE PLAYS

Following are the plays listed in the book to choose from for your Star Performer Action Plan. Check the boxes for the ones you want to practice.

Emotional Self-Control

The Coach's Corner: 8 Strategies for Emotional Self-Control

1. Self-Management ☐
2. Affect Labeling ☐
3. The Emotional Audit ☐
4. Putting On the Brakes ☐
5. Mindfulness ☐
6. Shuttling: Internal and External Awareness ☐
7. Identifying Triggers ☐
8. Reappraisal ☐

Self-Confidence

Star Profile: Henrik Fisker, CEO, Fisker Coachbuild, LLC

1. Take Private Time (p. 112) ☐
2. Get Third Opinions (p. 113) ☐
3. Evaluate Capacities (p. 113) ☐
4. Shoot from the Hip (p. 113) ☐
5. Go with That Gut Feeling (p. 114) ☐
6. Take Initiative (p. 114) ☐
7. Identify Your Strengths and Weaknesses (p. 114) ☐
8. Take Responsibility for Your Mistakes (p. 115) ☐
9. Reinforce People (p. 115) ☐
10. Be Willing to Make Decisions That Are Exceptions to the Rule (p. 115) ☐

The Coach's Corner: 10 Strategies for Self-Confidence

1. Being on Your Case vs. Being on Your Side (p. 117) ☐
2. Reflections on Thinking (p. 122) ☐
3. Busting Perfection: Creating Realistic Expectations (p. 124) ☐

Teamwork and Collaboration

The Coach's Corner: 23 Strategies for Teamwork and Collaboration

9. Ongoing Learning and Recognition (p. 154) ☐

10. Mentor Others (p. 155) ☐

11. Meeting Mastery and Meeting Menace (p. 155) ☐

12. Snapshot Management: "The One-Hand Rule" (p. 158) ☐

13. Meeting Menace Checklist (p. 160) ☐

14. Team Meetings (p. 162) ☐

15. Guidelines for Running a Great Meeting (p. 164) ☐

16. How to Establish Roles Within a Team Meeting (p. 164) ☐

17. "Stand-Ups"—Short Team Meetings (p. 165) ☐

18. The Meeting Checklist (p. 166) ☐

19. "Nails" Teambuilding Activity (p. 173) ☐

20. "Performance and Accountability" Teambuilding Activity (p. 177) ☐

21. "Expectations" Activity (p. 180) ☐

22. Team Assessment (p. 182) ☐

23. Teamwork Ingredients Survey (p. 184) ☐

Developing Others

Star Profile: Mark French, University of California at Santa Barbara (UCSB) Retired Head Coach, Women's Basketball Team

1. Leader's Point of View (POV): Basketball as a Metaphor for Life (p. 195) ☐

2. Practice (p. 195) ☐

3. Bonding and Team Meetings (p. 196) ☐

4. Recruiting Stars (p. 197) ☐

5. Building Effective Relationships (p. 198) ☐

6. Self-Assessments and Goal Setting (p. 199) ☐

7. One-on-Ones (p. 200) ☐

8. Supportive Learning (p. 200) ☐

9. Timely Feedback (p. 201) ☐

Communication and Empathy

**The Coach's Corner: 12 Strategies for Enhancing
Communication and Empathy**

1. Empathy Skills (p. 258)   ☐
2. Listening and Rapport-Building Skills (p. 264)   ☐
3. White Space Issues (p. 269)   ☐
4. Intention/Interpretation Gap (p. 272)   ☐
5. Power of Language: Metaphors, Stories, and Words (p. 277)   ☐
6. Clarity: Connecting the Dots to a Better Future (p. 282)   ☐
7. Giving Feedback: SSBIR (p. 284)   ☐
8. Assumption Ladder: Arriving and Delivering
   Communication (p. 289)   ☐
9. Balancing Inquiry and Advocacy (p. 295)   ☐
10. The Left-Hand Column (p. 297)   ☐
11. Dialogue vs. Discussion (p. 298)   ☐
12. Dialogue Roles (p. 300)   ☐

In order to make the best decisions, ask yourself the following questions and fill in your answers.

1. What are the one or two things you can do now that will bring you and your team the greatest benefit(s)?

2. Who are your support people that will keep you accountable?

3. What do you see as your biggest obstacle to this goal?

4. How will you get over this?

5. What will keep you motivated? What rewards will help?

6. What are your first steps?

7. When will you start?

KEEPING SCORE:
YOUR LEADERSHIP SCORECARD

Once you have chosen your specific goals and actions, keep a weekly scorecard to help you monitor your progress and stay on track. Here is an example from a new manager who wanted to implement two key activities from the Teamwork and Collaboration and Developing Others chapters. They are:

1. Team meetings

2. One-on-one meetings

His Scorecard for one week looked like this:

WEEK OF: JULY 7-11

GOAL OR ACTION	FREQUENCY	SUPPORT	SELF-RATING: 1-10
1. Hold team meeting	2 X month	Mgr, team	7
2. One-on-one w/ direct reports	1 X month	Mgr, team	5

Actions: 1. Get more input for the agenda

2. Schedule one-on-one a month ahead

At the end of the week he reviewed his actions and determined how well he had done and what he could do to improve. For his first goal he had two team meetings, one for training issues and the other for basic team information. He felt good about them, even though his team didn't do much talking. He decided that next time he would prepare the agenda ahead of time and get more of their involvement.

He didn't feel as good about the second goal, because he had one-on-ones with only two of his four people, while he had wanted to see all of them in the month. He decided to schedule himself a month ahead of time to ensure that he made enough time for everyone. Your support is important; the more people you involve in your actions, the more successful you will be.

As you evaluate yourself, be fair and just and not only "on your case." If you get in the 8-10 range for a month, you are doing great and probably have achieved your goals. If not, reread the appropriate section in the book and repeat another month before choosing more activities. Also, think of getting your supervisor to give you some mentoring or think about getting an Executive Coach to help you.

THE LEADERSHIP SCORECARD

Here is the LEADERSHIP SCORECARD. It is set up as a weekly template you can copy and put in a three-ring notebook or collect in a file. It's best done by hand instead of on the computer. At the end of the week, evaluate how well you did and mark your scores. Congratulate yourself and document if there are other ways to enhance your efforts.

Begin reviewing your Star Performer Action Plans today and kick off a new season of great leadership. These micro-initiatives, done consistently, will propel you into the top 10% and enhance your team's effectiveness.

On the following page is an example of a scorecard to use.

MONTH: _____

YEAR: _____

WEEK OF:

GOAL OR ACTION	FREQUENCY	SUPPORT	SELF-RATING: 1-10

Actions to enhance:

Being a leader is about your commitment to your growth and serving others. You are under the spotlight 24/7 and have more influence over others than you could ever imagine. Your disciplined actions can influence your team and organization to have many winning seasons. You hold the keys—use them wisely. Good luck.

NOTES

INTRODUCTION

1. W. Bennis, "The Challenges of Leadership in the Modern World," *American Psychologist* 62, no. 1 (2007): 2–5.

2. D. Lee, "Unemployment Rate Fall to 9.7%," *Los Angeles Times*, 2010.

3. S. L. Sladek, "Back to the Future," *Talent Management*, January 2010.

4. D. Rock, *Your Brain at Work: Strategies for Overcoming Distraction, Regaining Focus and Working Smarter All Day Long.* (New York: HarperCollins, 2009).

5. D. Siegel, *Mindsight: The New Science of Personal Transformation* (New York: Bantam Books, 2010).

6. D. Goleman, *Working with Emotional Intelligence* (New York: Bantam Books, 1998).

7. D. Goleman, *Social Intelligence: The New Science of Human Relationships* (New York: Bantam Books, 2006).

8. D. Goleman, *Social Intelligence* (New York: Bantam Books, 2006).

9. R. E. Kelley, *How to Be a Star at Work* (New York: Times Books, 1998).

10. R. E. Boyatzis and F. Ratti, "Emotional, Social and Cognitive Intelligence Competencies Distinguishing Effective Italian Managers and Leaders in a Private Company and Cooperatives," *Journal of Management Development* 28, no. 9 (2009): 821–838.

11. N. Dries and R. Pepermans, "Using Emotional Intelligence to Identify High Potential: A Meta Competency Perspective," *Leadership & Organization Development Journal* 28, no. 8 (2007): 749–770.

12. P. N. Lopes, D. Grewal, J. Kadis, M. Gall, P. Salovey, "Evidence That Emotional Intelligence Is Related to Job Performance and Affect and Attitudes at Work," *Psicothema* 18, Supl. (2006): 132–138.

13. S. Stein, *The EQ Factor: Does Emotional Intelligence Make You a Better CEO?* Special Report (Ontario, Canada: Innovators Alliance, November 2002).

14. T. Bradberry and J. Greaves, *Emotional Intelligence 2.0* (San Diego, CA: TalentSmart, 2009).

15. C. Cherniss and D. Goleman, *The Emotionally Intelligent Workplace: How to Select for, Measure, and Improve Emotional Intelligence in Individuals, Groups, and Organizations* (San Francisco: Jossey-Bass, 2001).

16. D. Goleman, *Working with Emotional Intelligence* (New York: Bantam Books, 1998), 5.

17. Ibid.

18. C. Cherniss and D. Goleman, *The Emotionally Intelligent Workplace* (San Francisco: Jossey-Bass, 2001), 21.

CHAPTER ONE

1. J. Zenger and J. Folkman, *The Extraordinary Leader* (New York: McGraw-Hill, 2002).

2. W. Bennis, "The Challenges of Leadership in the Modern World," *American Psychologist* 62, no. 1 (2007): 2–5.

3. K. Blanchard, *Critical Leadership Skills: Key Traits That Can Make or Break Today's Leaders* (San Diego: Ken Blanchard Companies, 2006).

4. A. Nancherla, "Please Boss Me Around," *Training and Development*, December 2009.

5. Center for Creative Leadership, *Driving Performance: Why Leadership Development Matters in Difficult Times* (January 2009).

6. Ibid.

7. Ibid.

8. G. Colvin, "Catch a Rising Star," *Fortune*, February 6, 2006, 50.

9. Ibid., 48.

10. Ibid.

11. Ibid., 50.

12. Ibid.

13. Ibid.

14. C. Raines, "Managing Millennials," from *Connecting Generations: The Sourcebook* (Menlo Park, CA: 2002).

15. R. E. Kelley, *How to Be a Star at Work* (New York: Times Books, 1998).

16. C. Cherniss and D. Goleman, *The Emotionally Intelligent Workplace* (San Francisco: Jossey-Bass, 2001).

17. Hay Group, *Inventory of Leadership Styles and Organizational Climate* Survey Certification material (Boston, MA: 2003).

18. C. Cherniss and D. Goleman, *The Emotionally Intelligent Workplace* (San Francisco: Jossey-Bass, 2001).

19. J. Zenger and J. Folkman, *The Extraordinary Leader* (New York: McGraw-Hill, 2002).

20. "Warren E. Buffett, CEO Compensation," Forbes.com (accessed February 23, 2009).

21. M. Buffett and D. Clark, *Warren Buffett's Management Secrets: Proven Tools for Personal and Business Success* (New York: Scribner Press, 2009).

22. A. Schroeder, "Please Hold for Mister Buffett," *BusinessWeek*, March 8, 2010.

23. Ibid.

24. M. Buffett and D. Clark, *Warren Buffett's Management Secrets* (New York: Scribner Press, 2009).

25. A. Schroeder, "Please Hold for Mister Buffett," *BusinessWeek*, March 8, 2010.

26. M. Buffett and D. Clark, *Warren Buffett's Management Secrets* (New York: Scribner Press, 2009).

27. A. Schroeder, "Please Hold for Mister Buffett," *BusinessWeek*, March 8, 2010.

28. M. Buffett and D. Clark, *Warren Buffett's Management Secrets* (New York: Scribner Press, 2009).

29. D. Everts, "Carly Fiorina Stumps for McCain," Cnet News, March 8, 2008, http://news.cnet.com (accessed February 5, 2010).

30. "50 Most Powerful Women," *Fortune*, October 2003.

31. *Wall Street Journal*, February 10, 2005.

32. "50 Most Powerful Women," *Fortune*, October 2003.

33. *Wall Street Journal*, February 10, 2005.

34. L. Kehoe, "Carly Fiorina," *Financial Times*, 2002.

35. *Wall Street Journal*, February 10, 2005.

36. "World's Most Admired Companies," *Fortune*, March 2010.

37. Fisher, "World's Most Admired Companies," *Fortune*, March 6, 2006.

38. J. Immelt, "Renewing American Leadership" (speech given to U.S. Military Academy at West Point, December 2009).

39. J. A. Byrne, "The Fast Company Interview: Jeff Immelt," *Fast Company*, July 2005.

40. Ibid.

41. Ibid.

42. "The Education of Jeff Immelt," *BusinessWeek* online, April 9, 2002.

43. Ibid.

44. J. A. Byrne, "The Fast Company Interview: Jeff Immelt," *Fast Company*, July 2005.

45. Ibid.

46. J. Immelt, "Renewing American Leadership" (speech given to U.S. Military Academy at West Point, December 2009).

47. Ibid

48. J. A. Byrne, "The Fast Company Interview: Jeff Immelt," *Fast Company*, July 2005.

49. Ibid.

50. "World's Most Admired Companies," *Fortune*, March 2010.

51. D. A. Vise and M. Malseed, *The Google Story* (New York: Bantam Dell, 2008).

52. "Defining Google," *60 Minutes*, CBS News, January 2, 2005.

53. D. A. Vise and M. Malseed, *The Google Story* (New York: Bantam Dell, 2008), 20.

54. Ibid., 16.

55. Ibid.

56. Woopidoo.com, "Business Quotes" (accessed November 2005).

57. Google.com, "Corporate Information" (accessed November 2005).

58. S. Framer, "Carroll Goes for Bold Move," *LA Times*, March 19, 2010.

59. D. Wharton and G. Klein, *Conquest: Pete Carroll and the Trojans' Climb to the Top of the College Football Mountain* (Chicago: Triumph Books, 2005).

60. H. Halladay, "Lemonade from Lemons in the Rose Bowl," Leadernotes.com (January 6, 2006).

61. D. Wharton and G. Klein, *Conquest* (Chicago: Triumph Books, 2005), 42.

62. Ibid., 43.

63. Ibid., 47–48.

64. M. Whitman, *The Power of Many: Values for Success in Business and in Life* (New York: Crown Publishing, 2010).

65. P. Sellers, "eBay's Secret," *Fortune*, 2004.

66. M. Whitman, *The Power of Many* (New York: Crown Publishing, 2010).

67. P. Sellers, "eBay's Secret," *Fortune*, 2004.

68. Ibid.

69. M. Whitman, *The Power of Many* (New York: Crown Publishing, 2010).

70. P. Sellers, "eBay's Secret," *Fortune*, 2004.

71. *Santa Barbara News-Press*, June 15, 2002.

72. J. Conason, "The Third Term," *Esquire*, December 2005.

73. Bill Clinton, *My Life* (New York: Alfred A. Knopf, 2004).

74. E. A. Johnson, *32 Ways to Be a Champion in Business* (New York: Crown Business, 2008).

75. Ibid

76. Ibid.

77. Ibid.

78. Ibid.

79. Ibid.

80. D. Goleman, *Working with Emotional Intelligence* (New York: Bantam Books, 1998).

81. Ibid.

82. Ibid.

83. D. O. Clifton and P. Nelson, *Soar with Your Strengths* (New York: Delacorte Press, 1992).

84. J. Zenger and J. Folkman, *The Extraordinary Leader* (New York: McGraw-Hill, 2002).

85. D. O. Clifton and P. Nelson, *Soar with Your Strengths* (New York: Delacorte Press, 1992).

86. M. Buckingham, *The One Thing You Need to Know* (New York: Free Press, 2005).

87. J. Zenger and J. Folkman, *The Extraordinary Leader* (New York: McGraw-Hill, 2002).

88. C. Flora, "Mirror Mirror: Seeing Yourself as Others See You," *Psychology Today*, June 2005.

89. C. Cherniss and D. Goleman, *The Emotionally Intelligent Workplace* (San Francisco: Jossey-Bass, 2001).

90. www.keepem.com (accessed 2005).

91. J. Krueger and E. Killhan, "Why Dilbert Is Right," *Gallup Management Journal*, March 9, 2006.

92. "Positivity Increases Productivity," *Gallup Management Journal*, July 8, 2004.

93. Hay Group, *Inventory of Leadership Styles and Organizational Climate* Survey Certification material (Boston, MA: 2003).

94. J. Zenger and J. Folkman, *The Extraordinary Leader* (New York: McGraw-Hill, 2002).

95. Ibid., 5.

96. Ibid., 187–188.

97. M. Buckingham, *The One Thing You Need to Know* (New York: Free Press, 2005).

CHAPTER TWO

1. D. Goleman, *Working with Emotional Intelligence* (New York: Bantam Books, 1998).

2. Ibid.

3. Ibid.

4. C. Cherniss and D. Goleman, *The Emotionally Intelligent Workplace* (San Francisco: Jossey-Bass, 2001).

5. H. L. Thompson, "Emotional Intelligence, Stress, and Catastrophic Leadership Failure," in *Handbook for Developing Emotional and Social Intelligence*, ed. M. Hughes, H. L. Thompson, and J. B. Terrell (San Francisco: Pfeiffer, 2009).

6. Ibid.

7. Ibid.

8. D. Rock, *Your Brain at Work* (New York: HarperCollins, 2009).

9. H. L. Thompson, "Emotional Intelligence, Stress, and Catastrophic Leadership Failure," in *Handbook for Developing Emotional and Social Intelligence*, ed. M. Hughes, H. L. Thompson, and J. B. Terrell (San Francisco: Pfeiffer, 2009).

10. D. Rock, *Your Brain at Work* (New York: HarperCollins, 2009).

11. www.cnnpolitics.com (accessed September 2009).

12. J. Freedman and T. Everett, *A Business Case for Emotional Intelligence*, 2nd ed. (Freedom, CA: Six Seconds Publishing, 2008).

13. H. L. Thompson, "Emotional Intelligence, Stress, and Catastrophic Leadership Failure," in *Handbook for Developing Emotional and Social Intelligence*, ed. M. Hughes, H. L. Thompson, and J. B. Terrell (San Francisco: Pfeiffer, 2009).

14. "Larry King Live," CNN, 2009.

15. "Breakthrough Ideas for Tomorrow's Business Agenda," *Harvard Business Review*, April 2003.

16. M. D. Lieberman, N. I. Eisenberger, M. J. Crockett, S. M. Tom, J. H. Pfeifer, and B. M. Way, "Putting Feelings Into Words: Affect Labeling Disrupts Amygdala Activity in Response to Affective Stimuli," *Psychological Science* 18, no. 5 (2007).

17. D. Siegel, *Mindsight* (New York: Bantam Books, 2010).

18. D. Rock, *Your Brain at Work* (New York: HarperCollins, 2009).

19. Ibid.

20. D. Siegel, *Mindsight* (New York: Bantam Books, 2010).

21. Ibid.

22. Ibid.

23. Ibid.

CHAPTER THREE

1. D. Goleman, *Working with Emotional Intelligence* (New York: Bantam Books, 1998).

2. R. E. Boyatzis, *The Competent Manager: A Model for Effective Performance* (New York: Wiley, 1982).

3. D. Goleman, *Working with Emotional Intelligence* (New York: Bantam Books, 1998).

4. C. K. Holahan and R. R. Sears, *Self-Confidence in High-IQ People and Career Success in the Gifted in Later Maturity* (Stanford: Stanford University Press, 1995).

5. A. Howard and D. W. Bray, *Managerial Lives in Transition* (New York: Guilford Press, 1988).

6. D. Goleman, *Working with Emotional Intelligence* (New York: Bantam Books, 1998), 51.

7. W. Bennis, *Managing People Is Like Herding Cats* (Provo, UT: Executive Excellence Publishing, 1997).

8. D. Stauffer, "How Good Data Leads to Bad Decisions," *Harvard Management Update* 7, no. 12 (2002).

9. L. E. Anderson and W. K. Balzer, "The Effects of Timing of Leaders' Opinion on Problem-Solving Groups," *Group and Organizational Studies* 16 (1991).

10. D. Stauffer, "How Good Data Leads to Bad Decisions," *Harvard Management Update* 7, no. 12 (2002).

11. D. Goleman, *Working with Emotional Intelligence* (New York: Bantam Books, 1998).

12. Ibid.

CHAPTER FOUR

1. H. A. Elfenbein, "Team Emotional Intelligence," in *Linking Emotional Intelligence and Performance at Work*, ed. V. U. Druskat, F. Sala, and G. Mount (Mahwah, NJ: Lawrence Erlbaum Associates, 2006).

2. J. Kotter, *Leading Change* (Boston, MA: Harvard Business School Press, 1996).

3. P. Senge, *The Fifth Discipline: The Art and Practice of the Learning Organization* (New York: Doubleday, 1990).

4. Ibid., xix, xxi.

5. J. M. Kouzes and B. Posner, *Leadership Challenge* (San Francisco: Jossey-Bass, 1987).

CHAPTER FIVE

1. D. Goleman, *Working with Emotional Intelligence* (New York: Bantam Books, 1998).

2. Ibid.

3. Ibid.

4. C. Cherniss and D. Goleman, *The Emotionally Intelligent Workplace* (San Francisco: Jossey-Bass, 2001).

5. D. Smith and G. Bell, *The Carolina Way: Leadership Lessons from a Life of Coaching* (New York: Penguin Press, 2004).

6. Ibid.

7. M. A. Dalton and G. P. Hollenbeck, *How to Design an Effective System for Developing Managers and Executives* (Greensboro, NC: Center for Creative Leadership, 1996).

8. D. C. McClelland, "Identifying Competencies with Behavioral-Event Interviews," *Psychological Science* 9, no. 5 (1999): 331–339.

9. P. Falcone, *96 Great Interview Questions to Ask Before You Hire* (New York: American Management Association, 1997).

10. D. Grote, "Driving True Development," *Training*, July 2005.

11. Ibid.

12. D. O. Clifton and P. Nelson, *Soar with Your Strengths* (New York: Delacorte Press, 1992).

CHAPTER SIX

1. D. Goleman, *Working with Emotional Intelligence* (New York: Bantam Books, 1998).

2. Ibid.

3. Ibid.

4. J. L. Luckner and R. S. Nadler, *Processing the Experience* (Dubuque, IA: Kendall/Hunt Publishing, 1997).

5. H. Friedman and R. DiMatteo, *Interpersonal Issues in Healthcare* (New York: Academic Press, 1982).

6. B. K. Pilling and S. Eroglu, "An Empirical Examination of the Impact of Salesperson Empathy and Professionalism and Mercantile Salability on Retail Buyers' Evaluations," *Journal of Personal Selling and Sales Management* 14, no. 1 (1994): 55–58.

7. C. M. Steele, "A Threat in the Air: How Stereotypes Shape Intellectual Identity and Performance," *American Psychologist* 52 (1997): 613–629.

8. G. Combs and J. Freedman, *Symbol, Story and Ceremony: Using Metaphor in Individual and Family Therapy* (New York: W. W. Norton and Company, 1990).

9. Ibid.

10. J. L. Luckner and R. S. Nadler, *Processing the Experience* (Dubuque, IA: Kendall/Hunt Publishing, 1997).

11. M. A. Gass, *Book of Metaphors: A Descriptive Presentation of Metaphors for Adventure Activities*, vol. 2 (Dubuque, IA: Kendall/Hunt Publishing, 1995), xv.

12. G. Combs and J. Freedman, *Symbol, Story and Ceremony* (New York: W. W. Norton and Company, 1990).

13. M. Buckingham, "Great Managers Understand Their People," *Working Knowledge* (Cambridge, MA: Harvard Business School, April 11, 2005).

14. A. Robbins, *Anthony Robbins' Powertalk: Strategies for Lifelong Success* audiocassette (Robbins Research International, 1996).

15. P. Senge, C. Roberts, R. Ross, B. Smith, and A. Kleiner, *The Fifth Discipline Fieldbook: Strategies and Tools for Building a Learning Organization* (New York: Doubleday, 1994).

16. L. Ellinor and G. Gerard, *Dialogue: Rediscovering the Transforming Power of Conversation* (New York: John Wiley and Sons, 1998).

17. P. Senge, C. Roberts, R. Ross, B. Smith, and A. Kleiner, *The Fifth Discipline Fieldbook* (New York: Doubleday, 1994).

CHAPTER SEVEN

1. C. Cherniss and D. Goleman, *The Emotionally Intelligent Workplace* (San Francisco: Jossey-Bass, 2001).

2. J. Zenger and J. Folkman, *The Extraordinary Leader* (New York: McGraw-Hill, 2002).

3. Ibid.

4. Hay Group, *Inventory of Leadership Styles and Organizational Climate:* Survey Certification material (Boston, MA: 2003).

5. T. Rath and D. O. Clifton, *How Full Is Your Bucket?* (New York: Gallup Press, 2004).

6. Department of Labor, "Study on Job Satisfaction and Productivity," 1988.

7. Six Seconds website, 6seconds.org (accessed 2004).

8. Ibid.

9. J. B. Leslie and E. Van Velsor, *A Look at Derailment Today: North America and Europe* (Greensboro, NC: Center for Creative Leadership, 1996).

10. Center for Creative Leadership, ccl.org (accessed 2003).

BIBLIOGRAPHY

Alexander, J. "From the President," *Leadership in Action*, Volume 22, Number 4, September/October, 2002.

Anders, G. "How Traits That Helped the Executive Climb the Corporate Ladder Came to Be Fatal Flaws," *Wall Street Journal*, February 10, 2005.

Anderson, L.E. and Balzer, W.K. "The Effects of Timing of Leaders' Opinion on Problem-Solving Groups," *Group and Organizational Studies*, 16, 1991.

Answers.com. Who2 Personalities, GuruNet Corporation, 2005.

Auerbach, J. *Personal Executive Coaching: Complete Guide for Mental Health Professionals*. Ventura, CA: Executive Coach College Press, 2001.

Bennis, W. *Managing People Is Like Herding Cats*. Provo, Utah: Executive Excellence Publishing, 1997.

Bennis, W. "The Challenges of Leadership in the Modern World," *American Psychologist* 62, no. 1 (2007): 2–5.

Blanchard, K. *Critical Leadership Skills Key Traits That Can Make or Break Today's Leaders*. San Diego: Ken Blanchard Companies, 2006.

Boyatzis, R.E. *The Competent Manager: A Model for Effective Performance*. New York: Wiley, 1982.

Boyatzis, R.E. and McKee, A. *Resonant Leadership: Renewing Yourself and Connecting with Others Through Mindfulness, Hope and Compassion*. Boston, MA: Harvard Business Press, 2005.

Boyatzis, R.E., and Ratti, F. "Emotional, Social and Cognitive Intelligence Competencies Distinguishing Effective Italian Managers and Leaders in a Private Company and Cooperatives," *Journal of Management Development* 28, no. 9 (2009): 821–838.

Bradberry, T., and Greaves, J. *Emotional Intelligence 2.0*. San Diego, CA: TalentSmart, 2009.

"Breakthrough Ideas for Tomorrow's Business Agenda," *Harvard Business Review*, April 2003.

Buckingham, M. *The One Thing You Need to Know*. New York: Free Press, 2005.

Buckingham, M. "Great Managers Understand Their People," *Working Knowledge,* Cambridge, MA: Harvard Business School, April 11, 2005.

Buffett, M., and Clark, D. *Warren Buffett's Management Secrets: Proven Tools for Personal and Business Success.* New York: Scribner Press, 2009.

Byham, W., Smith, A., and Paese, M. *Grow Your Own Leaders.* Upper Saddle River, NJ: Financial Times Prentice Hall, 2002.

Byrne, J.A. "The Fast Company Interview: Jeff Immelt," *Fast Company,* July 2005.

Carkuff, R., *The Art of Helping.* (8th edition). Amherst, MA: Human Resource Development Press, 2000.

CBSNEWS.com. "Clinton Cheated 'Because I Could,'" June 17, 2004.

CBS News, 60 Minutes, *Defining Google,* January 2, 2005.

Center for Creative Leadership, ccl.org, 2003.

Center for Creative Leadership. *Driving Performance: Why Leadership Development Matters in Difficult Times.* January 2009.

Cherniss, C. and Goleman, D. *The Emotionally Intelligent Workplace: How to Select for, Measure, and Improve Emotional Intelligence in Individuals, Groups, and Organizations.* San Francisco: Jossey-Bass, 2001.

Clifton, D.O. and Nelson, P. *Soar with Your Strengths.* New York: Delacorte Press, 1992.

Colvin, G. "Catch a Rising Star," *Fortune,* February 6, 2006.

Combs, G. and Freedman, J. *Symbol, Story and Ceremony: Using Metaphor in Individual and Family Therapy.* New York: W.W. Norton and Company, 1990.

Conason, J. "The Third Term," *Esquire,* December 2005.

Covey, S. *The 7 Habits of Highly Effective People.* New York: Simon and Schuster, 1989.

CNN. "Smart, Savvy, Strong-Willed Rice Charts Her Own Course," 2001.

Csikszentmihalyi, M. *Good Business: Leadership, Flow and Making of Meaning.* New York: Penguin Group, 2003.

Dalton, M.A. and Hollenbeck, G.P. *How to Design an Effective System for Developing Managers and Executives.* Greensboro, NC: Center for Creative Leadership, 1996.

Department of Labor, "Study on Job Satisfaction and Productivity," 1988.

Dries, N., and Pepermans, R. "Using Emotional Intelligence to Identify High Potential: A Meta Competency Perspective," *Leadership and Organization Development Journal* 28, no. 8 (2007): 749–770.

Dunning, D., Heath, C., and Suls, J.M. "Picture Imperfect," *Scientific American Mind,* Volume 16, Number 4, 2005.

Ellinor, L. and Gerard, G. *Dialogue: Rediscovering the Transforming Power of Conversation.* New York: John Wiley and Sons, Inc., 1998.

Everts, D. "Carly Fiorina Stumps for McCain," Cnet News website, March 8, 2008, http://news.cnet.com (accessed February 5, 2010).

Falcone, P. *96 Great Interview Questions to Ask Before You Hire.* New York: American Management Association, 1997.

Flora, C. "Mirror Mirror: Seeing Yourself as Others See You," *Psychology Today,* June 2005.

Fortune, "50 Most Powerful Women," October 2003.

Framer, S. "Carroll Goes for Bold Move," *Los Angeles Times,* March 19, 2010.

Freedman, J., and Everett, T. *A Business Case for Emotional Intelligence.* 2nd ed. Freedom, CA: Six Seconds Publishing, 2008.

Friedman, H. and DiMatteo, R. *Interpersonal Issues in Healthcare.* New York: Academic Press, 1982.

Gallup Management Journal, "Positivity Increases Productivity," July 8, 2004.

Gallup Poll. *Approval Rating and Country Satisfaction.* September 12–18th, 2005.

Gallwey, T. *The Inner Game of Work,* New York: Random House, 2000.

Gass, M.A. *Book of Metaphors: A Descriptive Presentation of Metaphors for Adventure Activities. Volume II.* Dubuque, IA: Kendall/Hunt Publishing, 1995.

Gimein, M. "You Bought. They Sold." *Fortune,* September 2, 2002.

Goleman, D. *Emotional Intelligence.* New York: Bantam Books, 1995.

Goleman, D. *Social Intelligence: The New Science of Human Relationships.* New York: Bantam Books, 2006.

Goleman, D. *Working with Emotional Intelligence.* New York: Bantam Books, 1998.

Goleman, D., Boyatzis, R. and McKee, A. *Primal Leadership: The Hidden Driver of Great Performance.* Harvard Business Review, December 2001.

Goleman, D., Boyatzis, R. and McKee, A. *Primal Leadership: Realizing the Power of Emotional Intelligence.* Boston, MA: Harvard Business School Press, 2002.

Google.com, Corporate Information, November 2005.

Grote, D. "Driving True Development," *Training,* July 2005.

Hay Group. Certification Material. Boston, MA: 2001.

Hay Group. *Inventory of Leadership Styles and Organizational Climate.* Survey Certification material. Boston, MA: 2003.

Halladay, H. "Lemonade from Lemons in the Rose Bowl," Leadernotes.com, January 6, 2006.

Hersey, P., Blanchard, K.H., and Johnson, D.E. *Managing Organizational Behavior.* Upper Saddle River, NJ: Prentice Hall, 1996.

Holahan, C.K. and Sears, R.R. *Self-Confidence in High-IQ People and Career Success in the Gifted in Later Maturity,* Stanford: Stanford University Press, 1995.

Howard, A. and Bray, D.W. *Managerial Lives in Transition*. New York: Guilford Press, 1988.

Hymowitz, C. "Chiefs with Skill of a COO Gain Favor as Celebrity CEOs Fade," *Wall Street Journal*, April 7, 2005.

Ignatius, A. "In Search of the Real Google," *Time,* February 20, 2006.

Immelt, J. "Renewing American Leadership," speech given to U.S. Military Academy at West Point, December 2009.

Johnson, E.A. *32 Ways to Be a Champion in Business*. New York: Crown Business, 2008.

Kaplan, R.E. *Beyond Ambition: How Driven Managers Can Lead Better and Live Better*. San Francisco: Jossey-Bass, 1991.

Kaye, B. and Jordan-Evans, S. *Retention and Engagement Drivers Report*. Career Systems International, 2004.

Kaye, B. and Jordan-Evans, S. *Love It Don't Leave It*. San Francisco: Berrett-Koehler, 2003.

Kehoe, L. "Carly Fiorina," *Financial Times,* 2002.

Kellerman, B. *Bad Leadership: What It Is, How It Happens, Why It Matters*. Boston, MA: Harvard Business School Press, 2004.

Kelley, R.E. *How to Be a Star at Work*. New York: Times Books, 1998.

Kotter, J. *Leading Change*. Boston, MA: Harvard Business School Press, 1996.

Kouzes, J.M. and Posner, B. *Leadership Challenge*. San Francisco: Jossey-Bass, 1987.

Krueger, J. and Killhan, E. "Why Dilbert is Right," *Gallup Management Journal*, March 9, 2006.

Lee, D. "Unemployment Rate Falls to 9.7%," *Los Angeles Times*, 2010.

Leslie, J.B. and Van Velsor, E. *A Look at Derailment Today: North America and Europe*, Greensboro, NC: Center for Creative Leadership, 1996.

Lieberman, M.D., Eisenberger, N.I., Crockett, M.J., Tom, S.M., Pfeifer, J.H., and Way, B.M. "Putting Feelings Into Words: Affect Labeling Disrupts Amygdala Activity in Response to Affective Stimuli," *Psychological Science* 18, no 5, 2007.

Liedtke, M. "Oracle CEO to Settle Suit by Donating $100 Million," *Santa Barbara News-Press*, November 23, 2005.

Lipman-Blumen, J. *The Allure of Toxic Leaders*. New York: Oxford University Press, 2005.

Lopes, P.N., Grewal, D., Kadis, J., Gall, M., and Salovey, P. "Evidence That Emotional Intelligence Is Related to Job Performance and Affect and Attitudes at Work," *Psicothema* 18, Supl. (2006): 132–138.

Luckner, J.L. and Nadler, R.S. *Processing the Experience*. Dubuque, Iowa: Kendall/Hunt Publishing, 1997.

Marinucci, C. "Chevron Redubs Ship Named for Bush Aide," *San Francisco Chronicle,* May 5, 2001.

Maslow, A. *Toward a Psychology of Being*. Princeton, NJ: Van Nostrand, 1968.

McCaffrey, S. "Clintons Earn Big Bucks, But Have Big Bills," *Santa Barbara News-Press*, June 15, 2002.

McClelland, D.C. "Identifying Competencies with Behavioral-Event Interviews," *Psychological Science*, Volume 9, Number 5, (1999) 331–339.

Nadler, G. and Chandon, W.J. *Smart Questions*. San Francisco: Jossey-Bass, 2004.

Nadler, R.S. *Leaders' Playbook*. Santa Barbara, CA: Psyccess Press, 2007.

Nadler, R.S. "Teamwork Is an Unnatural Act," *PIHRA Scope*, Vol. XLXI, No. 6, June 1998.

Nancherla, A. "Please Boss Me Around," *Training and Development*, December 2009.

Peterson, D. and Hicks, M.D. *Development First*. Minneapolis, MN: Personnel Decisions International, 1995.

Pike, R.E. *Creative Training Techniques*, Amherst, MA: HRD Press, 2003.

Pilling, B.K. and Eroglu, S. "An Empirical Examination of the Impact of Salesperson Empathy and Professionalism and Mercantile Salability on Retail Buyers' Evaluations," *Journal of Personal Selling and Sales Management*, 14 no. 1 (1994): 55–58.

Plotz, D. "Condoleezza Rice: George W. Bush Celebrity Adviser," *Slate,* May 12, 2000.

Polman, D. "Dean's Victory Marks Historic Shift in Party," *Santa Barbara News-Press*, February 13, 2005.

Raines, C. "Managing Millennials," from *Connecting Generations: The Sourcebook.* 2002 (13).

Rath, T. and Clifton, D.O. *How Full Is Your Bucket?* New York: Gallup Press, 2004.

Robbins, A. *Anthony Robbins' Powertalk: Strategies for Lifelong Success*, audio-cassette, Robbins Research International, 1996.

Rock, D. *Your Brain at Work: Strategies for Overcoming Distraction, Regaining Focus and Working Smarter All Day Long.* New York: Harper Collins, 2009.

Salovey, P. and Mayer, J. *Emotional Intelligence, Imagination, Cognition and Personality.* 9(3), 185-211, 1990.

Santa Barbara News-Press, June 15, 2002.

Scholtes, P. *The Team Handbook*. Madison, WI: Joiner Associates, Inc., 1988.

Schroeder, A. "Please Hold for Mister Buffett," *BusinessWeek*, March 8, 2010.

Seligman, M.E.P. *Authentic Happiness*. New York: Free Press, 2002.

Sellers, P. "eBay's Secret," *Fortune*, October 18, 2004.

Senge, P. *The Fifth Discipline: The Art and Practice of the Learning Organization.* New York: Doubleday, 1990.

Senge, P., Roberts C., Ross R., Smith B., and Kleiner, A. *The Fifth Discipline Fieldbook: Strategies and Tools for Building a Learning Organization.* New York: Doubleday, 1994.

Siegel, D. *Mindsight: The New Science of Personal Transformation.* New York: Bantam Books, 2010.

Six Seconds website, 2004. *www.6seconds.org*

Sladek, S.L. "Back to the Future," *Talent Management,* January 2010.

Smith, D. and Bell, G. *The Carolina Way: Leadership Lessons from a Life of Coaching,* New York: Penguin Press, 2004.

Spencer, L.M. and Spencer, S.M. *Competence at Work: Models for Superior Performance.* New York: Wiley, 1993.

Stauffer, D. "How Good Data Leads to Bad Decisions," *Harvard Management Update,* Volume 7, Number 12, 2002.

Steele, C.M. "A Threat in the Air: How Stereotypes Shape Intellectual Identity and Performance," *American Psychologist,* Vol. 52, (1997): 613–629.

Stein, S. *The EQ Factor: Does Emotional Intelligence Make You a Better CEO?* (Special Report). Ontario, Canada: Innovators Alliance, November 2002.

Sullivan, D. *Pure Genius.* Niles, IL: Nightengale-Conant, 2002.

Thompson, H.L. "Emotional Intelligence, Stress, and Catastrophic Leadership Failure." In *Handbook for Developing Emotional and Social Intelligence,* edited by M. Hughes, H.L. Thompson, and J.B. Terrell. San Francisco: Pfeiffer, 2009.

Time, "Howard Dean," January 12, 2004.

Vise, D.A. and Malseed, M. *The Google Story,* New York: Bantam Dell.

Wall Street Journal, February 10, 2005.

"Warren E. Buffett, CEO Compensation." Forbes.com (accessed February 23, 2009).

Wharton, D. and Klein, G. *Conquest: Pete Carroll and the Trojans' Climb to the Top of the College Football Mountain.* Chicago: Triumph Books, 2005.

Whitman, M. *The Power of Many: Values for Success in Business and in Life.* New York: Crown Publishing, 2010.

Woopidoo.com, Business Quotes, November 2005.

"World's Most Admired Companies," *Fortune,* March 2010.

Zenger, J. and Folkman, J. *The Extraordinary Leader.* New York: McGraw-Hill, 2002.

Zenger, J., Sandholtz, K., and Folkman, J. *Leadership Under the Microscope.* Oren, UT: Extraordinary Performance Group, Inc., 2004.

ADDITIONAL RESOURCES

The following are resources to develop your Emotional Intelligence, including 360-degree feedback, research, tools, and training.

Authentic Happiness

The main site for the field of positive psychology and the work of Martin Seligman. The site has articles you can download and a series of free assessments.

www.authentichappiness.org

Center for Breakthrough Thinking

Provides trainings, products, and services in "Breakthrough Thinking, Question Forward, and Smart Questions."

www.breakthroughthinking.com

info@breakthroughthinking.com

Center for Social and Emotional Education

Developing leaders in Social and Emotional Education; has training institutes and speakers.

212-707-8799

www.csee.net

sel@csee.net

Collaborative Growth

Provides EQ certification for organizations and trainers. Sponsor of the EQ Symposium.

303-271-0021

ww.cgrowth.com

contact@cgrowth.com

Competency and Emotional Intelligence

A journal that comes out four times a year based in England.
> 44 (0) 20 8662-2000
>
> www.competencyandei.com

EI Consortium

Consortium for Research on Emotional Intelligence in Organizations, housed at Rutgers University. Organization created by Daniel Goleman, Cary Cherniss, and others for advancement, research, and practice related to Emotional Intelligence in organizations. The site has research articles and downloadable PDFs.
> www.eiconsortium.org

EI World

A center for research and development of Emotional Intelligence based in England. Offers three EI assessments—BarOn EQi, BarOn EQ-360™, and MSCEIT™—plus articles, products, and services.
> www.eiworld.org

EQ Alliance

An association of EI practitioners and allies to raise awareness of EI tools and best practices.
> www.nexusEQ.com/assoc

EQ Directory

A directory of Emotional Intelligence resources.
> 650-685-9880
>
> www.eq.org

EQ Europe Education

Network for trainers, teachers, and counselors who are interested in Emotional Quality and Human Respect.
> www.eqee.org
>
> network@eqee.org

EQ Map

Certifies professionals in the EQ Map. Stress management experts with 20 years of experience leading business from stress toward resiliency.
> 800-252-3774
>
> www.essisystems.com

EQ University

Offers online assessment, training, and development. Certifies people in BarOn EQi™ and BarOn EQ-360™.

877-700-3305

www.equniversity.com

Gallup Organization

Provides market research and consulting services around the world. Publisher of the Gallup Poll, a widely recognized barometer of American opinion. Gallup Consulting has great research articles and practices on leadership development, employee engagement, climate, and strength-based strategies.

www.gallup.com

Hay Group

Certifies professionals in the ECI360™, the Goleman and Boyatzis EI model presented in this book. They also have added assessments for professional trainers, the Inventory of Leadership Styles™ (ILS), and Organizational Climate Survey™ (OCS). Research articles are available on the site.

877-267-8375

http://ei.haygroup.com

Institute of HeartMath

Does research, education, and training on bringing the heart and brain into synchronization, which helps communication and performance.

831-338-8500

www.heartmath.org

Mark Goulston

Author, blogger, and speaker; offers free resources and the book Just Listen.

http://markgoulston.com/resources

Mindsight Institute

Trainings on Mindsight and Mindfulness.

310-447-0848

info@drdansiegel.com

Multi-Health Systems, Inc.

Distributes the BarOn EQi™, BarOn EQ-360™, and MSCEIT™, along with other clinical, educational, forensic, and organizational products and resources.

800-456-3003

www.mhs.com

6 Seconds

Brings EI into schools, organizations, and communities. The website has articles, a newsletter, and an EQ store.

650-685-9885

www.6seconds.org

The Success Principles

Jack Canfield, co-creator of Chicken Soup for the Soul®, which has sold over 80 million books, is also the co-author of The Success Principles. *The authors have created books, training, and ecoaching on the 64 principles of success.*

800-237-8326

www.thesuccessprinciples.com

TalentSmart

Developed its own 360-degree EI assessment, along with products and other assessments.

888-818-SMART

www.talentsmart.com

True North Leadership, Inc.

Developed a seven-day EI training and a two-day EI training based on Leading with Emotional Intelligence *for corporations and organizations. 360-degree feedback using the ECI and executive coaching. The website has FREE EI assessments EI tools, curriculums, and free downloads.*

805-683-1066

www.leadingwithei.com

INDEX

ABOUT THE AUTHOR

Dr. Reldan S. Nadler, educated as a clinical psychologist, has become a world-class executive coach and team trainer. He is the president and CEO of True North Leadership, Inc., an Executive and Organizational Development firm. Dr. Nadler brings his expertise in Emotional Intelligence to all his keynotes, consulting, coaching, and training. He has designed and led numerous multiday boot camps for high achievers.

A licensed psychologist and Master Executive Coach, Dr. Nadler has been working for more than 30 years with top executives and their teams to become "Star Performers." He is the author of two best-selling leadership and team performance books, and is a sought-after speaker and consultant on leadership, Emotional Intelligence, teambuilding, executive coaching, and experiential learning. His latest works are the *Leading with Emotional Intelligence* e-learning program and *Leadership Keys and Field Guide.* They are the first in a series of EI curriculums and toolkits for leaders and their direct reports to move into the top 10% of performance.

Dr. Nadler has coached CEOs, presidents, and their staffs, developed and delivered innovative leadership programs for such organizations as Anheuser-Busch, BMW, EDS, MCI, and Vanguard Health Systems, and created and facilitated team trainings for DreamWorks Animation, Comerica Bank, America Honda, and General Motors Defense. He is recognized around the world for his expertise in linking experiential learning and Emotional Intelligence to business objectives.

Dr. Nadler has worked for and consulted to Outward Bound Schools in North Carolina, Canada, Colorado, and Japan. He is the co-author of *Processing the Experience*, a "classic" in the field of Experiential Education. His concept of "Edgework" explains the power and steps of pushing past your comfort zone to new achievements, a core aspect of Outward Bound programs and being a successful leader and person.

Dr. Nadler received his B.A. from the University of Hartford and his M.A. in Confluent Education at the University of California, Santa Barbara. He received his Psy.D. in Counseling Psychology from the University of Northern Colorado. Dr. Nadler is on the faculty of The College of Executive Coaching, a post-graduate institute, training professionals in personal and executive coaching, and is certified in the use of Daniel Goleman's and the Hay Group's Emotional Competence Inventory. He has a popular weekly Voiceamerica.com show with Dr. Cathy Greenberg, "Leadership Development News," on top leadership practices.

Currently, Dr. Nadler's work is identifying, developing, and teaching tools for organizations, teams, and individuals to increase Emotional Intelligence and become "Star Performers."

HOW TO ENGAGE THE AUTHOR

TO BRING EMOTIONAL INTELLIGENCE COMPETENCIES INTO YOUR ORGANIZATION

Contact:

True North Leadership, Inc.

1170 Camino Meleno

Santa Barbara, CA 93111

805 683-1066   FAX 805 692-6738

Rnadler@truenorthleadership.com

RELLY NADLER IS AVAILABLE FOR CONSULTING, COACHING, AND TRAINING

- Keynotes and Presentations
- Multiday Leadership Development training for your teams, based on Emotional Intelligence
- Executive coaching—senior leaders and emerging leaders 360-degree feedback
- Teambuilding training for Executive teams and departments
- "Relly tele"—telecourses to help in utilizing the tools
- E-learning programs based on the book
- Organizational consulting
- Organizational assessments
- Succession planning

Visit our website for more information on these services, for free EI tools and to sign up for our mailing list:

www.leadingwithei.com

PRODUCTS

Bring the Leading with Emotional Intelligence *curriculum to your teams!*

EI LEARNNG

This e-learning is designed for managers, leaders, and coaches. It is a complete *turn-key curriculum* for a team leader or coach. It includes:

1. *Powerpoint presentations* with notes include:
   - EI introduction with political and CEO profiles
   - Teamwork and Collaboration tools
   - Developing Others tools: Feedback, delegation, and coaching tools
2. *PDFs* of the key tools and checklists to distribute to your teams
   - EI Star Profile™
   - Derailer Detector™
   - Meeting Menace Checklist™
   - The Meeting Checklist™
   - Teamwork Ingredients Survey™
   - Assumption Ladder™
   - Coaching for Performance™
   - Hiring Checklist™
   - Feedback Tool™
   - Delegation Tool™
   - And more
3. A *curriculum* for leaders to pass on to their team, where partners practice the specific skills
4. *Audio podcasts* of interviews with leadership gurus to support the learning, e.g., Richard Boyatzis, Ken Blanchard, Marshall Goldsmith, Marcus Buckingham, and more

Site licenses and affiliate programs available.

Go to our website for more information and for free EI assessments and tools and to sign up for our mailing list at **www. leadingwith ei.com.**

LEADERSHIP KEYS

These are 11 cue cards of some of the most powerful *Leading with Emotional Intelligence* tools and more.

Ideal for your team members to have readily available for immediate use and application. Great for coaches to give to their clients. Affiliate programs available.

Leadership Keys packages include:

- Exercises to practice the tools
- Four sets of the Leadership Keys
- iPhone application of Keys with video explanation

Relly Nadler, Psy.D.

1170 Camino Meleno

Santa Barbara, CA 93111

805 683-1066   FAX 805 692-6738

Rnadler@truenorthleadership.com

For more information, go to www.leadingwithei.com.